THE VIVĀHA
The Hindu Marriage Saṁskāras

The Vivāha

The Hindu Marriage Saṁskāras

PT. BHAIYĀRĀM ŚARMĀ

Translated by
DR. R.C. PRASAD

MOTILAL BANARSIDASS PUBLISHERS
PRIVATE LIMITED • DELHI

First Edition: Delhi, 1993
Reprint: Delhi, 1995, 1999

ISBN: 81-208-1132-1

Also available at:

MOTILAL BANARSIDASS

41 U.A. Bungalow Road, Jawahar Nagar, Delhi 110 007
8 Mahalaxmi Chamber, Warden Road, Mumbai 400 026
120 Royapettah High Road, Mylapore, Chennai 600 004
Sanas Plaza, 1302, Baji Rao Road, Pune 411 002
16 St. Mark's Road, Bangalore 560 001
8 Camac Street, Calcutta 700 017
Ashok Rajpath, Patna 800 004
Chowk, Varanasi 221 001

PRINTED IN INDIA
BY JAINENDRA PRAKASH JAIN AT SHRI JAINENDRA PRESS,
A-45 NARAINA, PHASE I, NEW DELHI 110 028
AND PUBLISHED BY NARENDRA PRAKASH JAIN FOR
MOTILAL BANARSIDASS PUBLISHERS PRIVATE LIMITED,
BUNGALOW ROAD, DELHI 110 007

Preface

Among the innumerable castes and communities in India only the *trivargas*—brāhmaṇas, kṣatriyas and vaiśyas—perform their rites strictly in accordance with the injunctions ordained by the Vedas. These rites aggregate into sixteen saṁskāras, of which the marriage ceremonies are still the most important. But what is regrettable is that all these sacraments, written or published so far, being in Sanskrit, are beyond the comprehension of common priests entrusted with the duty of conducting the rituals. Only the scholar has the key to the secrets of Sanskrit in his possession. It is to overcome this hardship that I have translated the Vivāha mantras compiled by Ramdatta into Hindi and offered them with saṁkalpas and modes of performing the ceremonies with explanatory meaning of the mantras. In spite of their differences of opinion about a number of important ideas the marriage saṁskāras of the Hindus, collected by Ramdatta in accordance with Pāraskara Gṛhyasūtra, are nonetheless wellnigh identical. The same rites and the mode of their performance are here poured into a Hindi mould without adding anything extraneous. With such a book accompanied by a Hindi rendering, any person, however ill-equipped otherwise, can without any trepidation conduct marriage ceremonies. Moreover, it is observed everywhere that while the priest, already in anxious haste, has other marriage rites to perform in other homes, the host is himself restlessly awaiting the completion of the ceremonies, as is evident when he says: "Hurry up, Sir, for the boys are dozing off". You fools, why are such boys married when they do not let the rituals be properly completed? The hosts, so pathetically naive or in most cases absolutely ignorant, are little aware of the mysterious and symbolic meaning of the sacraments nor of the sublime ideals enshrined in them. For the ignorant the rituals are just a mockery, marriage a mockshow. Their priests neither explain to them the meaning of the mantras nor acquaint them with the process of the ritual. It is for this reason that I have not only explained with all possible lucidity the processes of such rituals as saṁkalpa, etc., but have also given the Hindi meaning of the mantras, attaching considerable importance to the latter, so that those Hindi-knowing people not familiar with Sanskrit may also be benefitted. With this aim in view and inspired by some most adored friends, I have written this widely appealing Hindi commentary on Pandit Ramdatta's marriage sacraments for the benefit of the common reader. It is also noteworthy that I have not mentioned the names of the chaṁda ṛṣis for the simple reason that in the ritual modes according to Nārada it is said: अग्निहोत्रे वैश्वदेवे विवाहादिविधौ तथा । होमकाले न दृश्यन्ते प्रायश्छन्दर्षिदेवताः ॥ (agnihotre vaiśvadeve vivāhādī-vidhau tathā । homakāle na dṛśyante prāyaśchandarṣidevatāḥ ॥)

In other words, in such ceremonies as Agnihotra, Bali Vaiśvadeva, Marriage and Homa the application of chaṁda, ṛṣi and of the presiding deity is not found—that is, they are not mentioned in the ceremonies mentioned above. Now what remains is this:

विनियोगं विना मंत्र पङ्के गौरिव सीदति ।

(viniyogaṁ vinā maṅtra paṅkegauriva sīdati.)

This is all right. Our purpose is not to show disrespect to any Dharma-sūtra, but what harm would it cause if the same practice (of not mentioning the names of the chandas, etc.) is followed with regard to other ceremonial rites than those mentioned above? Both sentences would be correct. My last request to my discerning readers is that in case they come across any textual variation or stylistic solecism, they should correct it. Allrespectable persons are appreciative of merit.

Kaviratna Pandita Bhaiyārām Śarmā Śāstri
Mahopadeśaka Sanātanadharma

Introduction

Ceremonial rites and rituals occupy a place of ùtmost importance in the life of a devout Hindu. Others, who pride themselves on their western culture and newfangled, avant-garde ideas, often scoff at the saṁskāras, but even they and the members of their family are as afraid of flouting them as any average religious Hindu. Society, however urbanized and unorthodox, has not been able to ring out the old when every little work in the Hindu home, sacred or profane, begins with the performance of appropriate rites according to the prescribed code. This accounts for the existence of no less than forty saṁskāras according to the author of *Gautama Smṛti.* Maharṣi Aṁgirā has, on the other hand, brought down the number to twenty-five and incorporated into them all the saṁskāras mentioned in *Gautaṁa Smṛti.* In the first chapter of *Vyāsa Smṛti* the number of ceremonial rites has been reduced to sixteen, which shows that the number of the saṁskāras has been fluctuating in accordance with the degree of importance attached to them from time to time.

Before performing a particular ceremonial rite it is necessary to acquaint oneself with its mode of performance and its purpose, which can be of three kinds: *utkarṣakāraka, samavāya* and *bhuṣaṇa.* He who performs a saṁskāra attains glory, admiration, and honour in society and, like a physically unattractive person who looks attractive when adorned with ornaments, attains beauty as well. Unfortunately, however, the ignorance, selfishness and exploitative behaviour of some of the present-day purohitas have made a mockery of all the sacred rites and sacrificial ceremonies of the Hindus. Neither are the ceremonies properly performed nor are their performers sincere enough, for the latter and their priests are, in Swami Sāhajānanda's view, almost all ignorant. None of them knows what the rituals, ceremonies, saṁskāras and their mode of performance are. The self-styled pundits officiate at the rituals and ceremonies only to extort a handsome fee and fatten on varieties of sumptuous delicacies. It is, therefore, natural to lament the atrocious ignorance of some purohitas, their cupidity and their culpability which has deprived the Hindus of the real knowledge of the saṁskāras and the style of performing them in accordance with the prescribed code.

Rituals and ceremonies so permeate the life of an average Hindu that he does not even step out without muttering a mantra or two. His historical and economic situation may vary; a man may be born a feudal lord or labourer or a proletarian. What does not vary is the necessity for him to exist successfully and happily in the world with his gods and manes pleased with him and in prosperity for himself, his family and his progeny. It is in order to safeguard himself against all inauspicious omens, evil eyes and the displeasure of the gods and brāhmaṇas that he performs certain appropriate rites and propitiates not only the gods but also the forces of evil. Even today he looks at the world as the medieval man looked at it; it is still bewildering, overwhelming, and has purpose. If someone during a journey accidentally injures himself, even the average Hindu would infer that this accident was caused because the appropriate ceremony before leaving for the destination was not performed. In fact, in the Hindu world picture, there are no vital actions—birth, initiation, marriage, death, etc.—which can be allowed to be performed without its appropriate rite. In the Yajurveda there is, for example, a reference to the shaving ceremony which precedes a śrauta sacrifice. The ceremony consisted of prayers offered to the shaving razor and directions given to the barber. Lest one should belittle the importance of popular religious rites and ceremonies, it may here be affirmed that the Atharvaveda, in contradiction to the Saṁhitās, is strewn with valuable mantras for almost every end of human life. The searcher after mantras knows that there are so many wedding and funeral hymns in this last of the Vedas. It is not surprizing, therefore, that a full hymn of the Atharvaveda should be devoted to the praise of the Vedic celibate.[1] As a matter of fact, Atharvaveda is, for the author of *Hindu Saṁskāras*, a mirror of 'the faith and rites of the common people' rather than of the highly specialized religion of the priest. Countless Hindu families still believe in ceremonial observances and in propitiating the duties not only to attain happiness and prosperity in the world but also final beatitude thereafter. In this sense the influence of the Vedas on the Hindu mind continues to be deep and ineffaceable. There is a general feeling that the continuance of the age-old saṁskāras is a glaring reflection of the Hindu superstition-laden world-view. To him every action, albeit insignificant, is 'part of the design of providence' and is presided over by some duty. If the latter is unfavourable he must be propitiated; if favourable he should be invoked for benediction. Human endeavour, howsoever zealously pursued is not enough. Providence must be invoked and worshipped with due devotion, muttering of mantras and appropriate libation of sanctified water, basil leaves, ghee, waving of festal lamps, etc. To invoke and worship the gods is the goal of the ceremonies and the mantras. The world for the Hindu is still interrelated and his cosmology substantially Vedic and Sanātan insofar as the saṁskāras are concerned. He continues to believe with Manu that having performed the rite of initiation the teacher must first instruct the pupil in the rules of personal purification, of conduct, of the fire-worship, and of the twilight devotions.

The elaborate marriage ceremonies provide a good example of the Hindu world-view. As superstitiously inclined as the Hindus were, it is not difficult to presume why they made oblations to the planets and the elements and devised so many complicated saṁskāras. Every devout Hindu, whatever his order, was expected to be up early to perform his routine

---

1. R.B. Pandey, *Hindu Saṁskāras* (Delhi: Motilal Banarsidass, 1987).

morning ablutions with prayer and muttering of sacred mantras. He spent the better part of the day working and earning his livelihood. The intensely pious spent the evenings in prayer and Kirtana, while the worldly folk recourse to other relaxed modes, but almost all of them had glimpses that made them less forlorn. Those near the sea had sight of Sūrya rising from the sea or heard old Udgātṛ priests chanting Vedic ṛcās at Soma sacrifices. The Hindu student or householder did not face any religious crisis nor the chaotic state of the modern world 'due to man's abandonment of God'. Nor was it fashionable to talk glibly about the 'death of God'. The ritualist, the pandit, the householder's purohita, and the householder himself were all interested in *causes* and not in purposes.

The Hindu society, though thoroughly superstition-laden, was not promiscuous, it was a society well regulated and strictly ordered. The seers, the interpreters of the Vedas and Vedic injunctions, and the institutes of the sacred law proclaimed by Manu governed society. Even the earliest Ṛgvedic society emerges, as Dr. R.B. Pandey says: "with a well established home which could not have been possible in the pre-marital stage of sexual relation. There is no instance of promiscuity proper in the Vedic literature. The only reference to it is found in the Mahābhārata. There it is stated that women were free in early primitive times and they could have sexual relations with anybody they liked, even, though they were married. This revolting custom, however, was abolished by Svetaketu, son of Uddālaka. This story, at most, proved that the Aryans had passed through a stage of society when such intercourse was tolerated in society. Temporary sexual relations also are not to be found either in the Vedas or in the Gṛhyasūtras."

The Hindu view of life is nowhere better illustrated than in the marital rites the officiating priests conducted and made the householder perform during the marriage ceremonies. Whether it was the Gandharva or the Paiśāca form of marriage the rites were performed in the presence of fire. Manu enjoins that rituals should be performed in the case of a virgin for legalizing the marriage, legitimatizing children and avoiding public scandal. Other authorities, such as Mādhavācārya, decisively show and stress that the religious idea is supreme in the Hindu life and that the marriage tie should always be consecrated and the union made lasting by imparting sanctity to it. Some of the law-givers go to the extent of maintaining that the mythical gods Soma, Gandharva and Agni help the physical development of a girl and it is they who are the enjoyers of her person. Thus it was that the religious father of the girl became anxious to give her away in marriage before she was enjoyed by these gods. Before a matrimonial negotiations started the boy's father was reminded of Manu's instruction that one should not marry a girl who is named after a constellation, a tree, a river, a mountain, a bird, a smoke, etc. Such a prohibition did not imply any loathing of these natural objects. In fact, the Hindus were like so many Sigmunds who believed, like D.H. Lawrence's hero in *The Trespasser*, that "the darkness is a sort of mother, and the moon a sister, and the stars children, and sometimes the sea is a brother: and there's family in one house. . ."

In almost every form of nuptial ceremony the Hindu invoked the beneficent gods for boons and blessings and sent specific appeals to unseen powers with definite rites of sacrifice and prayer. He did not waver in his belief that "Divinatory elements are also religious in their character, because they seek to find out whether the higher powers are propitious at a particular time or not". Pantheism appears to have evolved *pari passu* with the Vedic religion and rites, including the nuptial ceremonies in which clay, grass, cowdung, sesamum seeds, foodgrains, barley, raw rice, clarified butter, fire, stone, parched rice, water, sandal, turmeric and lime, pigments, precious stones including gold and silver, polaśa and mango leaves, pots, etc. played a vital part. No ceremony, especially the nuptial one; could be deemed properly performed without the blessing of Agni and Sūrya. Nothing could be sanctified without the grace and benediction of Gaṇeśa made of cowdung. *Milk and Gura* (jaggery) were as much valued as the deities. When the bride left her father's house the benedictions pronounced remembered Indra and said: "Now from the noose of Varuṇa I free thee, wherewith the blessed Savitā has bound her. In the heaven of righteousness, in the world of virtue, be it pleasant for thee, accompanied by the wooer. Let Bhaga take thy hand and hence conduct thee." On the day of marriage the bride was bathed in water consecrated with Vedic verses. At an important stage she was made to stand on a stone, to represent not only 'the lap of earth' but also firmness and fidelity. Thus the ceremonies central to the marriage proper are all symbolic. Prayers are said to drive away demons and a chariot is blessed. The newly weds start on a marriage procession. Mantras are muttered, while the procession goes round, to the effect that the bride was first the wife of Soma, then of Gandharva, then of Agni who lastly bestowed her on her human husband. When the procession returned to the bridegroom's house whence the demons were exercised, the bride sat with her husband before the household fire. According to some authorities, she sat on a bull-skin on which was spread the Bulbaja grass and worshipped Agni with her husband. The purohitas—the officiating priests tell us that Viśvāvasu, the Gandharva attached to unmarried girls supplicated to go away from the bride's chamber before cohabitation followed with the recital of verses. It is, therefore, reasonable to expect that valiant sons will be prayed for and prayers will be offered to Agni for giving ten sons to the couple.

We need not multiply examples of the nuptial rites being symbolic and deeply religious. They are expectedly expressive of the Hindu view of life. They are still in vogue wherever the Hindus are. No matter how far from their native land they are, they, barring some, cannot ignore the fact that their ancestors practised them and muttered the nuptial formulas contained in this book. A believing Hindu, a Hindu rooted in his country's tradition, albeit 'during the perilaces nineteen-nineties' does not have to become a giant to save the world from complete relapse; he believes, as did his ancestors, that he must 'bind a harder, stronger civilization like steel about the world', and the thing which can bind all the peoples of the world like steel is faith, the ancient belief in the interrelatedness of all that exists and of all that happens. Such a faith alone will be a binding, abiding faith, the saviour, the emancipator of man in chains of Discord the killer of the Eagle.

The centuries during which these rituals were compiled must have had their own crisis, but the Hindus did not yield to what is called 'unheroic nihilism', to the sort of feeling expressed in T.S. Eliot's Hollow Men or by Samuel Beckett, whose characters are incapable of motion; they think about their past lives, wondering what it was all about. The ancient Hindus knew the meaning of the question 'Why should I do anything?' which hangs over Beckett's character for they believe in external reality and found some purpose and meaning inside themselves. It is, in a purposeless world that such events as the following are possible:

> THE DOMINANT MOOD of America in the 1960s was apocalyptic. Perpetual crisis seemed in many ways the rule. Throughout the decade the events reported daily by newspapers and magazines documented the sweeping changes in every sector of our national life and often strained our imaginations to the point of disbelief. Increasingly, everyday 'reality' became more fantastic than the fictional visions of even our best novelists. . . .
> Even more important were changes in life-style and in the values and attitudes of Americans that appeared fundamental and comprehensive. The drug culture. The sexual revolutions. The age of Aquarius. Such phrases became the watchwords to describe basic changes affecting every area of our national life. Young people and minority groups sought radical solutions to their problems and

rejected, at least in part, the American dream of material success. Turning their backs on wealth and work they found meaningless, college students were attracted to communal living, Eastern religions, and consciousness-altering drugs. By the mid-sixties, political groups of every stripe had developed as individuals sought alternative solutions to the problems that beset society.

The reader is invited to decode the symbols used by the authors of the Gṛhyasūtras, especially of those mantras, sūtras and ṛcās used during the performance of the Hindu vivāha. This book is the first attempt to interpret and comment on some of the relevant mantras. The attempt owes whatever merit it has to the willing and ungrudging co-operation of my friend and pupil Digvijay Narayan Singh, who helped me to correct the errors inadvertently committed in transliteration and in other places.

Contents

उपोद्घातः
(UPODGHĀTAḤ)

Introduction

ब्राह्मो दैवस्तथैवार्षः प्राजापत्यस्तथासुरः ।
गान्धर्वो राक्षसश्चैव पैशाचश्चाष्टमोऽधमः ॥ (मनुः)

brāhmo daivastathaivārṣaḥ prājāpatyastathāsuraḥ ।
gāndharvo rākṣasaścaiva paiśācaścāṣṭamo'dhamaḥ ॥

(Manuḥ)

In the course of his description of eight kinds of marriages, Manu deems Brāhmavivāha to belong to the best category. Its characteristics are as follows:

आच्छाद्य चार्चयित्वा च श्रुतिशीलवते स्वयम् ।
आहूय दानं कन्यायाः ब्राह्मो धर्मः प्रकीर्तितः ॥ (मनुः)

ācchādya cārcayitvā ca śrutiśīlavate svayam ।
āhūya dānaṁ kanyāyāḥ brāhmo dharmaḥ prakīrtitaḥ ॥

(Manuḥ)

In other words, Brāhmavivāha is that form of marriage in which the bridegroom, a virtuous person living strictly in accordance with the rules prescribed by the Vedas, is invited and with affectionate welcome with garments, etc. is respectfully married to the bride. The underlying meaning of the passage, however, is that of such holy marriages 'of true minds' are born excellent children, but for this one must also make sure that the boy and the girl—their appearance, worth, lineage, etc.—are ideally suited for marriage. In this the girl has to undergo a severer test, for attention has to be paid even to her name; this is deemed imperative because such ceremonies as the Nāmakaraṇa (name-giving) are now rarely performed by the Hindus. Even where the saṁskāra is observed, it is the boy for whom the name-giving ceremony is performed, not for the girl. As a result of this the girls are given some despicable names forbidden by the śāstras. Remember:

नोद्वहेत्कपिलां कन्यां नाधिकांगीं न रोगिणीम् ।
नालोमिकां नातिलोमां न वाचाटां न पिंगलाम् ॥
नर्क्षवृक्षनदीनाम्नीं नान्त्यपर्वतनामिकाम् ।
न पक्ष्यहिप्रेष्यनाम्नीं न च भीषणनामिकाम् ॥ (मनुः)

nodvahetkapilāṁ kanyāṁ nādhikāṁgiṁ na rogiṇīm ।
nālomikāṁ nātilomāṁ na vācāṭāṁ na piṁgalām ॥
narkṣavṛkṣanadīnāmnīṁ nāntyaparvatanāmikām ।
na pakṣyahipreṣyanāmnīṁ na ca bhīṣaṇanāmikām ॥
(Manuḥ)

In other words, do not marry a maiden with reddish hair, nor one who has a redundant member, nor one who is sickly, nor one either with no hair on the body or too much, nor one who is garrulous or has red eyes, nor one named after a constellation, a tree, or a river, nor one bearing the name of a low caste, or of a mountain, nor one named after a bird, a snake, or a slave, nor one whose name inspires terror. The maiden to be married should have auspicious manners and an auspicious name. It is said:

अव्यंगांगीं सौम्यनाम्नीं हंसवारणगामिनीम् ।
तनुलोमकेशदशनां मृद्वंगीमुद्वहेत् स्त्रियम् ॥

avyaṁgāṁgīṁ saumyanāmnīṁ haṁsavāraṇagāminīm ।
tanulomakeśadaśanāṁ mṛdvaṁgīmudvahet striyam ॥

That is, wed a female free from bodily defects, who has an agreeable name (like Subhadrā, Kauśalyā, etc.), the graceful gait of a haṁsa (swan) or the undulating grace of an elephant, a moderate quantity of hair on the body and on the head, small teeth and soft limbs. Just as the girl is to be subjected to a severe, microscopic test, so must the male's features be thoroughly examined (before conjugal union). The rule in this connection is this:

महान्त्यपि समृद्धानि गोजाविधनधान्यतः ।
स्त्रीसंबन्धे दशैतानि कुलानि परिवर्जयेत् ॥

हीनक्रियं निष्पुरुषं निच्छन्दो रोमसार्शसम् ।
क्षय्यामयाव्यपस्मारी चित्रकुष्ठिकुलानि च ॥

mahāntyapi samṛddhāni gojāvidhanadhānyataḥ ।
strīsaṁbandhe daśaitāni kulāni parivarjayet ॥
hīnakriyaṁ niṣpuruṣaṁ nicchando romasārśasam ।
kṣayyāmayāvyapasmārī citrakuṣṭhikulāni ca ॥

The meaning is, that in connecting himself with a wife, one must carefully avoid the following ten families, be they ever so great, or rich in kine, horses, sheep, grain, or other property.

The families to be avoided are the following ten:

1. One which neglects the sacred rites; 2. one in which there is no manliness and nothing exalted (but only measly, inglorious hermaphrodites); 3. one in which the Veda is not studied (so that everyone remains stupid and none is learned); 4. one the members of which have bearlike, thick hair on the body; 5. one in which people are subject to hemorrhoids; 6-10. those which are subject to phthisis, weakness of digestion, epilepsy, or white and black leprosy.

These blemishes are transmitted by parental sperm to the children. The sages state that—

सर्वे संक्रामिणो दोषा वर्जयित्वा प्रवाहिकाम् ।

sarve saṁkrāmiṇo doṣā varjayitvā pravāhikām ।

According to this medical theory, let not a maiden be married in a family afflicted with any of these blemishes. Before establishing a matrimonial relation, one must assure onself that there is no blood relationship between the bride's and the bridegroom's family. (Lest one should commit sin by marrying a Sagotra one must be sure of the *gotra* of the maiden and of the bridegroom-to-be. Intermarriages between families descended from the same ṛṣi and between families bearing the same name or known to be connected, are forbidden.)

असपिंडा च या मातुरसगोत्रा च या पितुः ।
सा प्रशस्ता द्विजातीनां दारकर्मणि मैथुने ॥
asapiṁḍā ca yā māturasagotrā ca yā pituḥ ।
sā praśastā dvijātīnāṁ dārakarmaṇi maithune ॥

A maiden, that is to say, who is neither a Sapiṁḍā[1] on the mother's side, nor belongs to the same family on the father's side, is recommended to twice-born men for wedlock and conjugal union.

In other words, she must not marry a person up to the seventh degree of relationship on the father's and mother's side. 'असपिंडा च या मातुः' (asapiṁḍā ca yā mātuḥ) has, however, a deeper meaning, for, according to the Mitākṣarā, the celebrated commentary on Yājñavalkya's Smṛti, the word 'aspiṁḍā' should be thus interpreted: 'असपिंडा, कोऽर्थः? समान एकः पिंडो देहो यस्याः सा सपिंडा न सपिंडा असपिंडा ताम्, सपिंडता च एकशरीरावयवान्वयेन भवति' (aspiṁḍā, ko'rthaḥ? samāna ekaḥ piṁḍo deho yasyāḥ sā sapiṁḍā na sapiṁḍā asapiṁḍā tām, sapiṁḍatā ca ekaśarīrāvayavānvayena bhavati.) That is, a body of different parts, a *piṁḍa,* is essentially one. The *gotra* tradition implies the existence of a single animating, virile principle in all the descendants. The implication, therefore, is that one should take a wife or a husband one who is not a sapiṁḍā relation of one's mother. For more useful information on the subject see the commentary on śloka 52 of the Ācārādhyāya in Yājñavalkya Smṛti. Kanyādāna (the gift of a daughter), if thus performed

1. The word 'asapiṁḍā' must be taken to refer to the father's side also. Thus intermarriages with the daughter of a paternal aunt or with the paternal grandfather's sister's descendants are forbidden. Sapiṁḍā-relationship ceases with the fifth or the seventh (ancestor). Almost all the metrical Smṛtis declare the marriages within the *gotra, ipso facto,* invalid. Such marriages could not be legalized, nor the children born of such wedlocks.

according to the sacred law, yields great fruit. It is performed in three[1] stages.

अत्र प्रथमं वाग्दाने विधिः
(atra prathamaṁ vāgdāne vidhiḥ)

The custom of *sagāī* (betrothal) prevalent here is the preliminary part of the marriage ceremonies and consists in the *vāgdānam* or oral giving away of the bride to the bridegroom. Since the ceremony precedes all marriages, it should take place at least a day before the marriage, if not many days earlier.[2]

---

1. वाग्दानं कन्यादानं खट्वादिपारिबर्हदानं च इति त्रिधा दानम् । यदाह वृद्धमनुः–वरं सम्पूज्य खार्जूरं फलं दत्त्वा मुखे तथा । तस्मिन्कालेऽग्निसान्निध्ये पिता तुभ्यं प्रदास्यति ॥१॥ इति प्रतिज्ञया यच्च कन्या भ्रातादिना च सा । वाचा यद्दीयते तुल्ये वाग्दानं प्रथमं स्मृतम् ॥२॥ वरं सम्पूज्य विधिना वेद्यामग्निं निधाय च । दात्रा प्रदीयते यच्च कन्या संकल्पवाक्यतः ॥३॥ द्वितीयं कन्यकादानं तत्तु प्रोक्तं महर्षिभिः । वधूवरौ च खट्वायां मंडपे सन्निवेश्य च ॥४॥ पारिबर्हं महद्दत्वा जलेन च विसर्जनम् । तृतीयं कन्याकादानं व्यासाद्या मुनयो जगुः ॥५॥ इति ।

Vāgdānaṁ kanyādānaṁ khaṭvādipāribarhadānaṁ ca iti tridhā dānam । yadāha vṛddhamanuḥ—varaṁ sampūjya khārjūraṁ phalaṁ datvā mukhe tathā । tasminkāle'gnisānnidhye pitā tubhyaṁ pradāsyati ॥ 1 ॥ iti pratijñayā yacca kanyā bhrātādinā ca sā । vācā yaddīyate tulye vāgdānaṁ prathamaṁ smṛtam ॥ 2 ॥ varaṁ sampūjya vidhinā vedyāmagniṁ nidhāya ca । dātrā pradīyate yacca kanyā saṁkalpavākyataḥ ॥ 3 ॥ dvitīyaṁ kanyakādānaṁ tattu proktaṁ maharṣibhiḥ । vadhūvarau ca khaṭvāyāṁ maṁḍape sanniveśya ca ॥ 4 ॥ pāribarha mahaddatvā jalena ca visarjanam । tṛtīyaṁ kanyakādānaṁ vyāsādyā munayo jaguḥ ॥ 5 ॥ iti ।

2. The custom of Kanyāvaraṇa has given way to Varavaraṇa, according to which the brother of the bride and brāhmaṇas go to the house of the bridegroom and offer him upavīta, fruit, flowers, clothes, etc. on the occasion of Varavaraṇa. At present this custom is popularly known as Tilaka. In the opinion of Gadādhara this ceremony should take place one day before the marriage, but generally it is performed many days before it. See R.B. Pandey, *Hindu Sṁskāras* (Delhi, Motilal Banarsidass, 1987), pp. 208 *et seq*.—

The ceremony of betrothal has been in vogue among the Hindus from time immemorial. Having decided upon a bridegroom suited to the maiden, her father, brother or other kinsmen perform this ceremony fully convinced that it must follow the sacred law laid down in the śāstras. It is improper to allow any person other than the family priest or a competent preceptor to conduct this important pre-marital ceremony. The barber must not do it. In the opinion of the śāstras, for the performance of the betrothal ceremony the maiden's brother or, in his absence, the priest or any virtuous brāhmaṇa should go to the bridegroom's house and perform this ritual in accordance with the sacred law, the dharmaśāstra:

तत्र कन्याभ्राता पुरोधा अन्यो ब्राह्मणो वा कश्चित् ।

(tatra kanyābhrātā purodhā anyo brāhmaṇo vā kaścit)

the meaning of which is that the maiden's brother or the priest or any virtuous brāhmaṇa (may perform the betrothal ceremony). The ritual has been thus described:

उदङ्मुखः प्रत्यङ्मुखो वा उपविश्य प्राङ्मुखस्य वरस्य गंधाक्षतैरर्चितस्य मुखदत्तखाजूर्रादिफलस्य स्वयं पूगीफलयज्ञोपवीतमादाय–

(udaṅmukhaḥ pratyaṅmukho vā upaviśya prāṅmukhasya varasya gaṁdhākṣatairarcitasya mukhadattakhājūrrādiphalasya svayaṁ pūgīphalayajñopavītamādāya—)

In other words, with his face towards the north or the west the bestower (*dātā*) lets the bridegroom, who has been given a date fruit[1] in his mouth, be seated facing the east.

1. पूज्यश्च प्राङ्मुखो यत्रोदङ्मुखः पूजको भवेत् । अर्चयेद् देवमभितः इति प्रत्यङ्मुखश्च सः ॥ इति मनुः । प्रत्यङ्मुखं स्थापयेत्तु देवं पूज्यं तथैव च । पूजकः सम्मुखस्तस्य इति धर्मानुशासनम् ॥ इति वरस्य पूज्यत्वेन प्रत्यङ्मुखत्वे संसिद्धेऽपि–प्रत्यङ्मुखं स्थापयेत्तु देवं पूज्यं वरं विना । वरस्तु प्राङ्मुखः पूज्यः पूजकः स्यादुदङ्मुखः ॥ इति व्यासस्मृतिः । प्रत्यङ्मुखान्पूजनीयदेवांस्तत्सम्मुखास्थितः । अर्चयेन्नित्यमेवेत्थं विधिरित्येव सम्मतः ॥ स्थित्वा चाभिमुखं नार्च्चेच्छम्भुं जामातरं तथा । इन्द्रं चोदङ्मुखं स्थाप्य स्वयं प्राङ्मुखसंस्थितः । उदङ्मुखोच्चरेद् दाता वेदिस्थं प्राङ्मुखं वरम् ॥ इति पराशरः ॥

pūjyaśca prāṅmukho yatrodaṅmukhaḥ pūjako bhavet ।

Then he marks his forehead with fragrant *rolī* (red powder)[1] and sprinkles dry rice grains (*akṣata*) and incense (*gaṁdha*) upon him. Then taking a reasonable amount of sacrificial fees (*dakṣiṇā*), betel nut and sacred thread in his hand, he should recite the following ceremonial verses:

तस्मिन्कालेऽग्निसान्निध्ये स्नातः स्नाते ह्यरोगिणि ।
अव्यङ्गेऽपतिते क्लीबे पिता तुभ्यं प्रदास्यति ॥ इति पठित्वा हस्ते दद्यात् ।

tasminkāle'gnisānnidhye snātaḥ snāte hyarogiṇi ।
avyaṅge'patite klībe pitā tubhyaṁ pradāsyati ॥
iti paṭhitvā haste dadyāt ।

What the verse means is this:

"In an auspicious hour of the marriage ceremony when you will have taken your bath near the sacrificial fire and become purified, free from all public censure, neither fallen[2]

---

arcayed devambhitaḥ iti pratyaṅmukhaśca saḥ ॥ iti manuḥ । pratyaṅmukhaṁ sthāpayethu devaṁ pūjyaṁ tathaiva ca । pūjakaḥ sammukhastasya iti dharmānuśāsanam ॥ iti varasya pūjyatvena pratyaṅmukhatve saṁsiddhe'pi—pratyaṅmukhaṁ sthāpayettu devaṁ pūjyaṁ varaṁ vina । varastu prāṅmukhaḥ pūjyaḥ pūjakaḥ syādudaṅmukhaḥ ॥ iti vyāsasmṛtiḥ । pratyaṅmukhānpūjanīya-devāṁstatsammukhasthitaḥ । arcayennityamevetthaṁ vidhi-rityeva sammataḥ ॥ sthitvā cābhimukhaṁ nārccecchambhuṁ jāmātaraṁ tathā । indraṁ codaṅmukhaṁ sthāpya svayaṁ prāṅmukhasaṁsthitaḥ । udaṅmukhoccared dātā vedisthaṁ prāṅmukhaṁ varam ॥ iti parāśaraḥ ॥

1. i.e. he applies the holy mark on his forehead.

2. किञ्चापतिते सति ॥ व्रह्महा मद्यपः स्तेनस्तथैव गुरूतल्पगः । एते महापातकिनो यश्च तैः सह संवसेत् ॥ ब्रह्महत्यादिके पापे जातिभ्रंशकरे तथा । वृषलीगमनेऽत्यर्थं सावित्रीविरहेऽपि च ॥ अभक्ष्यभक्षणे चैव पतितो भवति ध्रुवम् ॥

kiñcāpatite sati ॥ vrahmahā madyapaḥ stenastathaiva gurutalpagaḥ । ete mahāpātakino yaśca taiḥ saha saṁvaset ॥ brahmahatyādike pāpe jātibhraṁśakare tathā । vṛṣalīgamane-'tyarthaṁ sāvitrīvirahe'pi ca ॥ abhakṣyabhakṣaṇe caiva patito bhavati dhruvam ॥

from your caste nor impotent,[1] my father will bestow upon you his daughter endowed with auspicious features.

ॐ[2] ऋतवः स्थ ऋतावृध ऋतुष्ठाः स्थ ऋतावृधः ।
घृतश्च्युतो मधुच्युतो विराजो मान कामदुघाः अक्षीयमणाः ॥

Oṁ ṛtavaḥ stha ṛtāvṛdha ṛtuṣṭhāḥ stha ṛtāvṛdhaḥ ।
ghṛtaścyuto madhucyuto virājo nāma kāmadughāḥ akṣīyamaṇāḥ ॥

O guardians of the maiden! Be established in truth which may ever increase—that is, may all deem you righteous in keeping your word. Unflaggingly committed to performing excellent deeds, may you further the honour of your family! May your vows (*vratas*) overflow with *ghee* (clarified butter) and your homes with sweetness! May you be renowned for your noble deeds, may your wishes be fulfilled, and may there be no dearth of anything!

Uttered by the bridegroom, the verse exhorts the bestowers not to waver in their commitment nor to let the betrothal be anulled. He would have so great an abundance of sweet fares at the bride's place that all the wedding guests, the *barātīs*, are fully fed to satiety and pleased: let nothing be wanted. The reason why so much importance has been attached to keeping the date fruit in the mouth is that date palm is considered *tṛṇarāja*—the king of all *tṛṇas* (vegetable kingdom). Those well-versed in vegetable properties regard it as belonging to the highest species among the *tṛṇas* and quite auspicious on that account. It is, therefore, said:

नारिकेलफलं चैव तदन्तर्भक्ष्यमप्युत ।
खर्जूरादिफलं राजन् ! विवाहे मङ्गलप्रदम् ॥

---

1. भस्मनि होमकरणात् षण्ढे कन्याप्रदानतः । कुलधर्मपरित्यागान्नरके नियतं वसेत् ।
bhasmani homakaraṇāt ṣaṇḍhe kanyāpradānataḥ । kuladharmaparityāgānnarake niyataṃ vaset ॥

2. See Appendix I.

nārikelaphalaṁ caiva tadantarbhakṣyamapyuta ।
kharjūrādiphalaṁ rājan! vivāhe maṅgalapradam ॥

Before the betrothal is finalised the age of the girl like that of the bridegroom should also be ascertained. According to कन्याया द्विगुणं वरम् (*kanyāyā dviguṇaṁ varam*), the bridegroom's age must be double the age of the bride. The reason given is: मैथुनं चैकविंशते (*maithunaṁ caikaviṁśate*). In the opinion of the Āyurveda, one should go to bed with a woman twenty-one years one's junior.

According to the Gṛhyasūtras, betrothal marks the beginning of a life of responsibility for both the bridegroom and the bride; it is a great milestone in their lives, signalling that they have now entered the order of householders. Whatever a chaste and virtuous maiden will do hereafter will lead her to the heights attained by such ideal women as Sāvitrī and others. It is clear from the law books that for them no gift is more rewarding and conducive to heavenly happiness than the gift of a daughter (*kanyādāna*)[1]. Are not

---

1. तत्र कन्यादानमाहात्म्यम्–भूमिदानं वृषोत्सर्गो दानं गजसुवर्णयोः। उभयतो वदना गोश्च तुलाया दानमुत्तमम् ॥ कन्यादानं जीवदानं शरणागतपालनम् । वेददानं महाराज महादानानि वै दश । तत्रापि च महाबाहो कन्यादानमनुत्तमम् ॥ कन्यादानात्परं दानं न भूतं न भविष्यति ॥ इति राजमार्तण्डनिरूपणात् । युगान्तरेश्वमेधो यथा च क्रतुराण्मतः। विधिवत्कन्यकादानमश्वमेधसमं फले ॥ इति गोविन्दराजोक्तम् । तिस्रः कोट्योऽर्धकोटी च तीर्थानां वायुरब्रवीत् । दिवि भुव्यन्तरिक्षे च कलौ ते सन्ति जाह्नवि ॥ वेदतन्त्रप्रणीतानि यानि मन्त्राणि सर्वशः। वेदमातुर्जपे तेषां फलं प्रोक्तं कलौ युगे ॥ राजसूयोऽश्वमेधश्च महादानानि यानि च । तेषामपि फलं प्रोक्तं कन्यादाने कलौ युगे ॥ इति पद्मपुराणोक्तम् । चिन्तामणीनां गिरयः कल्पवृक्षाः सहस्रशः । व्रजाश्च कामधेनूनां तत्र गच्छेद् दुहितृदः ॥ काञ्चनानि च हर्म्याणि नद्यः पायसकर्दमाः। फलान्यमृतकल्पानि तत्र गच्छेद् दुहितृदः ॥ इति मार्कण्डेयप्रोक्तम् ।

tatra kanyādānamāhātmyam—bhūmidānaṁ vṛṣotsargo dānaṁ gajasuvarṇayoḥ । ubhayato vadanā, gośca tulāyā dānamuttamam ॥ kanyādānaṁ jīvadānaṁ śaraṇāgatapālanam । vedadānaṁ mahārāja mahādānāni vai daśa ॥ tatrāpi ca mahābāho kanyādānamanuttamam । kanyādānātparaṁ dānaṁ na bhūtaṁ na bhaviṣyati ॥ iti rājamārtaṇḍanirūpaṇāt । yugāntareśvamedho yathā ca kraturāṇmataḥ । vidhivatkanyakādānamaśvamedhasamaṁ phale ॥ iti govindarājoktam । tisraḥ koṭyo'rdhakoṭī ca tīrthānāṁ vāyurabravīt । divi bhuvyantarikṣe ca kalau te santi

such men extremely unfortunate who enjoy themselves by selling off their daughters for a price? They will certainly rot in the pools of blood in Kumbhīpāka, one of the stench-filled, deeply harrowing infernos. There is no man more detestable than one who offers one's daughter for sale, for, according to Sanatkumāra:

अपत्यविक्रयो दोषः कुलद्वयविनाशकः ।
अशास्त्रविहितस्तस्मान्नाचरेदास्तिकः क्वचित् ॥

apatyavikrayo doṣaḥ kuladvayavināśakaḥ ।
aśāstravihitastasmānnācaredāstikaḥ kvacit ॥

The seer brings home the truth that to have one's children up for sale is a grave sin and instrumental in ruining the two families—the family of the person who buys and that of the person who sells. The maiden bought, as if she were a vendible object, feels humiliated and with the passage of time becomes corrupt, her adultery consequently ending in the birth of hybrids and bastards. This alone is enough to ruin the two families and is the reason why the scriptures scorn the practice of selling off one's daughter. The Gītā has clearly directed that:

संकरो नरकायैव कुलघ्नानां कुलस्य च ।
पतन्ति पितरो ह्येषां लुप्तपिंडोदकक्रियाः ॥

saṁkaro narakāyaiva kulaghnānāṁ kulasya ca ।
patanti pitaro hyeṣāṁ luptapiṁḍodakakriyāḥ ॥

All bastards, according to this verse, drag their *kulas*—families—to hell rather than become inheritors and carriers

---

jāhnavi ॥ vedatantrapraṇītāni yāni mantrāṇi sarvaśaḥ । vedamāturjape teṣāṁ phalaṁ proktaṁ kalau yuge ॥ rājasūyo'śvamedhaśca mahādānāni yāni ca । teṣāmapi phalaṁ proktaṁ kanyādāne kalau yuge ॥ iti padmapurāṇoktam । cintāmaṇīnāṁ girayaḥ kalpavṛkṣāḥ sahasraśaḥ । vrajāśca kāmadhenūnāṁ tatra gacched duhitṛdaḥ ॥ kāñcanāni ca harmyāṇi nadyaḥ pāyasakardamāḥ । phalānyamṛtakalpāni tatra gacched duhitṛdaḥ ॥ iti mārkaṇḍeyaproktam ।

of their propitious family traditions. When such a thing happens the fathers also fall in the sphere of the manes (*pitṛloka*). Even Manu has clearly declared the sale of daughters immoral:

आददीत न शूद्रोऽपि शुल्कं दुहितरन्ददत् ॥
ādadita na śūdro'pi śulkaṁ duhitarandadat ॥

which means that śūdras, too, must not take even the smallest gratuity for their daughters. Nor must the twiceborn (*dvija*) accept a gratuity through avarice, for such a deed is extremely sinful. When the śūdras are forbidden to have their daughters up for sale, it follows that by selling their daughters the twiceborn must suffer the torments of hell. This is also the opinion of Maharṣi Āpastamba:

अल्पेनापि हि शुल्केन पिता कन्यां ददाति यः ।
रौरवे बहुवर्षाणि पुरीषं मूत्रमश्नुते ॥
alpenāpi hi śulkena pitā kanyāṁ dadāti yaḥ ।
raurave bahuvarṣāṇi purīṣaṁ mūtramaśnute ॥

He who marries off his daughter for the smallest price remains in the most dreadful of hells, subsisting on urine and faeces for years. The number of years spent in hell has not been counted, but what 'for years' means is thus described in the śāstras:

यावन्ति कन्यारोमाणि तावदब्दान्निरङ्कुशाः ।
लभन्ते यातनां पापाः कन्याविक्रयिणोऽधमाः ॥
yāvanti kanyāromāṇi tāvadabdānniraṅkuśāḥ ।
labhante yātanāṁ pāpāḥ kanyāvikrayiṇo'dhamāḥ ॥

It means that the wicked father who sells his daughter suffers the torments of hell for as many years as there are hairs on the body of the girl, which makes it clear that when sufferings to be endured depend on the number of hairs on the girl's body, then the number of years to be spent in hell will also vary. There is thus no escape at all from the tortures of hell for one who sells one's daughter;

his sufferings are endless, lasting, understandably, till Doomsday. Let us see what the lawbooks have to say in this regard:

अपत्यविक्रये कन्यावरावस्थाविवर्जनम् ।
लोभाऽभिभूतैः क्रियते धर्मायनविनाशनम् ॥

apatyavikraye kanyāvarāvasthāvivarjanam ।
lobhā'bhibhūtaiḥ kriyate dharmāyanavināśanam ॥

In other words, never should a maiden be married to a boy too small or to a person too old. The reason given is that where the suitability of the match is ignored or considered unimportant, the maiden remains childless or becomes a widow or an adulteress. That is to say, when a grown-up girl is married to a youngster, she is deprived of all conjugal happiness and, falling victim to many a wasting disease, soon becomes old. By the time the husband attains manhood with all the bloom of youth, her womb, devoid of all life and creative force, ceases to conceive a child. She is reduced to a state of barrenness, while the maiden married to an old man becomes a widow in the prime of life. The sins of her father, a homicidal criminal, are visited upon her to whom the stigma of widowhood attaches as long as she lives a life of incredibly endless miseries and shameful privations. If her husband is too young or too old, she may in bad company become an adulteress. Then are born the crossbreeds and bastards who bring about the ruin of their *kuladharma*, all the merits earned by the fathers. Nārada's words can be cited in support of this view:

वृद्धस्य तरूणी भार्या मृत्युरेव न संशयः ।
तथा बालो धवो नार्या मृत्युरेव न संशयः ॥

vṛddhasya taruṇī bhāryā mṛtyureva na saṁśayaḥ ।
tathā bālo dhavo nāryā mṛtyureva na saṁśayaḥ ॥

For one who is aged, a young wife is Death just as a child-husband is Death for a full-blown, young woman. In other words, such incompatible pairs, clearly unsuited to each other, are unlikely to have a successful relationship. Consequently, such unions result in grave sins and suffering, which all thinking homo sapiens—men and women—should ponder. Thus will they see before them 'a flowing river' of injustice. Nārada further adds:

बालाय च सुतां नत्वा तथा वृद्धाय मूढ धीः ।
नारीहत्यामवाप्नोति भ्रूणहत्यां विशेषतः ॥

bālāya ca sutāṁ natvā tathā vṛddhāya mūḍha dhīḥ ।
nārīhatyāmavāpnoti bhrūṇahatyāṁ viśeṣataḥ ॥

The stupid father who gives his daughter to a very callow child-husband or to a ripe old man is a criminal who may be charged with the offence of murdering a woman, especially with the crime of foeticide. What is something common and widely heard of is that many women married to child-husbands die of shame and many others married to haggard-looking, aged husbands spend their lives, which they deem meaningless, cursing their parents and sighing sadly in agony. Isn't this a grievous crime? It certainly is, this foeticide which is committed because a young women married to a mere fledgeling or to an old droopy cannot give birth to a child, a fact with which every person having some knowledge of medical science is thoroughly acquainted. Moreover, when God's creative activity which goes on unimpeded receives a setback, what follows as a matter of course is foeticide. To every person, truly wise and sagacious, it should be amply clear that even if a child were by any chance conceived by a woman whose husband is either too young or too old, it will die in the mother's womb or, if born, shortly afterwards. Even if such a child survives, it is extremely weak, a sluggish dunce, an unfortunate victim of imbecility, sickness and unhappiness. Young mothers groaning in pain and unable to get over their bereavement end their lives in unutterable grief, blinded by tearfloods. The sins here mentioned attach to the wicked who sell off their daughters—to those whom the śāstras describe as meaner than the meanest cāṇḍāla. An illuminating parable, related in the *Nārada Purāṇa,* is notable in this context: "Asked by her mother-in-law, a newly married cāṇḍāla woman went one day to a nearby city, about seven kilometres away, for shopping. She bought all she needed; with the remaining money she bought a knife and a quantity of wine for herself and for her husband. Before going back home, she quaffed some of it and proceeded homeward. On the way she found herself so drunk and hungry that she had to sit down wearily close to a cremation ground. Brooding about what to eat to appease her hunger, she stood up and began to look all around, her eyes wide open. In front of her was a dead dog and close to it a funeral pyre in flames. Overcome by hunger that made her feel a churning in her stomach, she made pieces of the dog's flesh with the knife, moistened a lump of earth with her spittle and, smearing the corpse's skull with it, began to cook a meal. She roasted the flesh in alcohol, using the burning pyre as a fireplace. Having done all this, she covered the skull with a piece of the dog's skin, stood in the middle of the roadway and began to shout to the passersby that they should avoid her kitchenette where her meal was getting ready. A high sage named Candra, who heard the Cāṇḍāla woman warn away all intruders in this manner, asked her who she was and what she was cooking in her kitchenette. The Cāṇḍālī then replied:

श्वमांसं सुरया सिक्तं नृकपाले शवाग्निना ।
पाकं करोमि धर्मज्ञ ! पात्रेऽस्मिन् चर्मणावृते ॥

śvamāṁsaṁ surayā siktaṁ nṛkapāle śavāgninā ।
pākaṁ karomi dharmajña! pātre'smin carmaṇāvṛte ॥

"O sage! I am cooking a flesh-meal mixed with alcohol in the skull of a corpse and have covered it with a piece of a dog's skin."

Stunned, the ascetic nervously asked her why she had used the dog's skin to cover the skull. The Cāṇḍāla woman said:

नीचपादरजःपातभीत्या मे चर्मणावृतम् ।
अन्यथा भोजनार्हं मे स्यादिदं न कथंचन ॥

nīcapādarajaḥpātabhītyā me carmaṇāvṛtam ।
anyathā bhojanārhaṁ me syādidaṁ na kathaṁcana ॥

"Lest the dust particles thrown up by the feet of some mean and debased person should fall into it, I have covered the skull with a piece of dog's skin. Food defiled by dust from the feet of some wretched pedestrian is not eatable."

Amazed beyond measure, Candramuni then questioned her: "O most wretched of women! Is there a person in the world meaner than you or a person the dust of whose feet will spoil your food which is already so disgusting and nauseating? Tell me, is there a woman baser than you or a person whose touch will pollute even you?"

Having heard this, the woman answered:

गोहन्ता देवभूहर्त्ता कन्याविक्रयकारकः ।
महापातकिनो लोके चांडालादधिकाऽधमाः ॥

gohantā devabhūharttā kanyāvikrayakārakaḥ ।
mahāpātakino loke cāṁḍālādadhikā'dhamāḥ ॥

"He who slaughters cows and grabs the land given to gods and brāhmaṇs and he who sells off his daughter are much more contemptible than the Cāṇḍālas."

Hearing this, the great sage Candra admitted that what she had said was no doubt true, and added: "I knew it as well, but I have made you repeat it because I wanted other men—wayfarers like me—to hear it."

So saying, the sage went his way accompanied by other travellers. The story here narrated confirms that even Cāṇḍālas are not so wretched and debased as those who sell their daughters. Such a sale is heinous and absolutely forbidded for the Cāturvarṇyas.

अथ

विवाहपद्धतिः

पण्डितभैयारामकृत-कर्मसुबोधिनीभाषाटीकासहिता

श्रीमता रामदत्तेन मन्त्रिणा तस्य सूनुना ।
पद्धतिः क्रियते धर्म्या रम्या वाजसनेयिनाम् ॥१॥

टीकाकर्तुः मंगलम् ॥

श्रीराधेशमपारश्यामलरुचिं सद्भक्तभृङ्गास्पदं
भक्तानां हृदयैकध्याननिलयं देवद्विजानां प्रियम् ।
गोपीचित्तचकोरचन्द्रममलं वेदान्तवेद्यं विभुं
वंशीनादलयानुगं श्रुतिधरं श्रीनन्दलालं भजे ॥१॥

गौडानां सुखबोधनाय च कृता श्रीरामदत्तेन या
मान्या वैदिकगृह्यसूत्रग्रथिता वैवाहिकी पद्धतिः ।
भैयारामसुजन्मना मतिमता तस्येयमानन्ददा
टीका कर्मसुबोधिनी सुसरला भाषा मया तन्यते ॥२॥

दोहा– श्रुति सम्मत शिष्टानुसरण, सुन्दर फल दातार ।
रामदत्त पंडित कहा, कर्म विवाह विचार ॥
उस ही कर्म विवाह की, भैयाराम उदार ।
तिलक सुखद भाषा करै, निज मति के अनुसार ॥

atha
vivāhapaddhatiḥ
paṇḍitabhaiyārāmakṛta-karmasubodhinībhāṣāṭīkāsahītā

śrīmatā rāmadattena mantriṇā tasya sūnunā ।
paddhatiḥ kriyate dharmyā ramyā vājasaneyinām ॥ 1 ॥

ṭīkākartuḥ maṁgalam ॥

śrīrādheśamapāraśyāmalarucim sadbhaktabhṛṅgāspadaṁ
bhaktānāṁ hṛdayaikadhyānanilayaṁ devadvijānāṁ priyam ।

gopīcittacakoracandramamalaṁ vedāntavedyaṁ vibhuṁ
vaṁśīnādalayānugaṁ śrutidharaṁ śrīnandalālaṁ
bhaje ॥ 1 ॥
gauḍānāṁ sukhabodhanāya ca kṛtā śrīrāmadattena yā
mānyā vaidikagṛhyasūtragrathitā vaivāhikī paddhatiḥ ।
bhaiyārāmasujanmanā matimatā tasyeyamānandadā
ṭīkā karmasubodhinī susaralā bhāṣā mayā tanyate ॥ 2 ॥

With due courtesy enjoined by the sacred texts, the śrutis, Paṇḍit Rāmadatta, son of Śrī Gaṇeśa, a gifted interpreter and singer of the Vedic texts, has chanted this invocation, which yields all the most delectable fruits, and has codified the rules and procedures of performing nuptial rites. Avoiding all ambiguity and circumlocution, he has plainly and with all the alluring charm of the text shown how the marriage ceremony and some of its related rites should be performed by the brāhmaṇas, kṣatriyas and vaiśyas who profess faith in the White Yajurveda, in its Mādhyandinī branch which the Vājasaneyins follow, and in the saṁhitās (Vedic mantras) and the Kātyāyana sūtras. No Vedic mantras are permitted to be chanted on the occasion of a śūdra's marriage. An evidence of this is provided by the Yājñavalkya smṛti in which the varṇas have been divided into four categories: brāhmaṇas, kṣatriyas, vaiśyas and śūdras.[1] Of these only the first three can have all their ceremonies from birth to death performed according to the Vedic rules, not the śūdras. Since women, too, are debarred from wearing the sacrificial cord, they must not be initiated into the Vedas. This is a theory propounded by Yājñavalkya the great seer.

तत्र कन्याहस्तेन षोडशहस्तमितं मंडपं विधाय तद्दक्षिणस्यां दिशि पश्चिमां दिशमाश्रित्य मंडपसंलग्नमुत्तराऽभिमुखं कौतुकागारं च

---

1. ब्रह्मक्षत्रियविट्शूद्रा वर्णास्त्वाद्यास्त्रयो द्विजाः । निषेकादिश्मशानान्तास्तेषां वै मन्त्रतः क्रियाः ॥
brahmakṣatrīyaviṭśūdrā varṇāstvādyāstrayo dvijāḥ । niṣekādiśmaśānāntāsteṣāṁ vai mantratah kriyāḥ ॥

मंडपाद्बहिरैशान्यां जामातृचतुर्हस्तपरिमितां सिकतादिपरिष्कृतां वेदीञ्च कारयेत् ।

tatra kanyāhastena ṣoḍaśahastamitaṁ maṁḍapaṁ vidhāya taddakṣiṇasyāṁ diśi pascimāṁ diśamāśritya maṁḍapasaṁlagnamuttarā'bhimukhaṁ kautukāgāraṁ ca maṁḍapādbahiraiśānyāṁ jāmātṛcaturhastaparimitāṁ sikatādipariṣkṛtaṁ vedīñca kārayet ।

Before the ceremony proper begins, a temporary sacrificial shed (maṁḍapa) measuring 24 x 16 aṁgulas or about 18 x 16 inches (or sixteen times the length between the bride's elbow and the tip of her middle finger) should be erected. Its door should be in the southern corner adjacent to the western quarter. In other words, it should be located in the south-west quarter, the *nirṛti koṇa*, and face the north. At such a place, splendidly decorated and festooned with beautiful festal things, should all the customary family rites be performed. Outside the maṁḍapa but close to it in the north-east quarter, an altar with four supporting poles measuring four times the area between the bridegroom's elbow and the tip of his middle finger should be constructed for the sacrificial fire. There should not be any inauspicious, forbidden object on the altar such as hair, husk or pieces of brick or stone. According to the sage Kātyāyana, a *tilaka maṁḍapa* for setting up the planets must also be constructed after the four-poled altar has been built for the sacrificial fire. What Brahmā says in the context of Vṛndā's marriage in the *Brahmāṇḍa Purāṇa* supports this instruction. When the sun is in the house of Virgo (*Kanyā rāśi*) or Leo (*Siṁha rāśi*) or Libra (*Tulā rāśi*), the supporting poles should be fixed in the north-east quarter; when the sun is in the house of Scorpio (*Vṛścika rāśi*), or Sagittarius (*Dhanu rāśi*) or Capricorn (*Makara rāśi*), they should be fixed in the north-west quarter; in the *rāśis* called Pisces (*Mīna*), Aries (*Meṣa*) and Aquarius (*Kumbha*) they should be planted in the south-west quarter; and when the sun is in the Taurus (*Vṛṣa*), Gemini (*Mithuna*) and Cancer

(*Karka*) *rāśis* the poles should be fixed in the south-east corner (*Agni Koṇa*) ruled over by Agni.[1] This is how the sacrificial pavilion for the marriage rites should be fixed. The Brahma Purāṇa confirms this[2] and says that for the elimination of all obstructions and for peace and happiness throughout one's various lives, the wise have a Maṁḍapa erected for marital festivities. What the Maṁḍapa should look like has been described thus[3]: it should have four *staṁbhas* or supporting poles and four magnificent gateways decked with various festoons and charming hangings and fringes. The Maṁḍapa should be decorated with all manner of jewels, ivory flowers showing birds of varied plumage buzzing and whistling in the rustling breeze.

---

1. सूर्येङ्गनासिंहघटेषु शैवे स्तंभोऽलिकोदंडमृगेषु वायौ । मीनाऽजकुंभे निर्ऋतौ विवाहे स्थाप्योऽग्निकोणे मृग्युगमकर्के ॥

sūryeṅganāsiṁhaghaṭeṣu śaive staṁbho'likodaṁḍamṛgeṣu vāyau । mīnā'jakuṁbhe nirṛtau vivāha sthāpyo'gnikoṇe mṛgyugamakarke ॥

2. विवाहोत्सवयज्ञेषु मंडपं कल्पयेत्सुधीः । सर्वविघ्नविनाशाय सर्वेषां चित्ततुष्टये ॥

vivāhotsavayajñeṣu maṁḍapaṁ kalpayetsudhīḥ । sarvavighnavināśāya sarveṣāṁ cittatuṣṭaye ॥

3. चतुःस्तम्भसमायुक्तं चतुर्द्वारं सुशोभनम् । अनेकवर्षिकायुक्तं तोरणैः समलंकृतम् ॥ विहंगैः कृत्रिमैर्जुष्टं कूजद्भिर्वातयोगतः । मनोहरद्भिः सर्वेषां प्रेक्षकाणां समन्ततः ॥ शिल्पकर्मातिनिपुणं विश्वकर्मविनिर्मितम् । चित्रितं चित्रकारैश्च रंजितं रागकारिभिः ॥ मंडितं मणिभिः पुष्पैर्दन्तैर्वस्त्रैरलंकृतम् । सवितानं विधातव्यं तत्प्रकृष्टेन वाससा ॥ दक्षिणस्यां पराभागे कल्पयेत् मंडपान्तिके । विवाहे कौतुकागारं नारीशालां तथाध्वरे ॥ मंडपाद्बहिरैशान्यां वेदीञ्चैवाग्निहेतवे । मंडलाद्वहिरैशान्यामित्यपि पाठः कलाविति विशेषः ।

catuḥstambhasamāyuktaṁ caturdvāraṁ suśobhanam । anekavarṣikāyuktaṁ toraṇaiḥ samalaṁkṛtam ॥ vihaṁgaiḥ kṛtrimairjuṣṭaṁ kūjadbhirvātayogataḥ । manoharadbhiḥ sarveṣāṁprekṣakāṇāṁ samantataḥ ॥ śilpakarmātinipuṇaṁ viśvakarmavinirmitam । citritaṁ citrakāraiśca raṁjitaṁ rāgakāribhiḥ ॥ maṁḍitaṁ maṇibhiḥ puṣpairdantairvastrairalaṁkṛtam । savitānaṁ vidhātavyaṁ tatprakṛṣṭena vāsasā ॥ dakṣiṇasyāṁ parābhāge kalpayet maṁḍapāntike । vivāhe kautukāgāraṁ nārīśālāṁ tathādhvare ॥ maṁḍapādbahiraiśānyaṁ vedīñcaivāgnihetave । maṁḍalādvahiraiśānyāmityapi pāṭhaḥ kalāviti viśeṣaḥ ।

Standing on its four supporting *stambhas* or posts and having four beautiful (triumphal) arches, the Maṁḍapa must also be decorated with newly-dyed gorgeous canopies pleasantly studded with jewels expressive of the divine artifice of Viśvakarmā himself. Towards the southern quarter and close to the pavilion a sort of pleasure-house (*Kohabara or Kautukāgāra*) for women should be set apart, an auspicious spot where the female guests and members of the family assemble. Then an altar for the sacrificial fire should be constructed in the north-east quarter outside the Maṁḍapa. While constructing it, all the directives of the śāstras must be strictly followed.[1] It should accord with such instructions as follows:

Having erected the Maṁḍapa first for such sacrificial festivities as those accompanying marriages, a beautiful spot to the west of it, all smeared with pure, dazzling white

---

1. यज्ञोत्सवविवाहेपु विधायादौ च मंडपम् । धर्मदिक्पश्चिमे भागे कौतुकागारमुत्तमम् ॥ लेपितं शुद्धमृदया शुद्धये च सुशोभनम् । अधिष्ठितं सुकुंभेन निश्छिद्रेण दृढेन च ॥ चतुराननदीपेनाधिष्ठितेन सुशोभना । घृतेन तिलतैलेन ज्वलता वा दिवानिशम् ॥ विधातृप्रतिमां तत्र कन्या प्रयतमानसा । ब्रह्मचर्यव्रतवती स्नाता चैकाग्रमानसा ॥ एकवस्त्रा च स्वमनः संयम्यालीसमन्विता । ध्यायेच्चतुर्मुखीमष्टभुजां च कमलासने ॥ तिष्ठतीं कर्मफलदां समर्था योगसेविताम् । रूपयौवनसौभाग्यलब्धये यशसे तथा ॥ गृहाधिपत्यसिद्ध्यर्थं वश्याय गृहपुष्टये । सर्वविघ्नविनाशाय विवाहे मंगलाय च ॥ पितुश्च श्वशुरस्यापि यशसे चार्थसिद्धये । विवाहकौतुकं हस्ते बिभ्रती कन्यकावृता । कौतुकागारमध्यासेदित्याहाथर्वणी श्रुतिः ॥

yajñotsavavivāheṣu vidhāyādau ca maṁḍapam । dharmadikpaścime bhage kautukāgāramuttamam ॥ lepitaṁ śuddhamṛdayā śuddhaye ca suśobhanam । adhiṣṭhitaṁ sukuṁbhena niśchidreṇa dṛḍhena ca ॥ caturānanadīpenādhiṣṭhitena suśobhanā । ghṛtena tilatailena jvalatā vā divāniśam ॥ vidhātṛpratimaṁ tatra kanyā prayatamānasā । brahmacaryavratavatī snātā caikāgramānasā ॥ ekavastrā ca svamanaḥ saṁyamyālīsamnvitā । dhyāyeccaturmukhīṃaṣṭabhujāṁ ca kamalāsane ॥ tiṣṭhatīṁ karmaphaladāṁ samarthā yogasevitām । rūpayauvanasaubhāgyalabdhaye yaśase tathā ॥ gṛhādhipatyasidhyartha vaśyāya gṛhapuṣṭaye । sarvavighnavināśāya vivāhe maṁgalāya ca ॥ pituśca śvaśurasyāpi yaśase cārthasiddhaye । vivāhakautukaṁ haste bibhratī kanyakāvṛtā । kautukāgāramadhyādityāhātharvaṇī śrutiḥ ॥

clay, should be set apart for the Kautukāgāra. Here the beautiful sacrificial pitcher (*kalaśa*), which has no aperture whatever in it, should be firmly placed. It should be brightly lighted with a quadrangular earthen lamp burning day and night with fragrant ghee or the oil of gingelly seeds. Having fixed the idol of Bhagavatī, the goddess of Fate or Destiny personified, the maiden should wash and bathe herself and, keeping the vow of chastity and dressed in pure, clean-washed robes, should not let her mind oscillate or run wild. Instead, she should meditate on the goddess Bhagavatī resplendent on her lotus seat. The four-faced and eight-armed goddess, on whom she must mentally concentrate, is the bestower of the fruit of action and of power. She should remain seated in the Kautukāgāra for winning over Gṛhādhipatya-Siddhi (dominance, power and control over the family of her husband which she will now be joining) for peace, prosperity and cementing the family ties, warding off all calamities, blessing the marital rites, and for fame and fulfilment of all desires by her father and father-in-law. The Atharvaveda śruti confirms this. Later, the seer Āpastamba enunciates the same theory[1] and declares that in a marriage or in a sacrifice one should construct a pavilion, first and then in the north-east quarter outside place the Maṁḍapa Kalaśa—the sacrificial pitcher on the altar. In the centre of the Maṁḍapa construct the tilaka maṁḍala and install Gaṇeśa therein. Having done this, let a fire on the altar be lit after duly worshipping Agni (who is a witness to every sacrificial act. To this Kaśyapa

१. विधाय मंडपं पूर्वं विवाहे चाध्वरे तथा । तदैशान्यां बहिस्तस्माद्वेदीं कुंभं च मंडपे ॥ गणेशं स्थापयेन्मध्ये कृत्वा तिलकमंडलम् । वेद्याञ्च स्थापयेद्वह्निं साक्षित्वायार्चनाय च ॥

vidhāya maṁḍapaṁ pūrvaṁ vivāhe cādhvare tathā । tadaiśānyāṁ bahistasmādvedīṁ kuṁbhaṁ ca maṁḍape ॥ gaṇeśaṁ sthāpayenmadhye kṛtvā tilakamaṁḍalam । vedyāñca sthāpayedvahniṁ sākṣitvāyārcanāya ca॥

and Parāśara[1] especially add that in the Satyayuga (or Kṛta), the golden age, Tretā and Dvāpara—the first three cosmic ages—the altar should be constructed outside the pavilion for the installation of fire (Agni) in such ceremonies as that of marriage. It means that *maṁdapādbahiraiśānyaṁ* should be pronounced as it is in the Satyayuga, Tretā and Dvāpara, but in the Kaliyuga it would just be *maṁḍalādbahiḥ*. In other words, in the first three cosmic ages—the Satyayuga, Tretā and Dvāpara—the 'p' was pronounced, but in the last degenerated age, the present Kaliyuga, 'p' is replaced by 'l'. What is meant by this is that the altar should be constructed in the maṁḍapa itself, not outside it, towards the north-east quarter adjacent to the *tilaka maṁḍala*. The seer Marīci supports this view and says[2] that in the first three cosmic ages, beginning with the Satyayuga, religious observances thrilled the hearts of the performers, expanded them, but in the last, dark age—the Kaliyuga—the thrill has undergone a sort of diminution (for people are rather reluctantly drawn towards such observances). What it proves is that in the present age when religious practices have suffered a kind of devaluation, it is advisable to construct the altar not outside the maṁḍapa but outside the *tilaka maṁḍala*.

---

1. मंडपाद्बहिरैशान्यां सदा कुर्याच्च वेदिकाम् । अग्न्यर्थञ्च विवाहादौ कृतादिषु युगेषु वै ॥ इति पकारस्थाने लकारोच्चारणं सर्वत्र वाक्येष्विति कलियुगे । अन्ययुगेषु च व्यवस्था महद्भिः स्थापिता सैव मन्तव्येत्यर्थः ।

maṁḍapādbahiraiśānyāṁ sadā kuryācca vedikām । agnyarthañca vivāhādau kṛtādiṣu yugeṣu vai ॥ iti pakārasthāne lakāroccāraṇaṁ sarvatra vākyeṣviti kaliyuge ॥ anyayugeṣu ca vyavasthā mahadbhiḥ sthāpitā saiva mantavyetyarthaḥ ।

2. कृते भोगे मनोमोद उदारत्वं गमिष्यति । कलौ जनस्तु संकोचं धर्मकार्ये विशेषतः ॥ देशधर्मादिसंकोचाद्वेदी स्याद् मंडलाद्बहिः ॥

kṛte bhoge manomoda udāratvaṁ gaṁiṣyati । kalau janastu saṁkocaṁ dharmakārye viśeṣataḥ ॥ deśadharmādisaṁkocādvedī syād maṁḍalādbahiḥ ॥

Kātyāyana is of the same view when he argues that in nuptial rites a maṁḍala called tilaka[1] should be made. Outside that maṁḍala but in the adjoining north-east quarter an altar should be constructed for the installation of Agni (Fire), which tantamounts to saying that the *tilaka maṁḍala* and the altar should be inside the maṁḍapa. That explains why it is not proper to construct the altar outside the maṁḍapa. A little further the seer Kātyāyana has described the Sarvatobhadra and *tilaka maṁḍala,*[2] saying that in the former (i.e. Sarvatobhadra) the planets, such as the sun, are in the centre and the gods, like Indra, in their own allotted quarters, but Gaṇeśa is resplendently present outside. The *tilaka maṁḍala* is that at the centre of which Gaṇeśa is stationed and no other deity and that around which all other gods are stationed in their respective quarter. This grand and glorious orb (*maṁḍala*) is fittingly called *tilaka maṁḍala.* According to this description, for offering oblation to Agni on the occasions of Navagraha, the worship of Durgā, inauguration of house-construction or plantation of trees, the Sarvatobhadra Maṁḍala should be made, but in marriages, it is advisable to make *tilaka maṁḍala.*[3] The excellent seer Marīci says,

---

1. विवाहादौ लिखेन्नित्यं तिलकं नाम मंडलम् ॥

vivāhādau likhennityaṁ tilakaṁ nāma maṁḍalam ॥

2. सूर्यादयो ग्रहा यत्र राजन्ते मध्यसंस्थिताः । इन्द्रादयो प्रतिदिशं स्वस्वभागेष्ववस्थिताः ॥ बहिः शिवसुताद्याश्च सर्वतोभद्रमुच्यते । विघ्नराजो भवेद्यत्र मध्ये नान्यस्तु कश्चन ॥ सुमहत्सुंदरं चैव तिलकं नाम मंडलम् । गृहारामप्रतिष्ठायां दुर्गाहोमे नवग्रहे । सर्वतोभद्रकं कुर्यात् विवाहे तिलकं लिखेत् ।

sūryādayo grahā yatra rājante madhyasaṁsthitāḥ । indrādayo pratidiśaṁ svasvabhāgeṣvavasthitāḥ ॥ bahiḥ śivasutādyāśca sarvatobhadramucyate । vighnarājo bhavedyatra madhye nānyastu kaścana ॥ sumahatsuṁdaraṁ caiva tilakaṁ nāma maṁḍalam । gṛhārāmapratiṣṭhāyāṁ durgāhome navagrahe । sarvatobhadrakaṁ kuryāt vivāhe tilakaṁ likhet ।

3. वेदी बहिः स्याद्यदि मंडपाच्च तत्तूर्यभागेन च वेदिका स्यात् । वेदी यदा मण्डलतो बहिः स्यात्सा वेदिका हस्तमिता प्रतिष्ठा ॥

vedī bahiḥ syādyadi maṁḍapācca tattūryabhāgena ca vedikā syāt । vedi yadā maṇḍalato bahiḥ syātsā vedikā hastamitā pratiṣṭhā ॥

adding, that the maṁḍapa measures sixteen times the length between the elbow and the tip of the middle finger (roughly, 24 ft); if the sacrificial altar is outside that maṁḍapa it should be a square, each side measuring six feet with a height of eighteen inches. It should be inside the maṁḍapa connected with the *tilaka maṁḍala*. Such is the shape of the altar which Manu conceived,[1] saying: An altar should everywhere be four *aṁgulas* high. (An *aṁgula* is a finger's breadth=eight barley corns.)

विवाहदिने कृतनित्यक्रियेण जामातृपित्रा मातृपूजापूर्वकमाभ्युदयिकं कर्तव्यम् । कन्यापिता शुचिः स्नात्वा शुक्लाम्बरः कृतनित्यक्रियो मातृपूजाभ्युदयिकं कृत्वा अथ चार्हणवेलायां मण्डपे आगत्य चोदङ्मुखः गणेशकलशगौर्यादिदेवानां पूजनं कुर्यात् । सङ्कल्पश्चैवं कर्तव्यः ।

vivāhadine kṛtanityakriyeṇa jāmātṛpitrā mātṛpūjā-pūrvakamābhyudayikaṁ kartavyam । *kanyāpitā śuciḥ snātvā śuklāmbaraḥ kṛtanityakriyo mātṛpūjābhyudayikaṁ kṛtvā atha cārhaṇavelāyāṁ maṇḍape āgatya codaṅmukhaḥ gaṇeśakalaśagauryādidevānāṁ pūjanaṁ kuryāt* । *saṅkalpaścaivaṁ kartavyaḥ* ।

Having performed all the auspicious daily rites and offered his evening prayer, the bridegroom's father should perform the Nāṁdīmukha Śrāddha[2] along with Mātṛpūjā

---

१. सर्वत्र वेदी चतुरंगुलोच्छ्रिता विनिर्मिता सैकतमृत्तिकादिभिः । द्विधा तु सा केवलवेदिकात्मिका परा युतास्तम्भचतुष्टयेन या ॥

sarvatra vedī caturaṁgulocchrita vinirmitā saikatamṛt-tikādibhiḥ । dvidhā tu sā kevalavedikātmikā parā yutāstambha-catuṣṭayena yā ॥

2. Śrāddha is "a ceremony in honour and for the benefit of dead relatives observed with great strictness at various fixed periods and on occasions of rejoicing as well as mourning by the surviving relatives. . . these ceremonies are performed by the daily offering of water and on stated occasions by the offering of Piṇḍas or balls of rice and meal. . . to three paternal and three maternal forefathers, i.e. to father, grandfather, and great grand-father; it should be borne in mind that a Śrāddha is not a funeral

on the wedding day. In like manner the bride's father also should take a bath while the bridegroom is being greeted with worshipful regard. Having performed his daily rites and offered his evening prayers, he should don new garments and perform the morning Ṣoḍaśamātṛkā Pūjana and Naṁdīmukha Śrāddha. Having done so, he should then come to the pavilion and facing the north should worship Gaṇeśa, the sacred vessel (*kalaśa*) and such deities as Gauri, etc. ('Ṣoḍaśamātṛkā' refers to the divine mothers or personified energies of the principal deities, sometimes reckoned as sixteen: *viz.* Gauri, Padmā, Śacī, Medhā, Sāvitrī, Vijayā, Jayā, Deva-Senā, Svadhā, Svāhā, Śānti, Pushṭi, Dhṛti, Tushṭi, Ātma-devatā and kula-devatā.)

His first resolution should be as follows:

देशकालौ सकीर्त्याऽमुकगोत्रोऽमुकशर्म्माहमस्या अमुकनाम्न्या मम कन्यायाः भर्त्रा सह धर्मप्रजोत्पादनगृह्यपरिग्रहधर्माचरणेष्वधिकारसिद्धिद्वारा श्रीलक्ष्मीनारायणप्रीत्यर्थं विवाहाख्यं कर्म करिष्ये । तदङ्गविहितं निर्विघ्नता-प्राप्तिकामनया गणपत्यादिपूजनस्वस्तिपुण्याहवाचनं मातृकापूजनञ्च करिष्ये इतिः संकल्पः । एवं कन्यापिता गणपत्यादिदेवान् संपूज्योदङ्मुखः प्राङ्मुखं वरमूर्ध्वजानुं संबोध्येत्युच्चारयेद् भवानपि देवानर्चयतु तत्पश्चाद्भवन्तमर्चयिष्यामः ।

deśakālau sakīrtyā'mukagotro'mukaśarmmāhamasyā amukanāmnyā mama kanyāyāḥ bhartrā saha dharma-prajotpādanagṛhyaparigrahadharmācaraṇeṣvadhikara-siddhidvārā śrīlakṣmīnārāyaṇaprityarthaṁ vivāhākhyaṁ

---

ceremony (*antyeṣṭi*) but a supplement to such a ceremony; it is an act of reverential homage to a deceased person performed by relatives, and is moreover supposed to supply the dead with strengthening nutriment after the performance of the previous funeral ceremonies has endowed them with ethereal bodies." (Monier-Williams)

Nāṁdīmukha Śrāddha is "a Śrāddha offered to a class of deceased ancestors (according to some the 3 ancestors preceding the great-grandfather)".

karma kariṣye । tadaṅgavihitaṁ nirvighnatāprāptikāmanayā gaṇapatyādipūjanasvastipuṇyāhavācanaṁ mātṛkā-pūjanañca kariṣye iti saṁkalpaḥ । evaṁ kanyāpitā gaṇapatyādidevān saṁpūjyodaṅmukhaḥ prāṅmukhaṁ varamūrdhvajānuṁ saṁbodhyetyuccārayed bhavānapi devānarcayatu tatpaścādbhavantamarcayiṣyāmaḥ ।

That is to say, uttering the above Saṁkalpa (determinations), the bride's father should first pay obeisance to Gaṇapati and other deities and then stand with his face towards the north. Addressing the bridegroom, who faces the east, he should ask him to worship the gods, adding that he too would follow suit by reverencing him.

एवं श्रुत्वा वरो गणपत्यादिपूजनविधौ चाक्षतान्गृहीत्वा संकल्पं कुर्यात् ।

evaṁ śrutvā varo gaṇapatyādipūjanavidhau cākṣa-tāngṛhītvā saṁkalpaṁ kuryāt ।

On the advice of the host and in keeping with the manner of worshipping such gods as Gaṇeśa, the bride-groom should utter the following Saṁkalpa:[1]

हरिः ॐ विष्णुः ३ इत्यादि० अद्य ब्रह्मणोऽह्नि द्वितीयपरार्द्धे श्रीश्वेतवाराहकल्पे वैवस्वतमन्वन्तरे अष्टाविंशतितमे कलियुगे कलिप्रथमचरणे जम्बूद्वीपे भरतखण्डे आर्यावर्तान्तर्गतब्रह्मावर्तैकदेशे कुमारिकानाम्नि क्षेत्रे रामराज्ये कुरुक्षेत्राद्बहिर्मंडलेऽमुकनाम्नि संवत्सरेऽमुकायने सूर्येऽमुकर्तौ अमुकमासेऽमुकपक्षेऽमुकतिथावमुकवासरे

---

1. The ceremonies preceding the marriage day are the following: In the beginning the most auspicious god Gaṇeśa is worshipped and his symbol is installed in the nuptial canopy erected according to the rules laid down in the scriptures. The bride's father as well as her mother wears auspicious robes and having seated himself, he sips water, restrains his breath, and offers prayer to place and time, making up his mind (Saṁkalpa) to perform Svastivacana, Maṇḍapa-pratiṣṭhā, Mātṛpūjana, Vasordhārāpūjana, Āyuṣyajapa and Nāndi-śrāddha as ancillary to marriage.

यथावर्तमाननक्षत्रयोगकरणमुहूर्तवर्तमाने यथास्थानस्थितेषु सर्वेषु ग्रहेषु सत्सु अमुकगोत्रोत्पन्नोऽमुकशर्म्माहं मम विवाहोत्सवकर्मप्रारम्भनिमित्तं निर्विघ्नेन धर्मार्थकामसिद्धिद्वारा श्रीपरमेश्वरप्रीतिपूर्वकगार्हस्थ्यसुखप्राप्ति-कामनया करिष्यमाणविवाहसंस्कारकर्मणि आदौ गणपत्यादिग्रहाणां समातृकाणां सकलशानामावाहनं प्रतिष्ठापूजनस्तवनं च करिष्ये ।

hariḥ aum viśṇuḥ 3 ityādi adya brahmaṇo'hni dvitīyaparārddhe śrīśvetavārāhakalpe vaivasvata-manvantare aṣṭāviṁśatitame kaliyuge kaliprathamacaraṇe jambūdvīpe bharatakhaṇḍe āryāvartāntargata-brahmāvartaikadeśe kumārikānāmni kṣetre rāmarājye kurukṣetrādbahirmaṁḍale'mukanāmni saṁvatsare-'mukāyane sūrye'mukartau amukamāse 'mukapakṣe-'mukatithāvamukavāsare yathāvartamānanakṣatra-yogakaraṇamuhūrtavartamāne yathāsthānasthiteṣu sarveṣu graheṣu satsu amukgotrotpanno'mukaśarmmāhaṁ mama vivāhotsavakarmaprārambhanimittaṁ, nirvighnena dharmārthakāmasiddhidvārā śrīparameśvaraprītipūrvaka-gārhasthyasukhaprāptikāmanayā kariṣyamāṇavivāha-saṁskārakarmaṇi ādau gaṇapatyādigrahāṇāṁ samātṛ-kāṇāṁ sakalaśānāmāvāhanaṁ pratiṣṭhāpūjanastavanaṁ ca kariṣye ।

अथ स्वस्तिवाचनम्

ॐ स्वस्ति न इन्द्रो वृद्धश्रवाः स्वस्ति नः पूषा विश्ववेदाः । स्वस्ति नस्ताक्ष्यो अरिष्टनेमिः स्वस्ति नो बृहस्पतिर्दधातु ॥१॥ पयः पृथिव्यां पय ओषधीषु पयो दिव्यन्तरिक्षे पयो धाः पयस्वतीः प्रदिशः सन्तु मह्यम् ॥२॥ विष्णो रराटमसि विष्णोः श्नप्त्रे स्थो विष्णोः स्यूरसि विष्णोर्ध्रुवोऽसि वैष्णवमसि विष्णवे त्वा ॥३॥ अग्निदेवता वातो देवता सूर्यो देवता चन्द्रमा देवता वसवो देवता रूद्रा देवतादित्या देवता मरुतो देवता विश्वेदेवा देवता बृहस्पतिर्देवतेन्द्रो देवता वरुणो देवता ॥४॥ द्यौः शान्तिरन्तरिक्ष्ँ शान्तिः पृथिवी शान्तिरापः शान्तिरोषधयः शान्तिः । वनस्पतयः शान्तिर्विश्वेदेवाः शान्तिर्ब्रह्म शान्तिः सर्वँ् शान्तिः शान्तिरेव शान्तिः सा मा शान्तिरेधि ॥५॥ विश्वानि देव सवितर्दुरितानि परासुव ।

यद्भद्रं तन्न आसुव ॥६॥ इमा रुद्राय तवसे कपर्दिने क्षयद्वीराय प्रभरामहे मतीः । यथा शमसद्द्विपदे चतुष्पदे विश्वं पुष्टं ग्रामे अस्मिन्ननातुरम् ॥७॥ एतं ते देव सवितर्यज्ञं प्राहुर्बृहस्पतये ब्रह्मणे । तेन यज्ञमव तेन यज्ञपतिं तेन मामव ॥८॥ मनो जूतिर्जुषतामाज्यस्य बृहस्पतिर्यज्ञमिमं तनोत्वरिष्टं यज्ञँ समिमं दधातु । विश्वेदेवास हि मादयन्तामों प्रतिष्ठ ॥९॥ एष वै प्रतिष्ठा नाम यज्ञो यत्रैतेन यज्ञेन यजन्ते सर्वमेव प्रतिष्ठितं भवति ॥१०॥ एवं स्वस्त्ययनोच्चारणं कृत्वा गणानांत्वेतिमन्त्रेण गणपत्याऽऽवाहनं कुर्यात् ।

ॐ गणानां त्वा गणपतिँ हवामहे प्रियाणां त्वा प्रियपतिँ हवामहे निधीनां त्वा निधिपतिँ हवामहे वसो मम । आहमजानि गर्भधमा त्वमजासि गर्भधम् ॥१॥ नमो गणेभ्यो गणपतिभ्यश्च वो नमो नमो व्रातेभ्यो व्रातपतिभ्यश्च वो नमो नमो गृत्सेभ्यो गृत्सपतिभ्यश्च वो नमो नमो विरूपेभ्यो विश्वरूपेभ्यश्च वो नमो नमः ॥२॥ ॐ सुमुखश्चैकदन्तश्च कपिलो गजकर्णकः । लम्बोदरश्च विकटो विघ्ननाशो विनायकः ॥१॥ धूम्रकेतुर्गणाध्यक्षो भालचन्द्रो गजाननः । द्वादशैतानि नामानि यः पठेच्छृणुयादपि ॥२॥ विद्यारम्भे विवाहे च प्रवेशे निर्गमे तथा । संग्रामे संकटे चैव विघ्नस्तस्य न जायते ॥३॥ गणपतये नमः । गजवक्त्र गणाध्यक्ष सर्वविघ्नविनाशन । लम्बोदर विरूपाक्ष आगच्छ गणनायक ॥ इति गणपतिमावाह्य पूजनं कुर्यात् । पाद्यम् अर्घ्यं स्नानं गंधम् अक्षतान् धूपं दीपं नैवेद्यं मुखवासार्थं ताम्बूलम् पूगीफलम् दक्षिणाद्रव्यम् नमस्कारं समर्पयामि । सर्वदेवपूजनेष्वेवं ज्ञातव्यम् ।

atha svastivācanam

aum svasti na indro vṛddhaśravāḥ svasti naḥ pūṣā viśvavedāḥ । *svasti nastārkṣyo ariṣṭanemiḥ svasti no bṛhaspatirdadhātu* ॥ 1 ॥ *payaḥ pṛthivyāṁ paya oṣadhīṣu payo divyantarikṣe payo dhāḥ payasvatiḥ pradiśaḥ santu mahyam* ॥ 2 ॥ *viṣṇo rarāṭamasi viṣṇoḥ śnaptre stho viṣṇoḥ syūrasi viṣṇordhuvo'si vaiṣṇavamasi viṣṇave tvā* ॥ 3 ॥ *agnirdevatā vāto devatā sūryo devatā candramā devatā vasavo devatā rudrā devatādityā devatā maruto devatā viśvedevā devatā bṛhaspatirdevatendro devatā varuṇo devatā* ॥ 4 ॥ *dyauḥ śāntirantarikṣaṁ śāntiḥ pṛthivī śāntirāpaḥ śāntiroṣadhayaḥ śāntiḥ* । *vanaspatayaḥ śāntirviśvedevāḥ śātirbrahma śāntiḥ, sarvaṁ śāntiḥ śāntireva śāntiḥ sā mā śāntiredhi* ॥ 5 ॥ *viśvānideva savitarduritāni parāsuva* । *yadbhadraṁ tanna āsuva* ॥ 6 ॥ *imā rudrāya tavase kapardine kṣayadvīrāya prabharāmahe matīḥ* । *yathā śamasaddvipade catuṣpade viśvaṁ puṣṭaṁ grāme asminnanāturam* ॥ 7 ॥ *etaṁ te deva savitaryajñaṁ prāhurbṛhaspataye brahmaṇe* । *tena yajñamava tena yajñapatiṁ tena māmava* ॥ 8 ॥ *mano jūtirjuṣ-atāmājyasya bṛhaspatiryajñamimaṁ tanotvariṣṭaṁ yajñaṁ samimaṁ dadhātu* । *viśvedevāsa iha mādayantāmoṁ pratiṣṭha* ॥ 9 ॥ *eṣa vai pratiṣṭhā nāma yajño yatraitena yajñena yajante sarvameva pratiṣṭhitaṁ bhavati* ॥ 10 ॥ *evaṁ svastyayanoccāraṇaṁ kṛtvā gaṇānāṁtvetimantreṇa gaṇapatyā"vāhanaṁ kuryāt* ।

aum gaṇānāṁ tvā gaṇapatiṁ havāmahe priyāṇāṁ tvā priyapatiṁ havāmahe nidhīnāṁ tvā nidhipatiṁ havāmahe vaso mama । *āhamajāni garbhadhamā tvamjāsi garbha-dham* ॥ 1 ॥ *namo gaṇebhyo gaṇapatibhyaśca vo namo namo vrātebhyo vrātapatibhyaśca vo namo namo gṛtsebhyo gṛtsapatibhyaśca vo namo namo virūpebhyo viśvarūpe-bhyaśca vo namo namaḥ* ॥ 2 ॥ *aum sumukhaścaikadantaśca kapilo gajakarṇakaḥ* । *lambodaraśca vikaṭo vighnanāśo vināyakaḥ* ॥ 1 ॥ *dhūmraketurgaṇādhyakṣo bhālacandro gajānanaḥ* । *dvādaśaitāni nāmāni yaḥ paṭhecchṛṇu-yādapi* ॥ 2 ॥ *vidyārambhe vivāhe ca praveśe nirgame tathā* । *saṁgrāme saṁkaṭe caiva vighnastasya na jāyate* ॥ 3 ॥ *gaṇapataye namaḥ* । *gajavaktra gaṇādhyakṣa sarvavighna vināśana* । *lambodara virūpākṣa āgaccha gaṇanāyaka* ॥ *iti gaṇapatimāvāhya pūjanaṁ kuryāt* । *pādyam arghyaṁ snānaṁ gaṁdham akṣatān dhūpaṁ dīpaṁ naivedyaṁ mukhavāsārthaṁ tāmbūlam pūgīphalam dakṣiṇādravyam namaskāraṁ samarpayāmi* । *sarvadevapūjaneṣvevaṁ jñātavyam* ।

अथ कलशस्थापनं पूजनं च

ॐ ऋग्वेदाय नमः । यजुर्वेदाय नमः । सामवेदाय नमः । अथर्ववेदाय नमः । कलशाय नमः । वरुणाय नमः । रुद्राय नमः । समुद्राय नमः ।

गंगायै नमः । यमुनायै नमः । सरस्वत्यै नमः । कलशकुम्भाय नमः । ब्रह्मणा निर्मितस्त्वं हि मन्त्रैरेवाऽमृतोद्भवैः । प्रार्थयामि च त्वां कुम्भ वाञ्छितार्थन्तु देहि मे ॥१॥ ॐ वरूणस्योत्तम्भनमसि वरूणस्य स्कम्भसर्जनी स्थो वरूणस्य ऋतसदन्यसि वरूणस्य ऋतसदनमसि वरूणस्य ऋतसदनमासीद । कलशस्य मुखे विष्णुः कंठे रूद्रः समाश्रितः । मूले तस्य स्थितो ब्रह्मा मध्ये मातृगणः स्थितः । कुक्षौ तु सागराः सप्त सप्तद्वीपा वसुन्धरा । ऋग्वेदोऽथ यजुर्वेदः सामवेदो ह्यथर्वणः । अंगैश्च सहिताः सर्वे कलशं तु समाश्रिताः । देवदानवसंवादे मथ्यमाने महोदधौ । उद्धृतोऽसौ तदा कुम्भः ब्रह्मणा च प्रतिष्ठितः ॥१॥

इति कलशपूजनम् ॥

atha kalaśasthāpanaṁ pūjanaṁ ca

aum ṛgvedāya namaḥ । yajurvedāya namaḥ । sāmavedāya namaḥ । atharvavedāya namaḥ । kalaśāya namaḥ । varuṇāya namaḥ । rudrāya namaḥ । samudrāya namaḥ । gaṁgāyai namaḥ । yamunāyai namaḥ । sarasvatyai namaḥ । kalaśakumbhāya namaḥ । brahmaṇā nirmitastvaṁ hi mantrairevā'mṛtodbhavaiḥ । prārthayāmi ca tvāṁ kumbha vāñchitārthantu dehi me ॥ 1 ॥ aum varuṇasyottambhanamasi varuṇasya skambhasarjanī stho varuṇasya ṛtasadanyasi varuṇasya ṛtasadanamasi varuṇasya ṛtasadanamāsīda । kalaśasya mukhe viṣṇuḥ kaṁṭhe rudraḥ samāśritaḥ । mūle tasya sthito brahmā madhye mātṛgaṇaḥ sthitaḥ । kukṣau tu sāgarāḥ sapta saptadvīpā vasundharā । ṛgvedo'tha yajurvedaḥ sāmavedo hyatharvaṇaḥ । aṁgaiśca sahitāḥ sarve kalaśaṁ tu samāśritāḥ । devadānavasaṁvāde mathyamāne mahodadhau । uddhṛto'sau tadā kumbhaḥ brahmaṇā ca pratiṣṭhitaḥ ॥ 1 ॥

iti kalaśapūjanam ॥

अथ रक्षाविधानम्

ॐ मा नःशँ् सो अररुषो धूर्तिः प्रणङ्मर्त्यस्य । रक्षा णो ब्रह्मणस्पते ॥१॥ ॐ यदाबध्नन्दाक्षायणा हिरण्यँ् शतानीकाय

सुमनस्यमानाः । तन्म अबध्नामि शतशारदायाऽऽयुष्माञ्जरदष्टिर्यथासम् ॥
इति पठन् रक्षां बध्नीयात् ।

atha rakṣāvidhānam

aum mā naḥśaṁ so araruṣo dhūrtiḥ praṇaṅmartyasya । *rakṣā ṇo brahmaṇaspate* ॥ 1 ॥ *aum yadābadhnandākṣāyaṇā hiraṇyaṁ śatānīkāya sumanasyamānāḥ* । *tanma ābadhnāmi śataśāradāyā" yuṣmāñjaradaṣṭiryathāsam* ॥ *iti paṭhan rakṣāṁ badhnīyāt* ।

अथ नवग्रहपूजनम्

ॐ सूर्याय नमः गन्धाक्षतपुष्पधूपदीपनैवेद्यं समर्पयामि भोः सूर्यदेवेहागच्छेह तिष्ठ सुप्रसन्नो भव मम पूजां गृहाण एवं सर्वत्र । ॐ आ कृष्णेन रजसा वर्तमानो निवेशयन्नमृतं मर्त्यञ्च । हिरण्ययेन सविता रथेना देवो याति भुवनानि पश्यन् ॥ सूर्याय नमः ॥१॥ ॐ इमं देवा असपत्नँ् सुवध्वम्महते क्षत्राय महते ज्यैष्ठ्याय महते जानराज्यायेन्द्रस्येन्द्रियाय । इमममुष्य पुत्रममुष्यै पुत्रमस्यै विश एष वोमी राजा सोमोऽस्माकम्ब्राह्मणानँ् राजा ॥ चन्द्रमसे नमः ॥२॥ ॐ अग्निमूर्द्धा दिवः ककुत्पतिः पृथिव्या अयम् अपाँ् रेताँ् सि जिन्वति–भौमाय नमः ॥३॥ ॐ उद्बुध्यस्वाग्ने प्रतिजागृहि त्वमिष्टापूर्ते सँ् सृजेथामयञ्च । अस्मिन्त्सधस्थेऽध्युत्तरस्मिन्विश्वेदेवा यजमानश्च सीदत–बुधाय नमः ॥४॥ ॐ बृहस्पतेऽतियदर्योऽर्हाद्द्युमद्विभाति क्रतुमज्जनेषु । यद्दीदयच्छवस ऋतप्रजात तदस्मासु द्रविणं धेहि चित्रम्–गुरवे नमः ॥५॥ अन्नात्परिस्रुतो रसम्ब्रह्मणा व्यपिबत्क्षत्रं पयः सोमं प्रजापतिः । ऋतेन सत्यमिन्द्रियं विपानँ् शुक्रमन्धस इन्द्रस्येन्द्रियमिदम्पयोमृतम्मधु–शुक्राय नमः ॥६॥ ॐ शन्नो देवीरभिष्टय आपो भवन्तु पीतये । शँय्योरभिस्रवन्तु नः–शनैश्चराय नमः ॥७॥ ॐ कयानश्चित्र आभुवदूती सदावृधः सखा । कया शचिष्ठया वृता–राहवे नमः ॥८॥ केतुं कृण्वन्नकेतवे पेशो मर्य्या अपेशसे । समुषद्भिरजायथाः–केतवे नमः ॥९॥ ब्रह्मा मुरारिस्त्रिपुरान्तकारी भानुः शशी भूमिसुतो बुधश्च । गुरुश्च शुक्रः शनिराहुकेतवः सर्वे ग्रहाः शान्तिकरा भवन्तु ॥ इति नवग्रहपूजा ॥

atha navagrahapūjanam

aum sūryāya namaḥ gandhākṣatapuṣpadhūpadīpanaivedyaṁ samarpayāmi bhoḥ sūryadevehāgaccheha tiṣṭha suprasanno bhava nama pūjāṁ gṛhāṇa evaṁ sarvatra । *aum ā kṛṣṇena rajasā vartamāno niveśayannamṛtaṁ martyañca* । *hiraṇyayena savitā rathenā devo yāti bhuvanāni paśyan* ॥ *sūryāya namaḥ* ॥ 1 ॥ *aum imaṁ devā asapatnaṁ suvadhvammahate kṣatrāya mahate jyaiṣṭhyāya mahate jānarājyāyendrasyendriyāya* । *imamamuṣya putramamuṣyai putramasyai viśa eṣa vomī rājā somo'smākambrāhmaṇānaṁ rājā* ॥ *candramase namaḥ* ॥ 2 ॥ *aum agnimūrddhā divaḥ kakutpatiḥ pṛthivyā ayam apāṁ retāṁ si jinvati—bhaumāya namaḥ* ॥ 3 ॥ *aum udbudhyasvāgne pratijāgṛhi tvam-iṣṭāpūrtte saṁ sṛjethāmayañca* । *asmintsadhasthe-'dhyuttarasminviśvedevā yajamānaśca sīdata—budhāya namaḥ* ॥ 4 ॥ *aum bṛhaspate'tiyadaryo'rhādyumadvibhāti kratumajjaneṣu* । *yaddīdayacchavasa ṛtaprajāta tadasmāsu draviṇaṁ dhehi citram—gurave namaḥ* ॥ 5 ॥ *annātparisruto rasambrahmaṇā vyapibatkṣatraṁ payaḥ somaṁ prajāpatiḥ* । *ṛtena satyamindriyaṁ vipānaṁ śukramandhasa indrasyendriyamidampayomṛtammadhu—śukrāya namaḥ* ॥ 6 ॥ *aumśanno devīrabhiṣṭaya āpo bhavantu pītaye* । *śāṃyyorabhisravantu naḥ—śanaiścarāya namaḥ* ॥ 7 ॥ *aum kayānaścitra ābhuvadūtī sadāvṛdhaḥ sakhā* । *kayā śaciṣṭhayā vṛtā—rāhave namaḥ* ॥ 8 ॥ *ketuṁ kṛṇvannaketave peśo maryyā apeśase* । *samuṣadbhirajāyathāḥ—ketave namaḥ* ॥ 9 ॥ *brahmā murāristripurāntakārī bhānuḥ śaśī bhūmisuto budhaśca* । *guruśca śukraḥ śanirāhuketavaḥ sarve grahāḥ śāntikarā bhavantu* ॥ *iti navagrahapūjā* ॥

अथ मातृकापूजनम्

गौरी पद्मा शची मेधा सावित्री विजया जया । देवसेना स्वधा स्वाहा मातरो लोकमातरः ॥ धृतिः पुष्टिस्तथा तुष्टिस्तथात्मकुलदेवताः ॥१६॥ गौर्यादिषोडशमातृभ्यो नमः ।

इति षोडशमातृपूजा ॥

atha mātṛkāpūjanam

gaurī padmā śachī medhā sāvitrī vijayā jayā । devasenā svadhā svāhā mātaro lokamātaraḥ ॥ dhṛtiḥ puṣṭistathā tuṣṭistathātmakuladevatāḥ ॥ 6 ॥ gauryādiṣoḍaśamātṛbhyo namaḥ ।

iti ṣoḍaśamātṛpūjā ॥

अथ ओङ्कारपूजनम्

ओङ्कारं बिन्दुसंयुक्तं नित्यं ध्यायन्ति योगिनः । कामदं मोक्षदं चव ओङ्काराय नमो नमः ॥ पञ्चोङ्कारेभ्यो नमः ॥

atha oṅkārapūjanam

oṅkāraṁ bindusaṁyuktaṁ nityaṁ dhyāyanti yoginaḥ । kāmadaṁ mokṣadaṁ cava oṅkārāya namo namaḥ ॥ pañcoṅkārebhyo namaḥ ॥

अथ वास्तुपूजनम्

ॐ नमोस्तु सर्पेभ्यो ये के च पृथिवीमनु । ये अन्तरिक्षे ये दिवि तेभ्यः सर्पेभ्यो नमः ॥ वासुक्याद्यष्टकुलनागेभ्यो नमः ॥

atha vāstupūjanam

aum namostu sarpebhyo ye ke ca pṛthivīmanu । ye antarikṣe ye divi tebhyaḥ sarpebhyo namaḥ ॥ vāsukyādyaṣṭakulanāgebhyo namaḥ ॥

अथ योगिनीपूजनम्

ॐ आवाहयाम्यहं देवीं योगिनीं परमेश्वरीम् । योगाभ्यासेन संतुष्टा परध्यानसमन्विता ॥१॥ दिव्यकुण्डलसंकाशा दिव्यज्वाला त्रिलोचना । मूर्तिमती ह्यमूर्ता च उग्रा चैवोग्ररूपिणी ॥२॥ अनेकभावसंयुक्ता संसारार्णवतारिणी । यज्ञं कुर्वंतु निर्विघ्नं श्रेयो यच्छन्तु मातरः ॥३॥ दिव्ययोगी महायोगी सिद्धयोगी गणेश्वरी । प्रेताशी डाकिनी काली कालरात्रिर्निशाचरी ॥४॥ हुंकारी सिद्धवेताली खर्परी भूतगामिनी । ऊर्ध्वकेशी विरूपाक्षी शुष्कांगी मांसभोजनी ॥ फूत्कारी वीरभद्राक्षी धूम्राक्षी कलहप्रिया । रक्ता च घोररक्ताक्षी विरूपाक्षी भयंकरी ॥५॥

चौरिका मारिका चंडी वाराही मुण्डधारिणी । भैरवी चक्रिणी क्रोधा दुर्मुखी प्रेतवासिनी ॥७॥ कालाक्षी मोहिनी चक्री कंकाली भुवनेश्वरी । कुण्डला तालकौमारी यमदूती करालिनी ॥८॥ कौशिकी यक्षिणी यक्षी कौमारी यंत्रवाहिनी । दुर्घटे विकटे घोरे कपाले विषलंघने ॥९॥ चतुःषष्टि समाख्याता योगिन्यो हि वरप्रदाः । त्रैलोक्ये पूजिता नित्यं देवमानुषयोगिभिः ॥ इति चतुःषष्टियोगिनीपूजनम् ।

atha yoginīpūjanam

aum āvāhayāmyahaṁ devīṁ yoginiṁ parameśvarīm । yogābhyāsena saṁtuṣṭā paradhyānasaman-vitā ॥ 1 ॥ divyakuṇḍalasaṁkāśā divyajvālā trilocanā । mūrtimatī hyamūrtā ca ugrā caivograrūpiṇī ॥ 2 ॥ anekabhāvasaṁyuktā saṁsārārṇavatāriṇī । yajñaṁ kurvaṁtu nirvighnaṁ śreyo yacchantu mātaraḥ ॥ 3 ॥ divyayogī mahāyogī siddhayogī gaṇeśvarī । pretāśī ḍākinī kālī kālarātrirniśācarī ॥ 4 ॥ huṁkārī siddhavetālī kharparī bhūtagāminī । ūrdhvakeśī virūpākṣī śuṣkāṁgī māṁsabhojanī ॥ phūtkārī vīrabhadrākṣī dhūmrākṣī kalahapriyā । raktā ca ghoraraktākṣī virūpākṣī bhayaṁkarī ॥ 5 ॥ caurikā mārikā caṁḍī vārāhī muṇḍa-dhāriṇī । bhairavī cakriṇī krodhā durmukhī pretavāsinī ॥ 7 ॥ kālākṣī mohinī cakrī kaṁkālī bhuvaneśvarī । kuṇḍalā tālakaumārī yamadū karālinī ॥ 8 ॥ kauśikī yakṣiṇī yakṣī kaumārī yaṁtravāhinī । durghaṭe vikaṭe ghore kapāle viṣalaṁghane ॥ 9 ॥ catuḥṣaṣṭi samākhyāta yoginyo hi varapradāḥ । trailokye pūjitā nityaṁ devamānuṣayogibhiḥ ॥ iti catuḥṣaṣṭiyoginīpūjanam ।

अथ सोमदक्षिणे लक्ष्मीपूजनम्

गन्धद्वारां दुराधर्षां नित्यपुष्टां करीषिणीम् । ईश्वरीं सर्वभूतानां तामिहोपह्वये श्रियम् ॥ इत्यावाह्य ॐ श्रीश्च ते लक्ष्मीश्च पत्न्यावहोरात्रे पार्श्वे नक्षत्राणि रूपमश्विनौ व्यात्तम् । इष्णन्निषाणमुम्मऽइषाण सर्वलोकम्म इषाण–इति लक्ष्मीपूजनम् ॥

atha somadakṣiṇe lakṣmīpūjanam

gandhadvārāṁ durādharṣāṁ nityapuṣṭāṁ karīṣiṇīm ।

īśvarīṁ sarvabhūtānāṁ tāmihopahvaye śriyam ॥ *ityāvāhya aum śrīśca te lakṣmīśca patnyāvahorātre pārśve nakṣatrāṇi rūpamaṁśvinau vyāttam* । *iṣṇanniṣāṇamumma'iṣāṇa sarvalokamma iṣāṇa—iti lakṣmīpūjanam* ॥

अथ ब्रह्मपूजनम्

ॐ ब्रह्म जज्ञानम्प्रथमं पुरस्ताद्वि सीमतः सुरूचो वेन आवः । स बुध्न्या उपमा अस्य विष्ठा स तस्य योनिमसतश्च विवः ॥ इति पाद्यादिभिर्ब्रह्माणमर्चयेत् ॥

atha brahmapūjanam

aum brahma jajñānamprathamaṁ purastādvi sīmataḥ suruco vena āvaḥ । *sa budhnyā upamā asya viṣṭhā sa tasya yonimasataśca vivaḥ* ॥ *iti pādyādibhirbrahmāṇamarcayet* ॥

अथ सप्तर्षिपूजनम्

कश्यपोऽत्रिर्भरद्वाजो विश्वामित्रोऽथ गौतमः ।
जमदग्निर्वसिष्ठश्च सप्तैते ऋषयः स्मृताः ॥

atha saptarṣipūjanam

kaśyapo'trirbharadvājo viśvāmitro'tha gautamaḥ ।
jamadagnirvasiṣṭhaśca saptaite ṛṣayaḥ smṛtāḥ ॥

अथ विष्णुपूजनम्

ॐ विष्णो रराटमसि विष्णोः श्नप्त्रे स्थो विष्णोः स्यूरसि विष्णोर्ध्रुवोसि वैष्णवमसि विष्णवे त्वा ॥

atha viṣṇupūjanam

aum viṣṇo rarāṭamasi viṣṇoḥ śnaptre stho viṣṇoḥ syūrasi viṣṇordhruvosi vaiṣṇavamasi viṣṇave tvā ॥

अथ शिवपूजनम्

ॐ नमः शंभवाय च मयोभवाय च नमः शंकराय च मयस्कराय च नमः शिवाय च शिवतराय च ॥

atha śivapūjanam

aum namaḥ śaṁbhavāya ca mayobhavāya ca namaḥ śaṁkarāya ca mayaskarāya ca namaḥ śivāya ca śivatarāya ca ॥

अथेन्द्रपूजनम्

ॐ त्रातारमिन्द्रमवितारमिन्द्रँ हवे हवे सुहवँ शूरमिन्द्रम् । ह्वयामि शकम्पुरुहूतमिन्द्रँ स्वस्ति नो मघवा धात्विन्द्रः ॥

athendrapūjanam

aum trātāramindramavitāramindraṁ have have suhavaṁ śūramindram । *hvayāmi śakampuruhūtamindraṁ svasti no maghavā dhātvindraḥ* ॥

अथ वायुपूजनम्

ॐ वायो ये ते सहस्त्रिणो रथासस्तेभिरागहि । नियुत्वान्सोमपीतये ॥ ॐ वातो वा मनो वा गन्धर्वाः सप्तविँ शतिः । ते अग्रेऽश्वमयुञ्जँस्ते अस्मिन् जवमादधुः ॥ ॐ वायवे नमः ॥

atha vāyupūjanam

aum vāyo ye te sahasriṇo rathāsastebhirāgahi । *niyutvānsomapītaye* ॥ *aum vāto vā mano vā gandharvāḥ saptaviṁ śatiḥ* । *te agre'śvamayuñjaṃste asmin javamādadhuḥ* ॥ *aum vāyave namaḥ* ॥

अथ धर्मपूजनम्

ॐ अग्ने सपत्नदम्भनमदब्धासो अदाभ्यम् । चित्रावसो स्वस्ति ते परामशीय ॥ धर्माय नमः ॥

ततो यजमानः कृतपूजनं वरं पूर्ववत्संबोध्येदं संकल्पं पठेत् ॥ ॐ विष्णुः ३ त्रिरुच्चार्य देशकालौ संकीर्त्याऽमुकगोत्रोमुकशर्माऽहं श्रुतिस्मृति-पुराणोक्तफलप्राप्त्यर्थममुकगोत्राया अमुकनाम्न्याः कन्याया विवाहोत्सवनिमित्तवरपूजनं करिष्ये इति संकल्पः ।

ॐ साधु भवानास्तामर्चयिष्यामो भवन्तमिति ब्रूयात् ।

atha dharmapūjanam

aum agne sapatnadambhanamadabdhāso adābhyam ।
citrāvaso svasti te pāramaśīya ॥ *dharmāya namaḥ* ॥

tato yajamānaḥ kṛtapūjanaṁ varaṁ pūrvavatsaṁbodhyedaṁ saṁkalpaṁ paṭhet ॥ *aum viṣṇuḥ 3 triruccārya deśakālau saṁkīrtyā'mukagotromukaśarmā'haṁ śrutismṛtipurāṇoktaphalaprāptyarthamamukagotrāya amukanāmnyaḥ kanyāyā vivāhotsavanimittavarapūjanaṁ kariṣye iti saṁkalpaḥ* ।

aum sādhu bhavānāstāmarcayiṣyāmo bhavantamiti brūyāt ।

The host should speak to the bridegroom thus: You are most adorable; please be seated comfortably; I'll adore and reverence you, for of all those who are venerable, six are specially suited.[1] This is what the authors of Karmakāṇḍas say and, according to the Mahābhāṣya, you are one of them.

अर्चयेति वरेणोक्ते वरोपवेशनार्थं शुद्धमासनं दत्त्वा विष्टरमादाय ।

arcayeti vareṇokte varopaveśanārthaṁ śuddhamāsanaṁ dattvā viṣṭaramādāya ।

When the bridegroom acquiesces and lets himself be venerated, the bride's father or the host (Yajamāna, the patron of the sacrifice) should offer him a pure, unsoiled seat. He should then offer him a Viṣṭara (a seat made of 25 shoots of Kuśa grass tied up in a sheaf), an injunction given by Manu.[2] The sage Marīci defines a pure seat[3] as that

1. षडर्ध्या भवन्ति–आचार्य ऋत्विग्वैवाह्यो राजा च प्रियस्नातक: इति ।

ṣaḍardhyā bhavanti—ācārya ṛtvigvaivāhyo rājā ca priyasnātakaḥ iti ।

2. पूजको यजमानस्तु दत्त्वादौ शुद्धमासनम् । तस्योपवेशनार्थं तु विष्टरं प्रददेत्पुन: ॥ यथान्यायं यथोद्दिष्ट वराय विधिपूर्वकम् ॥

pūjako yajamānastu dattvādau śuddhamāsanam । tasyopaveśanārthaṁ tu viṣṭaraṁ pradadetpunaḥ ॥ yathānyayaṁ yathoddiṣṭa varāya vidhipūrvakam ॥

3. शणासूत्रादिनोतं च निर्मितं शोधितै शरै: । मुख्यं स्थूलतमं रम्यं प्राहू: शुद्धसुखासनम् ॥

śaṇāsūtrādinotaṁ ca nirmitaṁ śodhi śaraiḥ । mukhyaṁ sthūlatamaṁ ramyaṁ prāhum । śuddhaṣukhāsanam ॥

comfortable object which is made of white reed or grass (Śaras) woven with hempen chords or strings. Such a seat is thick, unsullied and beautiful and is deemed comfortable. The sage Parāśara holds the same view,[1] adding that the seat should be made of metals like gold or either of smooth or rugged white reed or of grass or wood. The host should then hold in his hand a bunch of twenty-five Kuśa grass.

A Viṣṭara has been characterized in the Gṛhyapariśiṣṭa thus:[2] a bunch of fifty holy Kuśa grass is Brahmā, of twenty-five a Viṣṭara; that with upraised hair is Brahmā and with long ones a Viṣṭara, that which is wrapped from right is Brahmā and the one wrapped from left is a Viṣṭara. Holding that in his hand, the host should utter the following mantra:

ॐ विष्टरो विष्टरो विष्टर इत्यन्येनोक्ते ।

aum viṣṭaro viṣṭaro viṣṭara ityanyenokte ।

The host should intone "aum Viṣṭaro Viṣṭaro Viṣṭara" followed by "this is a Viṣṭara" three times.

---

1. सिंहासनं सुवर्णादिधातुना निर्मितं शुभम् । दारुर्भिनिर्मितं चाथ शरैर्वा शुद्धमासनम् ॥

simhāsanaṁ suvarṇādidhātunā nirmitaṁ śubham । dārubhirnirmitaṁ cātha śarairvā śuddhamāsanam ॥

2. पञ्चाशता भवेद् ब्रह्मा तदर्धेन तु विष्टरः । ऊर्ध्वकेशो भवेद् ब्रह्मा लम्बकेशस्तु विष्टरः । दक्षिणावर्तको ब्रह्मा वामावर्तस्तु विष्टरः ॥ यद्वा–पंचविंशतिदर्भाणां वेण्यग्रं ग्रन्थिभूषितम् ॥ विष्टरं : सर्वयज्ञेषु लक्षणं परिकीर्त्तितम् ॥ विष्टरस्त्रिवृता दर्भकूर्चक इति विष्टरदाने विधिर्यथा ॥ विष्टरप्रभृतीनन्यस्त्रिस्त्रिवारं वदेत्करे । दातुर्निरीक्ष्य दाता तु विष्टरः प्रतिगृह्यताम् ॥ विष्टरं प्रतिगृह्णामीत्यभिधायाददेद् वरः । तमुत्तराग्रमादाय मंत्रेणोपविशेत्स्वयम् ॥

pañcāśatā bhaved brahmā tadardhena tu viṣṭaraḥ । ūrdhvakeśo bhaved brahmā lambakeśastu viṣṭaraḥ । darṣiṇāvartako brahmā vāmārvatastu viṣṭaraḥ ॥ yadva—paṁcaviṁśatidarbhāṇāṁ veṇyagraṁ granthibhūṣitam । viṣṭaraṁ sarvayajñeṣu lakṣaṇaṁ parikīrttitam ॥ viṣṭarastrivṛtā darbhakūrcaka iti viṣṭaradāne vidhiryathā ॥ viṣṭaraprabhṛtīnanyastristrivāraṁ vadetkare । dāturnirīkṣya dāta tu viṣṭaraḥ pratigṛhyatāṁ ॥ viṣṭaraṁ pratigṛhṇāmītyabhidhāyādaded varaḥ । tabhuttarāgramādāya maṁtreṇopaviśetsvayam ॥

ॐ विष्टरः प्रतिगृह्यतामिति दाता वदेत् ।

aum viṣṭaraḥ pratigṛhyatāmiti dātā vadet ।

The person offering the bride (her guardian) shall then say: "Please accept and hold the Viṣṭara." Then the bridegroom should intone the following mantra:

ॐ विष्टरं प्रतिगृह्णामीत्यभिधाय वरो विष्टरमुदग्रमुभयपाणिभ्यामादाय ।

aum viṣṭaraṁ pratigṛhaṇāmītyabhidhāya varo viṣṭaramudagramubhayapāṇibhyāmādāya ।

"I take the Viṣṭara", so saying, the bridegroom takes the Viṣṭara with both hands from the host, the forepart of the seat facing the north. This is followed by the bridegroom uttering the following mantra:

ॐ वर्ष्मोऽस्मि समानानामुद्यतामिव सूर्यः । इमन्तमभितिष्ठामि यो मा कश्चाभिदासति–इत्यनेनैनमुदगग्रमासनोपरि निधायाभ्युपविशति ।

aum varṣmo'smi samānānāmudyatāmiva sūryaḥ । *imantamabhitiṣṭhāmi yo mā kaścābhidāsati—ityanenainamudagagramāsanopari nidhāyābhyupaviśati* ।

The meaning of this is that the venerable bridegroom offers prayers for his being so honoured (or he prays to his own Self, Ātmā, and for his own glorification), saying that like the sun, who on rising illumines all the stellar constellations, he deems himself supreme among his kinsmen considering their lineage, knowledge, behaviour, age, physical look, stars, etc. He who has designs on his life or plots to kill him is on palpable evidence at once trampled on and cowed down like this Viṣṭara. Uttering this mantra and keeping the front of the Viṣṭara in the north, he should take his seat with the Viṣṭara spread on it. The host should then keep a jar full of water on his joined palms.[1] The water jar

---

1. लाजा च कुंकुमश्चैव तंडुलाः पुष्पमेव च । सर्वौषधिसमायुक्तं पञ्चाङ्गं पाद्यमुच्यते ।

lājā ca kuṁkumaścaiva taṁḍulāḥ puṣpameva ca । sarvauṣadhisamāyuktaṁ pañcāṅgaṁ pādyamucyate ॥

should have in it an assortment of such auspicious things as parched paddy (*khīla* or *dhāna*) saffron, rice, flowers and all the available herbs.

ॐ पाद्यं पाद्यं पाद्यमित्यन्येनोक्ते पाद्यं प्रतिगृह्यतामिति दाता वदेत् ।

aum pādyaṁ pādyaṁ pādyamityanyenokte pādyaṁ pratigṛhyatāmiti dātā vadet ।

The bride's father should utter 'Pādyaṁ' three times and then add 'Pādyaṁ pratigṛhyatām'—please hold this water jar and wash your feet.

ॐ पाद्यं प्रतिगृह्णामीत्यभिधाय वरः यजमानाञ्जलितोऽञ्जलिना पाद्यमादाय ।

aum pādyaṁ pratigṛhṇāmītyabhidhāya va'raḥ yajamānāñjalito'ñjalina pādyamādāya ।

"I let my hands hold this water jar for washing my feet." Thus speaking, the bridegroom lifts the jar from the host and keeping it on his own open hands intones this mantra:

ॐ विराजो दोहोसि विराजो दोहमशीय मयि पाद्यायै विराजो दोहः— इति मंत्रेण दक्षिणपादं प्रक्षाल्यानेनैव मंत्रेण वामपादं प्रक्षालयेत् ।

aum virājo dohosi virājo dohamaśīya mayi pādyāyai virājo dohaḥ—iti maṁtreṇa dakṣiṇapādaṁ prakṣālyānenaiva maṁtreṇa vāmapādaṁ prakṣālayet ।

—which is addressed to the water contained in the bowl: O Water! You are the essential sweetness[1] of the elemental liquid born of Cosmic Infinitude, Bhagavān, who is the light of all souls and virtues, prāṇas and guṇas. O vital, resplendent Water! Pray grant me the same delicious beauty and embellish my feet with loveliness by washing them clean.

The feet should be washed while the mantra is being

1. आपो नारा इति प्रोक्ता आपो वै नरसूनवः ।
āpo nārā iti proktā āpo vai narasūnavaḥ ।

intoned, not at the end of its recital. The second foot also should be washed in this manner.

ब्राह्मण[1]श्चद्दक्षिणपादं प्रथमं प्रक्षालयेत् । क्षत्रिवैश्ययोर्वामपादं प्रथमं प्रक्षालयेत् ।

brāhmaṇaścaddakṣiṇapādaṁ prathaṁ prakṣālayet । *kṣatrivaiśyayorvāmapādaṁ prathamaṁ prakṣālayet* ।

If [the bridegroom is] a brāhmaṇa, let the right foot be washed first; if he is a kṣatriya or a vaiśya, the ritual should be performed with the left foot first.

ततः पूर्ववद्विष्टरान्तरं गृहीत्वा वर्ष्मोऽस्मीति मन्त्रेण पूर्वोक्तप्रकारेण चरणयोरधस्तादुत्तराग्रं वरः कुर्यात् ।

tataḥ pūrvavadviṣṭarāntaraṁ gṛhītvā varṣmo'smīti mantreṇa pūrvoktaprakāreṇa caraṇayoradhastāduttarāgraṁ varaḥ kuryāt ।

The bridegroom should now take the second Viṣṭara like the first one and shove it, while its front faces north, hard under his feet with the repetition of the above mantra beginning with the word 'varṣmo'smi'.

ततो दूर्वाक्षतपुष्पचन्दनयुतार्घपात्रं गृहीत्वा यजमानः ।
ॐ अर्घोऽर्घोऽर्घ इत्यन्येनोक्ते अर्घः प्रतिगृह्यतामिति दाता वदेत् ।[2]

tato dūrvākṣatapuṣpacandanayutārghapātraṁ gṛhītvā yajamānaḥ ।

---

1. ब्राह्मणो दक्षिणं पादं पूर्वं प्रक्षालयेत्सदा । क्षत्रादिः प्रथमं सव्यमिति धर्मानुशासनन् ।

brāhmaṇo dakṣiṇaṁ pādaṁ pūrvaṁ prakṣālayetsadā । kṣatrādiḥ prathamaṁ savyamiti dharmānuśāsanan ॥

2. अर्घतेऽनेनेत्यऽर्घ इत्याप एव मंत्रलिङ्गात् । अर्घशब्देनोदकपात्रमेवेति कर्काचार्यः । अन्यच्च– कुशचन्दनपुष्पाणि चाक्षता उदकं तथा । पयो दधि तथा रुक्ममष्टाङ्गोऽर्घः करग्रहे ॥ कांस्यपात्रं भवेद्विप्रे स्वर्णपात्रं तु भूमिपे । रौप्यपात्रं भवेद्वैश्ये लौहपात्रं च शूद्रके ॥

arghate'nenetya'rgha ityāpa eva maṁtraliṅgāt । arghaśabdenodakapātrameveti karkācāryaḥ । anyacca—kuśacandanapuṣpāṇi cākṣatā udakaṁ tathā । payo dadhi tathā rukmamaṣṭāṅgo'rghaḥ karagrahe ॥ kāṁsyapātraṁ bhavedvipre svarṇapātraṁ tu bhūmipe । raupyapātraṁ bhavedvaiśye lauhapātraṁ ca śūdrake ॥

aum argho'rgho'rgha ityanyenokte arghaḥ pratigṛh-yatāmiti dātā vadet ।

Then the host should take the water bowl with *dūrvā* grass, sacred rice, flower, and sandal mixed with the water and then read the following mantra:

Repeating 'aum arghaḥ' three times, the bride's father should thus request the bridegroom, "Pray take this oblation."

अर्घं प्रतिगृह्णामीत्यभिधाय वरो यजमानहस्तादर्घं गृहीत्वा शिरसा-ऽभिवन्द्य ।

arghaṁ pratigṛhṇāmītyabhidhāya varo yajamāna-hastādarghaṁ gṛhītvā śirasā'bhivandya ।

"I take it." So saying, the bridegroom should take the oblatory pitcher from the host's hand and with his head bowed to the container, read the following mantra:

ॐ आपः स्थ युष्माभिः सर्वान् कामानवाप्नवानि–इति शिरसि अक्षतादिकं क्षिपेत् ।

aum āpaḥ stha yuṣmābhiḥ sarvān kāmānavāpnavāni—iti śirasi akṣatādikaṁ kṣipet ।

the meaning of which is: "O Water! you are the mainspring of all nectar, clarified butter, milk, curd, honey, fruit, flowers, leaves, food grains and physical robustness and satiety; be the granter of all my wishes wherever I am, so that my yearnings are all gratified."

As he reads this mantra, the bridegroom takes out some flowers and rice grains from the pitcher and sprinkles them on his head. This ritual over, he recites following mantra:

ॐ समुद्रं वः प्रहिणोमि स्वां योनिमभिगच्छत । अरिष्टाऽस्माकं वीरा मा परासेचि मत् पयः ॥

aum samudraṁ vaḥ prahiṇomi svāṁ yonimabhi-gacchata । ariṣṭa'smākaṁ vīrā mā parāseci mat payaḥ ॥

O Waters! the ocean is the cause and source of your being which gratifies one's desires (i.e. helps one to attain one's goal). Urged by me, you flow on towards your source, fancying that it is not too distant away. Before you depart, however, pray bless my brothers and sons so that they do not indulge in violence or suffer from any illness. But this auspicious water sanctified by the most venerable goddess Ambā and others must not go.

इत्यर्घपात्रस्थजलमैशान्यां त्यजन् पठेत् ।

ityarghapātrasthajalamaiśānyāṁ tyajan paṭhet ।

Emptying the pitcher in the north-eastern quarter, the bridegroom should recite the preceding mantra.

ततो यजमान आचमनीयमादाय ॐ आचमनीयमाचमनीयमाचमनीय-मित्यन्येनोक्ते आचमनीयं प्रतिगृह्यतामिति दाता वदेत् । आचमनीयं प्रतिगृह्णामीत्यभिधाय वरो यजमानहस्तादाचमनीयं गृहीत्वा ।

tato yajamāna ācamanīyamādāya aum ācamanīyam-ācamanīyamācamanīyamityanyenokte ācamanīyaṁ pratigṛhyatāmiti dātā vadet । *ācamanīyaṁ pratigṛhṇā-mītyabhidhāya varo yajamānahastādācamanīyaṁ gṛhītvā* ।

The oblation ritual completed, the host is thereafter required to take a little pure water[1] contained in a Kamaṁḍalu (a mendicant's pitcher) or in some other clean pot for Ācamana. He should then repeat 'aum ācamanīyam' three times before entreating the bridegroom to take the Ācamana (sip the holy water). To this the bridegroom should thus reply, "I acknowledge the water fit for Ācamana." Thus speaking, he takes the Ācamana pot from the host, holds it in his left hand, and rehearses the mantra 'ā'mā 'gan'.

1. पूताभिः प्रकृतिस्थाभिर्हीनाभिः फेनबुद्बुदैः ॥ त्रिवारमद्भिराचामेद् द्विजादिः शुद्धिहेतवे ॥ इत्याचारचन्द्रोदये । अद्भिस्तु प्रकृतिस्थाभिर्हीनाभिः फेनबुद्बुदैः । हृत्कंठतालुगाभिश्च यथासंख्यं द्विजादयः ॥ इत्याचारादर्शे । द्विजादिः ब्रह्मतीर्थेन त्रिः पिबेदम्बु वीक्षितम् ।

pūtābhiḥ prakṛtisthābhirhīnābhiḥ phenabudbudaiḥ ॥ trivaramadbhirācāmed dvijādiḥ śuddhihetave ॥ ityācāra-candrodaye । adbhistu prakṛtisthābhirhīnābhiḥ phenabudbudaiḥ । hṛtkaṁṭhatālugābhiśca yathāsaṁkhyaṁ dvijādayaḥ ॥ ityācārādarśe । dvijādiḥ brahmatīrthena triḥ pibedambu vīkṣitam ।

ॐ आऽमाऽगन्यशसा संसृज वर्च्चसा । तम्मा कुरु प्रियं प्रजानामधिपतिं पशूनामरिष्टिं तनूनाम्–इत्यनेन सकृदाचामेत् द्विस्तूष्णीमाचामेत् ।

aum ā'mā'ganyaśasā saṁsṛja varccasā । *tammā kuru priyaṁ prajānāmadhipatiṁ paśūnāmariṣṭiṁ tanūnām—ityanena sakṛdācāmet dvistūṣṇīmācāmet* ।

With a look at the water set apart for ceremonial sipping (Ācamana), he offers prayer to Varuṇa thus: "O Lord of the Waters! Established in the manner described above you render me glorious and endow me with divine radiance (Brahma Teja). Let the best among your subjects give me love and affection. Let me be the master of such animals as cows and horses and let my body be free of illness and acts of violence.[1] The first Ācamana should be performed with the recitation of this mantra, two more without it.

ततो यजमानः कांस्यपात्रस्थदधिमधुघृतानि[2] समादायाऽन्येन कांस्यपात्रेण पिधाय रक्तसूत्रेण आवेष्ट्य कराभ्यामादायेति पठेत् ।

---

1. अनभ्यासस्तु वेदानां त्यागात् सत्कर्मणां गवाम् । गुरुगङ्गाम्बुविप्राणां निन्दागोहत्यया समा ॥
anabhyāsastu vedānāṁ tyāgāt satkarmaṇāṁ gavām । gurugaṅgāmbuviprāṇāṁ nindāgohatyayā samā ॥

2. संशोधितं दधि मधु कांस्यपात्रे स्थितं घृतम् । कांस्येनान्येन संछन्नं मधुपर्कमितीर्यते ॥ शोधनञ्च ॥ दधिक्राव्णेति दध्नश्च वस्त्रान्निष्कासनञ्च यत् । मधुव्वातेति तिसृभिर्मधुनः शोधनं स्मृतम् ॥ आज्यमग्नावधिश्रित्य वह्निनानुसृते घृते । घृतं घृतेति मंत्रेण वस्त्रपूतञ्च शोधनम् ॥ एतच्छोधनमेतेषां मधुपर्कविधौ श्रुतम् । अन्यत्र मधुपर्कात्तु वस्त्रपूतं हि केवलम् ॥ मधुपर्के दध्यादिप्रमाणम् यथा–सर्पिश्च पलमेकन्तु द्विपलं मधु कीर्तितम् । पलमेकं दधि प्रोक्तं मधुपर्कविधौ बुधैः ॥ इति बृहत्परिमाणम् ॥ सर्पिरेकगुणं प्रोक्तं शोधितं द्विगुणं मधु । मधुपर्कविधौ प्रोक्तं सर्प्पिषा च समं दधि ॥ इदि लध्वापस्तम्बेन लघुपरिमाणं दर्शितम् ॥ लघुपरिमाणमेवेदानीम् ॥
saṁśodhitaṁ dadhi madhu kāṁsyapātre sthitaṁ ghṛtam । kāṁsyenānyena saṁchannaṁ madhuhparkamitīryate ॥ śodhanañca ॥ dadhikrāvṇeti daghnaśca vastrānniṣkāsanañca yat । madhuvvāteti tisṛbhiramadhunaḥ śodhanaṁ smṛtam ॥ ājyamagnāvadhiśritya vahninānusṛte ghṛte । ghṛtaṁ ghṛteti maṁtreṇa vastrapūtañca śodhanam ॥ etacchodhanameteṣāṁ madhuparkavidhau śrutam । anyatra madhuparkāttu vastrapūtaṁ hi kevalam ॥ madhuparke dadhyādipramāṇam yathā—sarpiśca palamekantu dvipalaṁ madhu kīrtitam । palamekaṁ dadhi proktaṁ madhuparkavidhau budhaiḥ ॥ iti bṛhatparimāṇam ॥ sarpirekaguṇaṁ proktaṁ śodhitaṁ dviguṇaṁ madhu । madhuparkavidhau proktaṁ sarppiṣā ca samaṁ dadhi ॥ iti

tato yajamānaḥ kāṁsyapātrasthadadhimadhughṛtāni samādāyā'nyena kāṁsyapātreṇa pidhāya raktasūtreṇa āveṣṭya karābhyāmādāyeti paṭhet ।

Then the host should take a copper or brass container filled with curd (*dahi*), honey (*śahada*), and ghī (*ghṛta*), cover it with another copper or brass jar, and wrap it around with a red string or chord. Holding it with both hands, he should read the following mantra:

ॐ मधुपर्कों मधुपर्को मधुपर्क इत्यन्येनोक्ते ॐ मधुपर्कः प्रतिगृह्यता-मिति दाता वदेत् । मधुपर्कं प्रतिगृह्णामीत्यभिधायैव वरः ।

aum madhuparko madhuparko madhuparka ityanyenokte aum madhuparkaḥ pratigṛhyatāmiti dātā vadet । *madhuparkaṁ pratigṛhṇāmītyabhidhāyaiva varaḥ* ।

Having repeated 'aum madhuparkaḥ' three times, the host should request the bridegroom to receive the Madhuparka. The bridegroom, acknowledging, should thus reply, "I take the Madhuparka; I take it." The bridegroom's emphatic acknowledgement and grateful repetition of 'I take' are meant to honour the host; he must not take it from him; all he is expected to do is to look at it while it is still in the host's hands. A confirmation of this direction can be had from the text a little further where it also says that while casting looks at it, the following mantra should be read:

ॐ मित्रस्य त्वा चक्षुषा प्रतीक्षे–इति मंत्रेणोद्धाटितमधुपर्कं यजमानकरस्थमेव निरीक्ष्य[1] ।

---

laghvāpastambena laghuparimāṇaṁ darśitam ॥ laghuparimāṇamevedānīm ॥

1. pratigṛhītaṁ madhuparkaṁ pītvā tyāge yathā mahāghorapāpasaṁbhavastathaiva romakīṭādidūṣitamadhuparkapāne'pi mahāghorapāpa sambhavaḥ ॥ yathā—romabhistu bhavetkuṣṭhī makṣikābhirdaridratā । kīṭakaiśca bhavedandhastadarthaṁ hi nirikṣaṇam ॥ gavāṁ dugdhe tu romāṇi ghṛtamadhye tu makṣikāḥ । madhau ca kīṭakāḥ syurvai tadarthaṁ hi nirīkṣaṇam ॥ puṁbhiśca yatkṛtaṁ pāpaṁ bālyayauvanavārddhake । tatsarvaṁ nāśayetpāpaṁ madhuparkovakāśane ॥

aum mitrasya tvā cakṣuṣā pratikṣe—iti maṁtreṇod-dhāṭitamadhuparkaṁ yajmānakarasthameva nirīkṣya ।

O Madhuparka! I look at you with the eyes of the sun (i.e. with the eyesight given by the sun).

The Madhuparka, now uncovered with the utterance of this mantra, should remain in the hands of the host as the following mantra (devasya tvā') is read and the Madhuparka is received in the right hand.

ॐ देवस्य त्वा सवितुः प्रसवेऽश्विनोर्बाहुभ्यां पूष्णो हस्ताभ्यां प्रतिगृह्णामि—इत्यभिधाय वरो मधुपर्कं गृहीत्वा[1] वामहस्ते कृत्वा ।

aum devasya tvā savituḥ prasave'śvinorbāhubhyāṁ pūṣṇo hastābhyāṁ pratigṛhṇāmi—ityabhidhāya varo madhuparkaṁ gṛhītvā vāmahaste kṛtvā ।

O Madhuparka! By the grace of the sun and the power bestowed by Aśvinīkumāra and derived from the god Pūṣā, I accept you with my hands thus invigorated and energized.

Thus speaking, the bridegroom receives the Madhuparka with his left hand and with the ring finger of the right (with its thumb intact[2]) stirs it after uttering the following mantra:

---

1. मधुपर्कं समादाय देवस्य त्वेति मंत्रतः । यजमानदत्तं दक्षेण सव्ये पाणौ निधापयेत् ॥ दक्षिणहस्तामिकया त्रिः समालोडयेद्वरः । तन्मूलेऽङ्गुष्ठमादाय मधुपर्कं च सर्वगम् ॥ ॐ नमः श्यावास्यायेति मंत्रेणैव विचक्षणः ॥

madhuparkaṁ samādāya devasya tveti maṁtrataḥ । yajamānadattaṁ dakṣeṇa savye pāṇau nidhāpayet ॥ dakṣiṇa-hastāmikayā triḥ samāloḍayedvaraḥ । tanmūle'ṅguṣṭhamādāya madhuparkaṁ ca sarvagam । aum namaḥ śyāvāsyāyeti maṁtreṇaiva vicakṣaṇaḥ ॥

2. ॐ नमः श्यावास्यायेति मन्त्रेण अङ्गुष्ठलग्नमूलकया दक्षिणहस्ताऽनामिकया त्रिः प्रदक्षिणमालोड्यात्र षड्वारं मन्त्रपाठः, विलोडनत्रये त्रिवारं मन्त्रपाठः, विलोडनाऽनन्तरं भूमिनिःक्षेपणेऽपि त्रिवारं मन्त्रपाठः । याज्ञवल्क्यः ॥ संविधाय करस्थं तं मन्त्रेणालोड्य निक्षिपेत् । त्रिस्त्रिर्वारं भाष्यबलान्मंत्राभ्यासकृतिस्तथेति ॥

aum namaḥ śyāvāsyāyeti mantreṇa aṅguṣṭhalagnamūlakayā dakṣiṇahastā'nāmikayā triḥ pradakṣiṇamāloḍyātra ṣaḍvāraṁ mantrapāṭhaḥ, viloḍanatraye trivāraṁ mantrapāṭhaḥ, viloḍanā'nantaraṁ bhūminiḥkṣepaṇe'pi trivāraṁ mantrapāṭhaḥ । yājñavalkyaḥ ॥ saṁvidhāya karasthaṁ taṁ mantreṇāloḍya nikṣipet । tristrirvāraṁ bhāṣyabalānmaṁtrābhyāsakṛtistatheti ॥

ॐ नमः श्यावास्यायान्नशने यत्त आविद्धं तत्ते निष्कृन्तामि—इति अनामिकया त्रिः प्रदक्षिणमालोड्य अनामिकाङ्गुष्ठाभ्यां भूमौ किञ्चिन्निक्षिप्य पुनस्तथैव द्विः प्रत्येकं निक्षिपेत् ।

aum namaḥ śyāvāsyāyannaśane yatta āviddhaṁ tatte niṣkṛntāmi—iti anāmikayā triḥ pradakṣiṇamālodya anāmikāṅguṣṭhābhyāṁ bhūmau kiñcinnikṣipya punastathaiva dviḥ pratyekaṁ nikṣipet ।

Addressing the digestive stomach-fire (*jaṭharāgni*), the bridegroom shall thus speak, "O ape-coloured Fire! I do homage to you and take out from your food that which is forbidden and uneatable, so that you may be fed on what is absolutely pure and unadulterated."

Uttering this mantra, the bridegroom shall then take out a few drops of Madhuparka with his ring finger and thumb and sprinkle them on the ground and then again in the same manner twice. The procedure to be followed is that he should join the thumb to the root of his ring finger and stir the Madhuparka with the latter three times.

तत आचारान्मधुपर्कं किञ्चित्कन्यायै द्रष्टुं दद्यात् ।

tata ācārānmadhuparkaṁ kiñcitkanyāyai draṣṭuṁ dadyāt ।

This should be followed by letting the bride, now sitting in the Kautukāgāra, have a look at the Madhuparka at least once. This ritual, in no manner negligible, should be observed in accordance with the custom prevailing in the region and family. It signifies that the bride should also have a close look at the Madhuparka, for women, possessed of great skill in minute observation, are also credited with having the most astute observant mind. In order to assure oneself that nothing impure has profaned the sacred substance—Madhuparka—one must show it to the bride. The stigma attached to not counting it an indispensable item is not as serious as that attached to the consumption of impure Madhuparka. This explains why one should strictly follow the customs and saṁskāras enjoined by tradition and culture. According to the instructions of the śāstras, even if the family custom and national[1] culture are antagonistic to scriptural rules, they must not be abjured.

The mantra beginning with 'yanmadhuno madhavyam' which follows enjoins that the Madhuparka should be taken three times.

ॐ यन्मधुनो मधव्यं परमँ्रूपमन्नाद्यं तेनाहं मधुनो मधव्येन परमेण रूपेणान्नाद्येन परमो मधव्योऽन्नादोऽसानि–इति अनेनैव वारत्रयं मधुपर्कप्राशनम् । प्रतिप्राशने चैतन्मंत्रपाठः । ततो मधुपर्कशेषमसंचरे देशे धारयेत् ।

aum yanmadhuno madhavyaṁ paramaṁ rūpamannādyaṁ tenāhaṁ madhuno madhavyena parameṇa rūpeṇānnādyena paramo madhavyo'nnādo'sāni—iti anenaiva vāratrayaṁ madhuparkaprāśanam । *pratiprāśane caitanmaṁtrapāṭhaḥ* । *tato madhuparkaśeṣamasaṁcare deśe dhārayet* ।

As you repeat this mantra ('aum yanmadhuno', etc.) take a little of the Madhuparka. Repeat it again and yet again. (In all, take the drink three times.) Would you consider the leavings of the sacred potion impure when a part of it has already been drunk? Does a person forfeit his right to a mantra after tasting a stale, impure drink? The dilemma is resolved by bearing in mind that a brāhmaṇa does not become impure (*ucchiṣta*) by drinking Madhuparka and Soma, however stale or leftover. The mantra ('aụm yanmadhuno', etc.) is a tribute to the purity and sweetness of Madhuparka: "O celestial beings! The luscious sweetness which lights up the body despite all the strokes (of time and circumstance); which is the quintessence of the honeyed juice of flowers (*makaranda*); which is the material cause (*upādāna kāraṇa*) of all vital foodgrains, and which irradiates the beauty of honey itself is most suited to

---

1. वेदधर्मान्देशधर्मान्कुलधर्म्मांश्च शश्वतान् । धर्मशास्त्रविरुद्धांश्च न त्यजेद्ज्ञानदुर्बलः ॥
vedadharmāndeśadharmānkuladharmmāṁśca śāśvatān । dharmaśāstraviruddhāṁśca na tyajedjñānadurbalaḥ ॥

Madhuparka, the manifold qualities of which are all centred in the food I eat."

Drink the Madhuparka three times, and as you drink it, keep on repeating the mantra not exceeding this number. The potion left over in the Madhuparka bowl after use may be handed to any of the disciples present or it may be kept at a lonely, untrodden place in the eastern quarter.

ततस्त्रिराचामेद्वरः । ॐ वाङ्मे आस्येऽस्तु । नसोर्मे प्राणोऽस्तु । अक्ष्णोर्मे चक्षुरस्तु । कर्णयोर्मे श्रोत्रमस्तु । बाह्वोर्मे बलमस्तु । ऊर्वोर्मे ओजोऽस्तु । अरिष्टानि मेऽङ्गानि तनूस्तन्वा मे सह सन्तु—इति प्रत्येकं सर्वगात्राणि संस्पृशेत् ।

tatastrirācāmedvaraḥ । *aum vāṅme āsye'stu* । *nasorme prāṇo'stu* । *akṣṇorme cakṣurastu* । *karṇayorme śrotramastu* । *bāhvorme balamastu* । *ūrvorme ojo'stu* । *ariṣṭāni me'ṅgāni tanūstanvā me saha santu—iti pratyekaṁ sarvagātrāṇi saṁspṛśet* ।

Having done this, perform Ācamana[1] (by sipping water) three times. (The ritual act of sipping water three times constitutes a single Ācamana. Three Ācamanas would therefore mean sipping water nine times.) Sip water of Brahma Tīrtha[2] (aromatic water smelling of a kind of ginger) and

---

1. आचामेदाचमनं कृत्वा इत्यादिपदैस्त्रिवारमेव जलभक्षणं कर्तव्यम् । अतएव मूलकारेण ततस्त्रिराचामेदित्याचमनस्वरूपाऽभिधानमेव कृतं न तु नववारं जलभक्षणमिति । पादयोर्द्विगृहीत्वा तु सुप्रक्षालितपाणिना । त्रिराचम्य ततः शब्दं स्मृत्वा विष्णुं सनातनम् ॥

ācāmedācamana kṛtvā ityādipadaistrivārameva jalabhakṣaṇaṁ kartavyam । ataeva mūlakāreṇa tatastrirācāmedityācamanasvarūpā'bhidhānameva kṛtaṁ na tu navavāraṁ jalabhakṣaṇamiti । pādayodviṁgṛhītvā tu suprakṣālitapāṇinā । trirācamya tataḥ śabdaṁ smṛtvā viṣṇu sanātanam ॥

2. हस्तगं प्रथमात्तीर्थाद्दक्षिणात् त्रिः पिबेज्जलम् । अशब्दमनवस्रावमबहिर्जान्वबुद्बुदम् ॥ दक्षिणन्तु करं कृत्वा गोकर्णाकृतिवत्पुनः । त्रिः पिबेद्वीक्षितं तोयमास्यं द्वि परिमार्जयेत् ॥ अद्भिस्तु प्रकृतिस्थाभिर्हीनाभिः फेनबुद्बुदैः । हृत्कण्ठतालुगाभिश्च यथासंख्यं द्विजादयः ॥ शुद्ध्येयुः स्त्री च शूद्रश्च सकृत्स्पृष्टाभिरन्ततः । अन्तत ओष्ठप्रान्तेनेत्यर्थः ॥ ब्राह्मणः विप्रस्तीर्थेन नित्यकालमुपस्पृशेत् ॥ कायत्रैः दशिकाभ्यां वा न पित्र्येण कदाचन । कनिष्ठादेशिन्यङ्गुष्ठमूलान्यग्रकरस्य च । प्रजापतिपितृब्रह्मदेवतीर्थान्यनुक्रमात् ॥

hastagaṁ prathamāttirthāddakṣiṇāt triḥ pibejjalam । aśabdamanavastrāvamabahirjānvabudbudam ॥ dakṣiṇantu karaṁ

then perform Aṅganyāsa by adhering to the Aṅganyāsa technique.

(Aṅganyāsa is the ceremony of touching certain parts of the body.) Touch the vital sense organs:

vāṁme āsye'stu—"Let there be speech in my mouth." So saying, touch your mouth with the first three fingers of your hand.

nasorme prāṇo'stu—"Let there be breath in my nostrils." Having said this, touch your nostrils with your thumb and forefinger at once.

akṣṇorme cakṣurastu—"Let there be vision in my eyes." With this, touch your eyes with your middle finger and tumb.

karṇayorme śrotramastu—"Let my ears hear." Touch your right ear first and then the left ear with your ring finger and thumb.

bāhvorme balamastu—Having said, "Let me be sturdy-armed," touch your right arm first and then the left one with your thumb and little finger.

ūrvorme ojo'stu—Having said, "Let my thighs be strong and muscled," touch your right thigh first and then the left one with all your fingers.

ariṣṭāni me'ṅgāni tanūstanvā me saha santu—"Let my physical organs be rid of all debilitating illnesses at once." Touch your body from head to foot with both hands. This is how Aṅganyāsa should be performed.

ततो वरः गोस्तुतिं करोति ।

tato varaḥ gostutiṁ karoti ।

---

kṛtvā gokarṇākṛtivatpunaḥ । triḥ pibedvīkṣitaṁ toyamāsyaṁ dvi parimārjayet ॥ adbhistu prakṛtisthābhirhīnābhiḥ phenabudbudaiḥ । hṛtkaṇṭhatālugābhiśca yathāsaṁkhyaṁ dvijādayaḥ ॥ śuddhyeyuḥ strī ca śūdraśca sakṛtspṛṣṭābhirantataḥ । antata oṣṭhaprānte-netyarthaḥ ॥ brāhmaṇaḥ viprastīrthena nityakālamupaspṛśet ॥ kāyatraiḥ daśikābhyāṁ vā na pitryeṇa kadācana । kaniṣṭhā-deśinyaṅguṣṭhamūlānyagra karasya ca । prajāpatipitṛbrahma-devatīrthānyanukramāt ॥

Then bowing to the cow the bridegroom should perform the following sacrament:

ततो यजमानद्वारा गौर्गौर्गौरित्यभिहिते । अत्र वर-यजमानाभ्यां तृणच्छेदनमाचारो न तु विधिः अत एवं पद्धतिषु । ततो वरस्तृणं यजमानेन सह गृहीत्वाऽग्रिमं मंत्रं पठेत् ।

tato yajamānadvārā gaurgaurgaurityabhihite । *atra vara-yajamānābhyāṃ tṛṇacchedanamācāro na tu vidhiḥ ata evaṁ paddhatiṣu* । *tato varastṛṇaṁ yajamānena saha gṛhitvā-'grimaṁ maṁtraṁ paṭhet* ।

Here 'Tṛṇachedana' by the bridegroom and the host is just a custom and not a rule. That is why the law books are silent on this point while the manuals or handbooks (*paddhatis*) mention it. Thereafter the host has to repeat 'gaurgaurgauḥ' three times and let a piece of straw (*tṛṇa*) be picked up by the bridegroom and himself (to indicate that they are protectors of the cow and that they look upon its meat as little more than worthless trash).

ॐ माता रुद्राणां दुहिता वसूना॑ स्वसादित्यानामृत्तस्य नाभिः । प्रनु वोचं चिकितुषे जनाय मा गामनागामदितिं वधिष्ट—मम चामुष्य च पाप्मा हतः ।

aum mātā rudrāṇāṁ duhitā vasūnāṁ svasādityānāmamṛtasya nābhiḥ । *pranu vocaṁ cikituṣe janāya mā gāmanāgāmaditiṁ vadhiṣṭa—mama cāmuṣya ca pāpmā hataḥ* ।

(ahaṁ cikituṣe cetanāvate janāya ko'rthaḥ yajamānāya) I tell the sensible host (nu iti tarke pravocaṁ bravīmi) that he must not kill this innocent living cow for my sport and pleasure; she is the mother of the Rudras (rudrāṇāṁ mātā) and the daughter of the Vasus (vasūnāṁ duhitā). She was born of the ocean on the occasion of its legendary churning by gods and demons. She is the sister of the celestial deities called the Ādītyas (ādityānāṁ svasā), all sons of Nārāyaṇa, as she is the source of the nectar of milk (amṛtasya nābhiḥ).

So she is unslaughterable and fit to be nursed by me. May she destroy my transgressions as well as my host's.

ॐ उत्सृजत तृणान्यत्तूद्धृत्योत्सृजेत् इति ब्रूयात् । उत्सृजेत्तु तामिति तृणं छिन्द्यादित्युत्सृजेत् ।

aum utsṛjat tṛṇānyattūddhṛtyotsṛjet iti brūyāt । utsṛjettu tāmiti tṛṇaṁ chindyādityutsṛjet ।

Bowing to the cow with the repetition of 'aum mātā rudrāṇāṁ', the bridegroom snatches the straw with sudden force and snaps it asunder. Then he says, "May my most venerable cow, whom I look after with loving care, feed on this grass!"

ततो यजमानः वराय[1] गोदानं दद्यात्संकल्पं चैव कुर्यात् ।

---

1. In this Kali Age (*Kaliyuga*) some dull-witted people question the propriety of making the gift of cows to the brāhmaṇa and of his acceptance of the offer. "Why should the bridegroom be debarred from receiving the gift?" one may ask. Those who level such allegations are blind to the fact that the three *varṇas* to which the non-brāhmaṇas belong have no right to receive *dānas* or gifts.

One should keep one's eyes open and see for himself the exegesis on the Vedic mantra *ko'dātkasmādāt,* on the basis of which the bridegroom says, "Blessed is Love the Conqueror of the World who compels even those (the kṣatriyas, etc.) who never accept gifts, to accept the gift of a maiden—kanyādāna. The mantra is expressive of the remorse and embarrassment of a non-brāhmaṇa bridegroom. If the gift of a maiden so embarrasses a *traivarṇika* bridegroom and fills him with remorse, then how can a non-brāhmaṇa bridegroom accept the gift of a cow? Moreover, in the expression 'varāya godānaṁ dadyāt', the word 'vara' does not signify the bridegroom being married but stands for 'excellence', *śreṣtha.* That is why in the Saṁkalpa a little further 'śarmaṇe varāya' has been used, 'śarmā' being the title of a brāhmaṇa. What 'varāya ko'rthah śreṣthabrāhmaṇāya godānaṁ dadyāt', therefore, means is that the gift of the cow (godāna) should be made to a worthy brāhmaṇa, not to any and every Tom, Dick, and Harry, who appears for marriage. If the gift of the cow is made

tato yajamānaḥ varāya godānaṁ dadyātsaṁkalpaṁ caivaṁ kuryāt ।

The host should then gift the cow to the bridegroom

ॐ विष्णुः ३ अद्येत्यादि देशकालौ संकीर्त्य० एवं ग्रहगुण-विशेषणविशिष्टायां महापुण्यतिथौ अमुकगोत्रोऽमुकशर्म्माहमिमां मधुपर्कसंबन्धिनीं गां तन्मौल्योपकल्पितां दक्षिणां वाऽमुकगोत्राया-ऽमुकशर्मणे वराय तुभ्यं संप्रददे । स्वस्तीति वरो ब्रूयात् । ततो गोदानप्रतिष्ठार्थं दक्षिणां च दद्यात् ।

aum viṣṇuḥ 3 adyetyādi deśakālau saṁkīrtya० evaṁ grahaguṇaviśeṣaṇaviśiṣṭāyāṁ mahāpuṇyatithau amuka-gotro'mukaśarmmāhamimāṁ madhuparkasaṁbandhinīṁ gāṁ tanmaulyopakalpitāṁ dakṣiṇāṁ vā'mukagotrāyā-'mukaśarmaṇe varāya tubhyaṁ saṁpradadade । *svastīti varo brūyāt* । *tato godānapratiṣṭhārthaṁ dakṣiṇāṃ ca dadyāt* ।

This done (the saṁkalpa uttered), the bridegroom should thus address the host: "I wish you well." The process of positioning the sacrificial fire by the bridegroom is as follows:

ततो वेदिकायास्तुषकेशशर्कराभस्मादिरहितां चतुरस्त्रां भूमिं कुशैः परिसमुह्य तानैशान्यां परित्यज्य गोमयोदकेनोपलिप्य स्पयेन स्त्रुवमूलेन वा प्रागग्रप्रादेशमितमुत्तरोत्तरक्रमेण त्रिरुल्लिख्योल्लेखनक्रमेणाऽनामिकाङ्-गुष्ठाभ्यां मृदमुद्धृत्य जलेनाभ्युक्ष्य तत्र तूष्णीं कांस्यपात्रेण पिहितं शुद्धपुरुषेणाऽन्येनानीतमग्निं दृष्ट्वा वरः संकल्पं कुर्यात् ।

tato vedikāyāstuṣakeśaśarkarābhasmādirahitāṁ caturasrāṁ bhūmiṁ kuśaiḥ parisamuhya tānaiśānyāṁ parityajya gomayodakenopalipya spayena sruvamūlena vā prāgagraprādeśamitamuttarottarakrameṇa trirullikhyol-

---

to a brāhmaṇa bridegroom, it is twice blessed, for the person receiving the gift is not only a brāhmaṇa but also meritorious and worthy.

lekhanakrameṇā' nāmikāṅguṣṭhābhyāṁ mṛdamuddhṛtya jalenābhyukṣya tatra tūṣṇīṁ kāṁsyapātreṇa pihitaṁ śuddhapuruṣeṇā'neynānītamagniṁ dṛṣṭvā varaḥ saṁkalpaṁ kuryāt ।

The quadrilateral space, a cubit in length (i.e. the length of the arm from the elbow to the tip of the middle finger), around the first sacrificial altar should be meticulously swept clean with a broom made of kuśa grass. Once the altar is tidied and the impurities of hair, pebbles, ashes, chaff and other forbidden objects are removed, it is smeared with cowdung and water and three oblique lines running from east to west are drawn upon it with a *sruva* (a small wooden ladle). Start cutting the patterns (i.e. drawing the lines) one after another from right (*dakṣiṇa*) to left (*uttara*). Then the same process should be adopted while throwing away the loosened[1] soil with the ring finger and the thumb. Having completed this ritual, spray the altar with water and then, silently glancing at the fire kept in a brass container (screened with another jar made of the same metal) which has been brought by another person who is spotlessly clean, the bridegroom should utter the following Saṁkalpa.

अद्येत्यादि० अमुकगोत्रोत्पन्नोऽमुकशर्माऽहं धर्मार्थकामसिद्धिद्वारा श्रीपरमेश्वरप्रीतये ब्राह्मविधिना विवाहकर्मकर्तुं पञ्चभूसंस्कार-पूर्वकमग्निस्थापनं करिष्ये इति सङ्कल्प्य स्वयं प्राङ्मुखो वरः यस्मिन्पात्रे स्थितोऽयमग्निः तत्पात्रं प्रत्यङ्मुखं स्थापयित्वाऽग्निपूजनं कुर्यात् ।

adyetyādi० amukagotrotpanno'mukaśarmā'haṁ dharmārthakāmasiddhidvārā śrīparameśvaraprītaye brāhmavidhinā vivāhakarmakartuṁ pañcabhūsaṁskāra-pūrvakamagnisthāpanaṁ kariṣye iti saṅkalpya svayaṁ prāṅmukho varaḥ yasminpātre sthito'yamagniḥ tatpātraṁ pratyaṅmukhaṁ sthāpayitvā'gnipūjanaṁ kuryāt ।

---

1. i.e. in the process of using the *sruva* to draw lines on the altar or cut the pattern of lines on it.

Having done so, the bridegroom should turn to the east by himself, keep the fire in front and do obeisance to it with the citation of the following mantra:

ॐ जयन्ती मंगला काली भद्रकाली कपालिनी । दुर्गा क्षमा शिवा धात्री स्वाहा स्वधा नमोऽस्तु ते ॥१॥ पश्चात्पात्रस्थमग्निं वेदिकायां संस्थाप्य तद्रक्षार्थं कञ्चिन्नियुज्य कौतुकागाराद्वरः वाद्यशब्दपूर्वकं कन्यां मंडपे आनीय स्वदक्षिणतः सत्कारपूर्वकमुपवेशयेत् ।

aum jayantī maṁgalā kālī bhadrakālī kapālinī । durgā kṣamā śivā dhātrī svāhā svadhā namo'stu te ॥ 1 ॥ paścāt-pātrasthamagniṁ vedikāyāṁ saṁsthāpya tadrakṣārthaṁ kañcinniyujya kautukāgārādvaraḥ vādyaśabdapūrvakaṁ kanyāṁ maṁḍape ānīya svadakṣiṇataḥ satkāra-pūrvakamupaveśayet ।

After the obeisance has been paid, the fire, till now contained in the brass receptacle, should be kept on the altar and well protected by feeding it with *palasa* leaves or by posting a guard to keep watch. It is at this stage that the bridegroom should lead the bride from the Kautukāgāra to the pavilion to the accompaniment of music and respectfully seat her on his right. The śāstras enjoin that the bridegroom himself should lead the maiden out of the Kautukāgāra, but the practice has ceased to find popular favour, which prefers the maternal uncle of the maiden to do what the bridegroom should have done. As it has the approval of custom and a rationale, there is nothing improper about it, for, as the saying goes, *yadyapi śuddhaṁ lokaviruddhaṁ nācaraṇīyam,* that is, even the purest of rules are not worth following if they conflict with custom.

ततः कन्या संकल्पं कुर्यात्
tataḥ kanyā saṁkalpaṁ kuryāt

Then must the maiden utter the following Saṁkalpa for the worship of the various divinities, *Devapūjana.*

अद्येत्यादि० मम विवाहोत्सवकर्मणि निर्विघ्नेन वरप्राप्तिपूर्वकपुत्र-

पौत्रादिफलप्राप्तये गणेशादिकृपया अखंडसौभाग्यफलप्राप्त्यर्थं च गणेशादिग्रहाणां सुप्रतिष्ठितानां पूजनमहं करिष्ये । ततो गणपत्यादीनां पूजनं ओमादिनमोन्तकैस्तत्तन्मत्रैर्वा कुर्यात् । ततो यजमानः मौड्याः पटकस्य पूजनं कृत्वा कन्याशिरसि शब्दपूर्वकं मौडीबंधनं विधाय वराय वस्त्रचतुष्टयं प्रयच्छति । संकल्पस्त्वेवम्-देशकालौ संकीर्त्य० अद्याऽमुकगोत्रोत्पन्नोऽहं मम सकलकामनासिद्धये एतत् वस्त्रचतुष्टयं अमुकगोत्रायाऽमुकशर्मणे वराय तुभ्यं संप्रददे-स्वस्तीति वरो ब्रूयात् । प्रथमस्तु वरस्तेषु मध्ये द्वयं कन्यायै दद्यात् ।

adyetyādi° mama vivāhotsavakarmaṇi nirvighnena varaprāptipūrvakaputrapautrādiphalaprāptaye gaṇeśādi-kṛpayā akhaṁḍasaubhāgyaphalaprāptyarthaṁ ca gaṇeśādi-grahāṇāṁ supratiṣṭhitānāṁ pūjanamahaṁ kariṣye । tato gaṇapatyādīnāṁ pūjanaṁ kṛtvā kanyāśirasi śabda-pūrvakaṁ mauḍībaṁdhanaṁ vidhāya varāya vastra-catuṣṭayaṁ prayacchati । saṁkalpastvevam-deśakālau saṁkīrtya° adya'mukagotrotpanno'haṁ mama sakala-kāmanāsiddhaye etat vastracatuṣṭayaṁ amukagotrāyā-'mukaśarmaṇe varāya tubhyaṁ saṁpradade-svastīti varo brūyāt । prathamastu varasteṣu madhye dvayaṁ kanyāyai dadyāt ।

Having uttered the above Saṁkalpa, the maiden should worship Gaṇeśa and the planets (which influence the destinies of men and are either auspicious or inauspicious) already installed there symbolically. Each of these should be worshipped with 'aum' as the first and 'namaḥ' as the last word of the incantation. In between the two, name the divinity being worshipped. This should be done in a general way or else with propitiatory mantras with which they are honoured in the holy texts. Then the host should do obeisance to the ornamental diadem (*maurī*) and tie it around the bride's head. This is followed by the offer of four pieces of clothing by the bride's father for the bridegroom with the repetition of the above Saṁkalpa. The bridegroom should offer two of these to the bride.

ततः परिधानम्

tataḥ paridhānam

The bridegroom should then offer new undergarments[1] to the bride, saying:

ॐ जरां गच्छ परिधत्स्व[2] वासो भवाकृष्टीनामभिशस्तिपावा । शतञ्च जीव शरदः सुवर्चा रयिञ्च पुत्राननुसंव्ययस्वाऽऽयुष्मतीदं परिधत्स्व वासः– इति मन्त्रेण वरः कन्यायै अधोवस्त्रं दद्यात् ।

aum jarāṁ gaccha paridhatsva vāso bhavākṛṣṭīnāmabhiśastipāvā । śatañca jīva śaradaḥ suvarcā rayiñca putrānanusaṁvyayasvā''yuṣmatīdaṁ paridhatsva vāsaḥ—iti mantreṇa varaḥ kanyāyai adhovastraṁ dadyāt ।

O maiden blessed with longevity! May you live long and never suffer dearth of clothes. May you be a woman of winning charms (tvaṁ ākṛṣṭī bhava ākṛṣyante manolocanāni anayetyākṛṣṭī arthāt manoharā) and alluring temperament and may you shed all your childhood playfulness and insensibility and be sociable and tender to your kindreds like your father-in-law. May you also be the best among women and live as long as I would do and may you radiate the splendour of fidelity and be the source of wealth and male progeny.

With this mantra the bridegroom should let the bride have new undergarments.

अथोत्तरीयं वासः समादाय वरोऽग्रिममंत्रेण परिधापयेत् । ॐ या अकृन्तन्नवयन् या अतन्वत । याश्च देवीस्तन्तूनभितो ततन्थ । तास्त्वा देवीर्जरसे संव्ययस्वाष्मतीदं परिधत्स्व वासः ॥

1. अधौतवस्त्रो यः कुर्यान्नित्यनैमित्तिकीं क्रियाम् । न क्रियाफलमाप्नोति वृथा तस्य परिश्रमः ॥
adhautavastro yaḥ kuryānnityanaimittikīṁ kriyām । na kriyāphalamāpnoti vṛthā tasya pariśramaḥ ॥

2. सदशं नूतनं वस्त्रं मञ्जिष्ठादिसुरञ्जितम् । अहतं तद्विजानीयादित्युक्तं पूर्वसूरिभिः ॥ २ वासोलक्षणेन शुभं ज्ञातये–ईषद्धौतं नव श्वेतं सदशं यन्न धारितम् । अहतं तद्विजानीयात् सर्वकर्मसु पावनम् ॥
sadaśaṁ nūtanaṁ vastraṁ mañjiṣṭhādisurañjitam । ahataṁ tadvijānīyādityuktaṁ pūrvasūribhiḥ ॥ 2 vāsolakṣaṇena śubhaṁ jñāyate—īṣaddhautaṁ nava śvetaṁ sadaśaṁ yanna dhāritam । ahataṁ tadvijānīyāt sarvakarmasu pāvanam ॥

athottarīyaṁ vāsaḥ samādāya varo'grimamaṁtreṇa paridhāpayet । aum yā akṛntannavayan yā atanvata । yāśca devīstantūnabhito tatantha । tāstvā devīrjarase saṁvyayasvāṣmatīdaṁ paridhatsva vāsaḥ ॥

The meaning of the mantra is stated in terms of the craft and skill involved in the meaning of cloth. What it says is that the uppergarment given to the bride is a sacred piece of cloth divinely textured by celestial maidens and goddesses. It is these *devīs* who placed the set of yarns lengthwise in the loom, crossed it by and intersected it with the weft. Thus to them goes the credit for forming the lengthwise threads in the fabric and for getting the cloth woven. (They unrolled and rolled the yarns according to expediency and skilfully completed the whole process.) Being bestowers of power and talent, they are giving you this garment, their own handiwork (svakāryarūpavadidaṁ vāsaḥ), so that you may live long (jarase dīrghakālanirduṣṭajīvanāya saṁvyayaṣva paridhāpayanti). O *Āyuṣmati* (Maiden blessed with a long life)! For this reason put on this uppergarment. With this incantation, let the bride wear it.

ततो वरः स्वयं परिधत्ते

tato varaḥ svayaṁ paridhatte

The bridegroom should also take two pieces of clothing and wear them with the citation of the following mantras:

ॐ परिधास्यै यशोधास्यै दीर्घायुष्ट्वाय जरदष्टिरस्मि । शतञ्च जीवामि शरदः पुरूची रायस्पोषमभिसंव्ययिष्ये ॥ इति मंत्रेणाऽधोवस्त्रं वरः परिधत्ते ।

aum paridhāsyai yaśodhāsyai dīrghāyuṣṭvāya jaradaṣtirasmi । śatañca jīvāmi śaradaḥ purūcī rāyaspoṣamabhisaṁvyayiṣye ॥ iti maṁtreṇā'dhovastraṁ varaḥ paridhatte ।

O dress deities! I wear this garment for both fair fame and long life free from all defilements. It is by your grace that I, a mortal, will live my full life. This garment is the augmentor of wealth and bestower of a long life of hundred years.

The bridegroom should wear the undergarment with the citation of this mantra:

ॐ यशसा मा द्यावापृथिवी यशसेन्द्राबृहस्पती । यशो भगश्च माऽविन्दद्यशो मा प्रतिपद्यताम्–इति मन्त्रेण वर उत्तरीयं च धत्ते ।

aum yaśasā mā dyāvāpṛthivī yaśasendrābṛhaspatī । yaśo bhagaśca mā'vindadyaśo mā pratipadyatām—iti mantreṇa vara uttarīyaṁ ca dhatte ।

O dress deities! May I acquire the honour and glory of the heavens and the earth, of Indra and Bṛhaspati and of the gracious Lord, the sun (tathā ca bhagaḥ sūryo'pi yaśasā yukto māvindat). I may attain the glory all these gods have accumulated (taccaitaiḥ sampāditaṁ yaśo mā māṁ pratipadyatāṁ māṁ prāpnuyāt mayi sarvadā tiṣṭhatvititātparyam).

The uppergarment should be worn with the recitation of this mantra:

ततः कन्याया वरस्य च द्विराचमनम् ॥ ततः कन्याप्रदेन परस्परं समंजेथामिति प्रेषितयोः परस्परं सम्मुखीकरणम् ।

tataḥ kanyāyā varasya ca dvirācamanam । tataḥ kanyāpradena parasparaṁ samaṁjethāmiti preṣitayoḥ parasparaṁ sammukhīkaraṇam ।

Thereafter the bridegroom and the bride should perform two Ācamanas each. This done, the bride's father should let the bridegroom and the bride face each other (athainau vadhūvarau kanyāpitā samañjayati parasparaṁ sammukhīkaroti—'samaṁjantu viśvedevā' iti mantreṇa) with the repetition of 'samaṁjantu viśvedevā' (samaṁjanaṁ ca yuvāṁ parasparaṁ samañjethāmiti preṣitayoḥ parasparaṁ sammukhīkaraṇam). 'Samaṁjana' is but looking at each other by the bridegroom and the bride when instructed by the bride's father (or when brought face to face with each other by him).

It is incumbent upon him[1] to bring them together to face each other and upon the bridegroom to read the following mantra:

ॐ समञ्जन्तु विश्वेदेवाः समापो हृदयानि नौ । सम्मातरिश्वा सन्धाता समुदेष्ट्री दधातु नौ–इति वरः पठेत् ।

aum samañjantu viśvedevāḥ samāpo hṛdayāni nau । *sammātariśvā sandhātā samudeṣṭrī dadhātu nau—iti varaḥ paṭhet* ।

O maiden![2] All the gods of the world (viśvedevāḥ samastadevatāḥ) may, like pure water, purge your mind as well as your *saṁskāras* (mental impressions on the mind of acts done in a former state of existence) of the taint of sin while letting you retain all the best (womanly) qualities.

---

1. वासांसि परिधायैतावाचान्तौ यदि तिष्ठतः । सम्मुखीकरणं कुर्यात्तयोस्तु दुहितुः पिता ॥ सुमन्तुरपि–पिता तु प्रेषणेनैव सम्मुखीकरणञ्चरेत् । मन्त्रलिंगात्तु मन्त्रस्तु पठनीयो वरेण च ॥ इति सत्यपि कारितत्वे वरस्यैव मंत्रपाठो मंत्रलिङ्गात् । कारितत्वञ्च सन्निधानात्कन्यापितुरेव सन्निहितत्वं ह्यस्य तु प्रदातृत्वात् । मन्त्रपाठोऽपि कन्यासम्मुखमेव ।

vāsāṁsi paridhāyaitāvācāntau yadi tiṣṭhataḥ । sammukhīkaraṇaṁ kuryāttayostu duhituḥ pitā ॥ sumanturapi—pitā tu preṣaṇenaiva sammukhīkaraṇañcaret । mantraliṁgāttu mantrastu paṭhanīyo vareṇa ca ॥ iti satyapi kāritatve varasyaiva maṁtrapāṭho maṁtraliṅgāt । kāritatvañca sannidhānātkanyāpitureva sannihitatvaṁ hyasya tu pradātṛtvāt । mantrapāṭho'pi kanyāsammukhameva ।

2. आप्रदानाद्भवेत्कन्या चाभिषेकाद्वधूः स्मृता । सुमङ्गल्या चतुर्थ्यां तु यथात्रेर्वचनं यथा ॥ अभिषेकानन्तरं सुमङ्गलीवधूशब्दप्रवृत्तिः । तथा च नारदः–दशवर्षा भवेत्कन्या सम्प्रदाने वधूर्भवेत् । साङ्गुष्ठग्रहणे भार्या पत्नी चातुर्थकर्मणि ॥ एतच्छब्दप्रयोजनमाह ॥ कन्यादर्शनमात्रं स्याद्वरस्य वचनं न हि । बध्वा दर्शनसंस्पर्शभाषणं मुनिभिः स्मृतम् ॥ वामभागे स्थितिः प्रोक्ता भार्याया धर्मकर्मसु । सर्वं भोगविलासादि पत्न्या सह समाचरेत् ॥

āpradānādbhavetkanyā cābhiṣekādvadhūḥ smṛtā । sumaṅgalyā caturthyāṁ tu yathātrervacanaṁ yathā ॥ abhiṣekānantaraṁ sumaṅgalīvadhūśabdapravṛttiḥ । tathā ca nāradaḥ—daśavarṣā bhavetkanyā sampradāne vadhūrbhavet । sāṅguṣṭhagrahaṇe bhāryā patnī cāturthakarmaṇi ॥ etacchabdaprayojanamāha ॥ kanyādarśanamātraṁ syādvarasya vacanaṁ na hi । badhvā darśanasaṁsparśabhāṣaṇaṁ munibhiḥ smṛtam ॥ vāmabhāge sthitiḥ proktā bhāryāyā dharmakarmasu । sarvaṁ bhogavilāsādi patnyā saha samācaret ॥

Like a propitious wind (sammātariśvā anukūlo vāyuḥ), let Prajāpati be favourable and lead us to righteousness and help us attain wealth, potency and liberation. Let the god of the Gāyatrī mantra grant us the four goals of life: dharma, artha, kāma and mokṣa (nau hṛdayāni dadhātu dharmārthakāmamokṣeṣu susthitāni karotu).

Some carping critics may object to the use of 'samañjantu' and to the exhortation 'O maiden'. Such an address does not imply any facetiousness, for till now the maiden is just an unmarried girl and not a bride (*vadhū*). What the maiden says is that the youth performing the marital rituals is like all other young men before his marriage (i.e. before the rituals are performed *in extenso*), which, in other words, means, "So long as we are unmarried, I remain unrelated to you, nor can I claim you as mine." It is for this reason that there is nothing objectionable, much less absurd, about addressing the bride as 'maiden', she is still a maiden before the gift (*dāna*) is completed.

ततः कन्याप्रदकर्तृकं ग्रन्थिबन्धनम् । ततः सपत्नीको यजमानः कन्यादानं कुर्यात् ।

tataḥ kanyāpradakartṛkaṁ granthibandhanam । *tataḥ sapatnīko yajamānaḥ kanyādānaṁ kuryāt* ।

Having completed the ritual of 'saṁmukhīkaraṇa' or of bringing the bridegroom and the bride to eye each other, the host giving the maiden in marriage shall take some coins, flowers, fruits, raw rice, etc. and keep them in the bride's clothes, one end of which should be tied to the bridegroom's garment in a knot[1] (kanyāpradakartṛkaṁ

---

1. तथा च योगी याज्ञवल्क्यः–कन्याकासुदशे पार्श्वे द्रव्यपुष्पाक्षतानि च । निक्षिप्य तानि सम्बद्ध्वा वरवस्त्रेण संयुजेत् ॥ वस्त्रैः संयोज्य तौ पूर्वं कन्यादानं समाचरेत् । दानेन युक्तयोः पश्चाद्विदध्यात् पाणिपीडनम् ॥ इति ।

tatha ca yogī yājñavalkyaḥ—kanyakāsudaśe pārśve dravyapuṣpākṣatāni ca । nikṣipya tāni sambaddhvā varavastreṇa saṁyujet ॥ vastraiḥ saṁyojya tau pūrvaṁ kanyādānaṁ samācaret । dānena yuktayoḥ paścādvidadhyāt pāṇipīḍanam ॥ iti ।

granthibandhanam—kanyāpradātā kartā yasya tat granthibandhanam dravyapuṣpaphalākṣatādi kanyāvāsasi nikṣipya granthi badhvā varavastreṇa kanyāprado granthibandhanaṁ kuryāt ।) The host and his wife should then perform the ceremony of Kanyādāna in keeping with the prescribed code.

यजमानः कन्याहस्तौ पीतौ कृत्वा जामातृदक्षिणकरोपरि कन्यादक्षिणकरं निधाय मौलिबन्धनं विधायेमं मंत्रं पठेत् । ॐ दाताऽहं वरुणो राजा द्रव्यमादित्यदैवतम् । वरोऽसौ विष्णुरूपेण प्रतिगृह्णात्वयं विधिः ॥ इति दाता पठेत् ।

yajamānaḥ kanyāhastau pītau kṛtvā jāmātṛ-dakṣiṇakaropari kanyādakṣiṇakaraṁ nidhāya maulibandhanaṁ vidhāyemaṁ maṁtraṁ paṭhet । *aum dātā'haṁ varuṇo rājā dravyamādityadaivatam* । *varo'sau viṣṇurūpeṇa pratigṛhṇātvayaṁ vidhiḥ* ॥ *iti dātā paṭhet* ।

Of the right and left palms of the maiden, both of which should be dyed yellow by the host the right one must be placed on the right palm of the bridegroom. A read thread (nālā or kalāvā which is tied on the wrist by the Hindus on auspicious occasions) should then be wrapped around the joined palms and the mantra beginning with 'aum dātā'haṁ' be repeated. (All this has to be done by the host, who claims, according to the mantra, that he is Varuṇa the king, the maiden being offered as *dāna* is like the resplendent sun or is possessed of the surpassing brilliance of the sungod, and the bridegroom is like Viṣṇu. He ends with the request that the bridegroom should accept the bride.) This is the holy sacrament of Kanyādāna; it is incumbent upon the host to bear this in mind.

अथ शाखोच्चारः

अर्थात् मंगलाष्टकपठनपूर्वकगोत्रोच्चारविधिं कृत्वा पश्चात् कन्यादानसंकल्पं कुर्यात् । प्रथमं वरपक्षे गोत्रोच्चारपूर्वकं मंगलाष्टकम् ।

atha śākhoccāraḥ

arthāt maṁgalāṣṭakapaṭhanapūrvakagotroccāravidhiṁ kṛtvā paścāt kanyādānasaṁkalpaṁ kuryāt । *prathamaṁ varapakṣe gotroccārapūrvakaṁ maṁgalāṣṭakam* ।

Before uttering the Saṁkalpa for Kanyādāna (marriage proper), the two ceremonies still to be performed are Gotroccāraṇa and Maṁgalāṣṭaka. It is the bridegroom's side, however, that performs the ceremony of Gotroccāraṇa along with Maṁgalāṣṭaka as follows:

भास्वान् काश्यपगोत्रजोऽरूणचिर्यः सिंहराशीश्वरः
षट्त्रिस्थो दशशोभनो गुणशशीभौमेषु मित्रं समा ।
शुक्रो मन्दरिपुः कलिङ्गजनितश्चाऽग्नीश्वरौ दैवते
मध्ये वर्तुलपूर्वदिग्दिनकरः कुर्यात्सदा मङ्गलम् ॥१॥

अद्याऽमुकगोत्रस्याऽमुकप्रवरस्य यजुर्वेदान्तर्गतमाध्यन्दिनीशाखाध्यायिनोऽमुकसूत्रिणोऽमुकशर्म्मणः प्रप्रौत्राय० आयुष्मते चिरजीविने कन्यार्थिने वराय ।

चन्द्रः कर्कटकः प्रभुः सितनिभश्चात्रेयगोत्रोद्भव-
श्चाग्नेय्यां चतुरस्त्रवारुणमुखश्चारोप्युमाधीश्वरः ।
षट्सप्ताऽग्निदशैकशोभनफलो नोरिर्बुधार्कप्रियः
स्वामी यामुनदेशजो हिमकरः कुर्यात्सदा मङ्गलम् ॥२॥
भौमो दक्षिणदिग्त्रिकोणयमदिग्विघ्नेश्वरो रक्तभः
स्वामी वृश्चिकमेषयोः सुरगुरुश्चार्कः शशी सौहृदः ।
ज्ञोरिः षट्त्रिफलप्रदश्च वसुधास्कन्दौ क्रमाद्देवते
भारद्वाजकुलोद्भवः क्षितिसुतः कुर्यात्सदा मङ्गलम् ॥३॥
सौम्योदङ्मुखपीतवर्णमगधश्चात्रेयगोत्रोद्भवो
बाणेशानदिशः सुहृच्छनिभृगुः शत्रुः सदा शीतगुः ।
कन्यायुग्मपतिर्दशाष्टचतुरः षण्णेत्रगः शोभनो
विष्णुः पौरुषदैवते शशिसुतः कुर्यात्सदा मंगलम् ॥४॥
जीवश्चाङ्गिरगोत्रजोत्तरमुखो दीर्घोत्तरासंस्थितः
पीताश्वत्थसमिच्च सिन्धुजनितश्चापोऽथ मीनाधिपः ।

सूर्येन्दुक्षितिजप्रियो बुधसितौ शत्रुः समाश्चापरे
सप्ताङ्कः द्विभवः शुभः सुरगुरुः कुर्यात्सदा मंगलम् ॥५॥
शुक्रो भार्गवगोत्रजः सितनिभः प्राचीमुखः पूर्वदिक्
पञ्चाङ्गो वृषभस्तुलाधिपमहाराष्ट्राधिपोदुम्बरः ।
इन्द्राणी मघवानुभौ बुधशनी मित्रेऽर्कचन्द्रौ रिपू
षष्ठो द्विर्दशवर्जितो भृगुसुतः कुर्यात्सदा मंगलम् ॥६॥
मन्दः कृष्णनिभस्तु पश्चिममुखः सौराष्ट्रकः काश्यपः
स्वामी वै मृगकुम्भयोबुर्धसितौ मित्रे समश्चाङ्गिराः ।
स्थानं पश्चिमदिक् प्रजापतियमौ देवौ धनुष्यासनः
षट्त्रिस्थः शुभकृच्छनी रविसुतः कुर्यात्सदा मंगलम् ॥७॥
राहुः सिंहलदेशजश्च निर्ॠतिः कृष्णाङ्गशूर्पासनो
यः पैठीनसिसंभवश्च समिधो दूर्वामुखो दक्षिणः ।
यः सर्पाद्यधिदेवते च निर्ॠतिप्रत्याधिदेवः सदा
षट्त्रिस्थः शुभकृच्च सिंहिकसुतः कुर्यात् सदा मंगलम् ॥८॥
केतुर्जैमिनिगोत्रजः कुशसमिद्वायव्यकोणे स्थित-
श्चित्राङ्गध्वजलाञ्छनो हिमगुहा यो दक्षिणाशामुखः ।
ब्रह्मा चैव सचित्रचित्रसहितः प्रत्याधिदेवः सदा
षट्त्रिस्थः शुभकृच्च बर्बरपतिः कुर्यात्सदा मंगलम् ॥९॥
इत्येतद् ग्रहमंगलाष्टनवकं लोकोपकारप्रदं
पापौघप्रशमं महच्छुभकरं सौभाग्यसंवर्द्धनम् ।
यः शुद्धः शृणुयाद्विवाहसमये श्रीकालिदासोदितं
स्तोत्रं मंगलदायकं शुभकरं प्राप्नोत्यभीष्टं फलम् ॥१०॥

bhāsvān kāśyapagotrajo'ruṇaruciryaḥ siṁharāśīśvaraḥ ṣaṭtristho daśaṣobhano guṇaśaśībhaumeṣu mitraṁ samā ।
śukro mandaripuḥ kaliṅgajanitaścā'gnīśvarau daivate madhye vartulapūrvadigdinakaraḥ kuryātsadā maṅgalam ॥ 1 ॥
adyā'mukagotrasyā'mukapravarasya yajurvedāntar-gatamādhyandinīśākhādhyāyino'mukasūtriṇo'muka-

śarmmaṇaḥ praprautrāya॰ āyuṣmate cirajīvine kanyārthine varāya ।

candraḥ karkaṭakaḥ prabhuḥ sitanibhaścātreyagotrod bhava-
ścāgneyyāṁ caturasravāruṇamukhaścāropyum-ādhīśvaraḥ ।
ṣaṭsaptā'gnidaśaikaśobhanaphalo norirbudhārkapriyaḥ
svāmī yāmunadeśajo himakuraḥ kuryātsadā maṅgalam ॥ 2 ॥

bhaumo dakṣiṇadigtrikoṇayamadigvighneśvaro raktabhaḥ
svāmī vṛścikameṣayoḥ suraguruścārkaḥ śaśī sauhṛdaḥ ।
jñoriḥ ṣaṭtriphalapradaśca vasudhāskandau kramād-devate
bhāradvājakulodbhavaḥ kṣitisutaḥ kuryātsadā maṅgalam ॥ 3 ॥

saumyodaṅmukhapītavarṇamagadhaścātreyagotrod-bhavo
bāṇeśānadiśaḥ suhṛcchanibhṛguḥ śatruḥ sadā śītaguḥ ।
kanyāyugmapatirdaśāṣṭacaturaḥ ṣaṇṇetragaḥ śobhano
viṣṇuḥ pauruṣadaivate śaśisutaḥ kuryātsadā maṁgalam ॥ 4 ॥

jīvaścāṅgiragotrajottaramukho dīrghottarāsaṁsthitaḥ
pītāśvatthasamicca sindhujanitaścāpo'tha mīnādhipaḥ ।
sūryendukṣitijapriyo budhasitau śatruḥ samāścāpare
saptāṅkaḥ dvibhavaḥ śubhaḥ suraguruḥ kuryātsadā maṁgalam ॥ 5 ॥

śukro bhārgavagotrajaḥ sitanibhaḥ prācīmukhaḥ pūrvadik
pañcāṅgo vṛṣabhastulādhipamahārāṣṭrādhipodum-baraḥ ।
indrāṇī maghavānubhau budhaśanī mitre'rkacandrau ripū
ṣaṣṭho dvirdaśavarjito bhṛgusutaḥ kuryātsadā maṁgalam ॥ 6 ॥

mandaḥ kṛṣṇanibhastu paścimamukhaḥ saurāṣṭrakaḥ kāśyapaḥ

svāmī vai mṛgakumbhayorbudhasitau mitre samaś-cāṅgirāḥ ।
sthānaṁ paścimadik prajāpatiyamau devau dhanu-ṣyāsanaḥ
ṣaṭtristhaḥ śubhakṛcchanī ravisutaḥ kuryātsadā maṁgalam ॥ 7 ॥
rāhuḥ siṁhaladeśajaśca nirṛtiḥ kṛṣṇāṅgaśūrpāsano
yaḥ paiṭhīnasisaṁbhavaśca samidho dūrvāmukho dakṣiṇaḥ ।
yaḥ sarpādyadhidevate ca na nirṛtipratyādhidevaḥ sadā
ṣaṭtristhaḥ śubhakṛcca siṁhikasutaḥ kuryātsadā maṁgalam ॥ 8 ॥
keturjaiminigotrajaḥ kuśasamidvāyavyakoṇe sthita-ścitrāṅgadhvajalāñchano himaguhā yo dakṣiṇāś-āmukhaḥ । *brahmā caiva sacitracitrasahitaḥ pratyā-dhidevaḥ sadā ṣaṭtristhaḥ śubhakṛcca barbarapatiḥ kuryātsadā maṁgalam* ॥ 9 ॥
ityetad grahamaṁgalāṣṭanavakaṁ lokopakārapradaṁ
pāpaughapraśamaṁ mahacchubhakaraṁ saubhāgya-saṁvarddhanaṁ ।
yaḥ śuddhaḥ śṛṇuyādvivāhasamaye śrīkālidāsoditaṁ
stotraṁ maṁgaladāyakaṁ śubhakaraṁ prāpnotya-bhīṣṭaṁ phalaṁ ॥ 10 ॥

अथ कन्यापक्षे मङ्गलाष्टकं प्रारभ्यते

इभमुखोब्जभवः कमलापतिः शिवशिवाऽनुगतारकदर्पहाः ।
खगपतिर्विबुधा विबुधस्त्रियः शुभगतिं प्रदिशन्तु सदा हि नः ॥१॥
दिनकरोऽत्रिजभूमिजचन्द्रजाः सुरगुरुर्भृगुदैत्यगुरुस्तथा ।
रविजचन्द्ररिपुर्ग्रहकेतवः शुभगतिं प्रदिशन्तु सदा हि नः ॥२॥
नदनदीशधराधरणीधराः वरुणवायुधनेशवनेचराः ।
मदनपावकदिग्गजपन्नगाः शुभगतिं प्रदिशन्तु सदा हि नः ॥३॥
त्रिपथगा यमुना च सरस्वती, शुभनदी सरयूर्मलहारिणी ।
मधुमती गिरिका च दृषद्वती शुभगतिं प्रदिशन्तु सदा हि नः ॥४॥
नृहरिकूर्मसुमत्स्यवराहकाः कपिलवामनधर्मदिगीश्वराः ।
दशरथः ससुतोङ्गदमारुती शुभगतिं प्रदिशन्तु सदा हि नः ॥५॥

यदुपतिर्बलबुद्धिजिनेश्वराः कलियुगान्तकरो जमदग्निजः ।
मनुमरीचिवशिष्ठकुमारकाः शुभगतिं प्रदशिन्तु सदा हि नः ॥६॥
पुलहकश्यपगौतमगाधिजाः सरभकुंभजवल्मिकसंभवाः ।
लिखितहारितशंखकुशादयः शुभगतिं प्रदिशन्तु सदा हि नः ॥७॥
ऋषभनारददक्षपराशराः शुनकशौनकगालवकर्दमाः ।
हरिकलांशकलाः पृथिवीश्वराः शुभगतिं प्रदिशन्तु सदा हि नः ॥८॥
अभयरामबुधेन जयाष्टकं शुभमिदं करहंसपुरे कृतम् ।
पठति यो हि विवाहसुमङ्गले भवतु सौख्यकरं वरकन्ययोः ॥९॥
ग्रामे श्रीकरहंसनाम्नि विमले भैयादिरामेण य-
च्छ्रीमद्भूसुरकुञ्जलालतनुजेनेदं कृतञ्चाष्टकम् ।
तच्छीघ्रं वरकन्ययोर्ददतु शं पाणिग्रहे सर्वदा
नित्यं ये प्रपठन्ति सादरतया तेषां सदा मङ्गलम् ॥१०॥

atha kanyāpakṣe maṅgalāṣṭakam prārabhyate

ibhamukhobjabhavaḥ kamalapatiḥ śivaśivā'nugatāraka-darpahāḥ ।
khagapatirvibudhā vibudhastriyaḥ śubhagatiṃ pradiśantu sadā hi naḥ ॥ 1 ॥
dinkaro'trijabhūmijacandrajāḥ suragururbhṛgudaitya-gurustathā ।
ravijacandraripurgrahaketavaḥ śubhagatiṁ pradiśantu sadā hi naḥ ॥ 2 ॥
nadanadīśadharādharaṇīdharāḥ varuṇavāyudhane-śavanecarāḥ ।
madanapāvakadiggajapannagāḥ śubhagatiṁ pradiśantu sadā hi naḥ ॥ 3 ॥
tripathagā yamunā ca sarasvatī, śubhanadī sarayūrmala-hāriṇī ।
madhumatī girikā ca dṛṣadvatī śubhagatiṁ pradiśantu sadā hi naḥ ॥ 4 ॥
nṛharikūrmasumatsyavarāhakāḥ kapilavāmanadharma-digīśvarāḥ ।
daśarathaḥ sasutoṅgadamārutī śubhagatiṁ pradiśantu sadā hi naḥ ॥ 5 ॥

yadupatirbalabuddhijineśvarāḥ kaliyugāntakaro jamad-
agnijaḥ ।
manumarīcivaśiṣṭhakumārakāḥ śubhagatiṁ pradiśantu
sadā hi naḥ ॥ 6 ॥
pulahakaśyapagautamagādhijāḥ sarabhakuṁbhajaval-
mikasaṁbhavāḥ ।
likhitahāritaśaṁkhakuśādayaḥ śubhagatiṁ pradiśantu
sadā hi naḥ ॥ 7 ॥
ṛṣabhanāradadakṣaparāśarāḥ śunakaśaunakagālavakar-
damāḥ ।
harikalāṁśakalāḥ pṛthivīśvarāḥ śubhagatiṁ pradiśantu
sadā hi naḥ ॥ 8 ॥
abhayarāmabudhena jayāṣṭakaṁ śubhamidaṁ kara-
haṁsapure kṛtam ।
paṭhati yo hi vivāhasumaṅgale bhavatu saukhyakaraṁ
varakanyayoḥ ॥ 9 ॥
grāme śrīkarahaṁsanāmni vimale bhaiyādirāmeṇa
yacchrimadbhūsurakuñjalālatanujenedaṁ kṛtañcāṣṭa-
kam ।
tacchīghraṁ varakanyayordadatu śaṁ pāṇigrahe
sarvadā
nityaṁ ye prapaṭhanti sādaratayā teṣāṁ sadā
maṅgalam ॥ 10 ॥

अथ कन्यादानविधिः

ततो यजमानः स्वस्त्रिया सह ग्रन्थिबन्धनं विधाय शंखस्थ-दूर्वाक्षतफलपुष्प-चन्दनजलसहितं सहिरण्यं कन्याकराङ्गुष्ठं गृहीत्वा वरस्य वामकरं ताम्रमय्यां पृथिव्यां संस्थाप्य कन्यादानसंकल्पं कुर्यात् ।

atha kanyādānavidhiḥ

tato yajamānaḥ svastriyā saha granthibandhanaṁ vidhāya śaṁkhasthadūrvakṣata phala puṣpa candana jala sahitaṁ sahiraṇyaṁ kanyākarāṅguṣṭhaṁ gṛhītvā varasya vāmakaraṁ tāmramayyāṁ pṛthivyāṁ saṁsthāpya kanyādānasaṁkalpaṁ kuryāt ।

This accomplished, the host (or the person marrying off

the maiden) and his wife should have their garments tied together and perform the following ceremony:

Keep a few blades of *dūrbā* grass (*dūba*), raw rice, fruits, flowers, sandal, water, and some substance like gold in the centre of a conch. Hold the right-hand thumb of the bride. The left hand of the bridegroom should be kept on a few loose pieces of copper coins placed on the ground. Then he (the host) should have the following Saṁkalpa uttered. (tatra kanyādāne vidhiḥ—dātā śaṁkhasthetyādi pratigṛhṇātvayaṁ vidhiriti dātā paṭhedityantaṁ mūlakāreṇaina darśitaḥ ।) That is, according to the original text itself, the host, who is the donor, should collect in a conch the materials mentioned above and let the bride-groom accept them. There is also an evidence to support this statement.[1]

---

1. तथा च बृहत्पाराशरः–कन्यादानसमारम्भे दाता शंखे समाददेत् । दूर्वाक्षतफलं पुष्पं चन्दनं जलमेव च ॥ जामातृदक्षिणकरोपरि कन्यादक्षिणकरं निधाय कृत्वा दाताहमित्यादि वाक्यं दाता पठेत् ॥ कन्यादानं ततः कुर्याद्यथोक्तं प्रब्रुवन् वच इति ॥ वचः संकल्पादिवाक्यम् इति । संकल्पवाक्येऽपि विशेषमाह ऋष्यशृङ्गः– अद्येत्यादि यथाकालज्ञानं कृत्वा तु दैशिकम् । सप्तम्यन्तन्तु षष्ठ्यन्तं गोत्रं प्रवरमेव च ॥ वेदादिवत्समुच्चार्य प्रपितामहपूर्वकम् ॥ संज्ञाऽभिधानं चार्घस्य चतुर्थ्यन्तं वरन्तथा । द्वितीयान्तन्तु कन्याया नाम संकीर्तयेद् बुधः ॥ पितृगोत्रादिवत्याश्च फलसकीर्तनं ततः । पत्नीत्वेन तुभ्यमहं ददे इति समुत्सृजेत् ॥ ननु सर्वत्र वाक्ये तु पितृपूर्वकसम्बन्धकथनाऽभिधानत्वे सिद्धे प्रपितामहपूर्वकमिति वाक्ये कथमिति चेत् तत्राह ॥ प्रपितामहपूर्वकमेव विवाहादौ वाक्यमृषिभिः प्रोक्तं प्रमाणं तत्र ब्रह्मपुराणे–नान्दीमुखे विवाहादौ प्रपितामहपूर्वकम् । वाक्यमुच्चारयेत्प्राज्ञोऽप्यन्यत्र पितृपूर्वकमिति ॥ प्रपितामहादिसंबन्धनिरूपणमपि अमुकगोत्रस्य० प्रपौत्रायेत्यादिकमपि यत् तत् त्रिवारं वाक्यं पठेत् तथैव निरूपणात् ॥ तथा च कर्मदीपिकायाम् ॥ कन्यावरौ युतौ कृत्वा दाता स्वर्गादिसिद्धये । कन्यादानस्य वाक्ये तु द्वयोः सम्बन्धकीर्तनम् ॥ प्रपितामहादिमारभ्य गोत्रप्रवरादिसंयुतम् । कुलसंबन्धकरणं त्रिस्त्रिवारमुदीरणमिति ॥ कर्मकन्दल्यामपि–संबन्धमाभाषणपूर्वमाहुरिति आभाषणं परस्परमभिमुखीभूय पुनः पुनर्वार्ताकरणं तदेव पूर्वं मुख्यं यत्र तत् सम्बन्धमाहुरित्यर्थः । अन्यत्राऽपि– मैत्री सप्तपदा प्रोक्ता सप्तवाक्याऽथवा भवेत् । सत्तराणान्तु त्रिपदी सत्तमानां पदे पदे ॥ इति वचनात् ॥ द्वयोर्योनि- सम्बन्धजमैत्रीकरणे त्रिवारोच्चारणमेव । योनिसम्बधजा मैत्री तत्तुल्या नापरा स्मृता । अन्याश्चोत्पद्य नश्यन्ति नित्या मैत्रीयमुच्यते ॥ योनिसम्बन्धजा मैत्री वैरत्वेऽपि न नश्यति–इति धर्मवचनात् सम्बन्धानान्तु सर्वेषां योनिसम्बन्धमुत्तमम् । अन्यत्क्रोधे विनश्येत इदं तु न विनश्यति ॥ इति भृगुवचनात् ।

tathā ca bṛhatpārāśaraḥ—kanyādānasamārambhe dātā śaṁkhe samādadet । dūrvākṣataphalaṁ puṣpaṁ candanaṁ jalameva ca ॥ jāmātṛdakṣiṇakaropari kanyādakṣiṇakaraṁ nidhāya kṛtvā dātāhamityādi vākyaṁ dātā paṭhet ॥ kanyādānaṁ tataḥ kuryādyathoktaṁ prabruvan vaca iti ॥ vacaḥ saṁkalpādivākyam iti । saṁkalpavākye'pi viśeṣamāha ṛṣyaśṛṅgaḥ—adyetyādi yathākālajñānaṁ kṛtvā tu daiśikam । saptamyantantu ṣaṣṭhyantaṁ

अथ द्विजवर्णकन्यादानं[1] संकल्पः

हरिः ॐ विष्णुर्विष्णुर्विष्णुरपवित्रः पवित्रो वा सर्वाऽवस्थाङ्गतोऽपि वा । यः स्मरेत्पुण्डरीकाक्षं स बाह्याऽभ्यन्तरः शुचिः ॥ श्रीपुण्डरीकाक्षः

---

gotraṁ pravarameva ca ॥ vedādivatsamuccārya prapitāmahapūrvakam । saṁjña'bhidhānaṁ cārghasya caturthyantaṁ varantathā । dvitīyāntantu kanyāyā nāma saṁkīrtayed budhaḥ ॥ pitṛgotrādivatyāśca phalasakīrtanaṁ tataḥ । patnītvena tubhyamahaṁ dade iti samutsṛjet ॥ nanu sarvatra vākye tu pitṛpūrvaka sambandha kathanā'bhidhānatve siddhẹ prapitāmahapūrvaka miti vākye kathamiti cet tatrāha ॥ prapitāmahapūrvakameva vivāhādau vākyamṛṣibhiḥ proktaṁ pramāṇaṁ tatra brahmapurāṇe—nāndīmukhe vivāhādau prapitāmahapūrvakam । vākyamuccārayetprājño'pyanyatra pitṛpūrvakamiti ॥ prapitāmahādi saṁbandha nirūpaṇamapi amukagotrasya॰ prapautrāyetyādikamapi yat tat trivāraṁ vākyaṁ paṭhet tathaiva nirūpaṇāt ॥ tathā ca karmadīpikāyām ॥ kanyāvarau yutau kṛtvā dātā svargādisiddhaye । kanyānasya vākye tu dvayoḥ sambandhakīrtanam ॥ prapitāmahādimārabhya gotrapravarādisaṁyutam । kulasaṁbandhakaraṇaṁ tristrivāramudīraṇamiti ॥ karmakandalyāmapi—saṁbandhamābhāṣaṇapūrvamāhuriti ābhāṣaṇaṁ parasparamabhimukhībhūya punaḥ । punarvārtākaraṇaṁ tadeva pūrvaṁ mukhyaṁ yatra tat sambandhamāhurityarthaḥ । anyatrā'pi-maitrī saptapadā proktā saptavākyā'thavā bhavet । sattarāṇāntu tripadī sattamānāṁ pade pade ॥ iti vacanāt ॥ dvayoryonisambandhajamaitrīkaraṇe trivāroccāraṇameva । yonisambandhajā maitrī tattulyā nāparā smṛtā । anyāścotpadya naśyanti nityā maitrīyamucyate ॥ yonisambandhajā maitrī vairatve'pi na naśyati—iti dharmavacanāt sambandhānāntu sarveṣāṁ yonisambandhamuttamam । anyatkrodhe vinaśyeta idaṁ tu na vinaśyati ॥ iti bhṛguvacanāt ।

1. अथ कन्यादानसंकल्पवाक्यं लिख्यते ॥ कन्यादानस्यैवोत्कृष्टत्वमुक्तम् । कन्यादानात्परं दानं न भूतं न भविष्यति । गौतमः । अश्वमेधः क्रतुवरो यथा यज्ञेषु चोत्तमः । एवं सर्वेषु दानेषु कन्यादानं प्रशस्यते ॥ सूतसंहितायाम्–अश्वमेधसहस्रस्य वाजपेयशतस्य च । एककन्याप्रदानेन फलमाप्नोति निश्चितम् ॥ सुमन्तुरपि । यत्पुण्यं कोटियज्ञानां वेदपारायणे फलम् । कोटितीर्थस्नानजञ्च कन्यादाने ततोऽधिकमिति ॥ एकविंशतिवंश्यानामात्मना सह भूपते । एकस्मात्कन्यकादानाद्ब्रह्मलोकमनश्वरम् ॥ एकस्मिन् कन्यादाने सर्व कर्म समाप्यते ॥ इति युधिष्ठिरं प्रति कृष्णवाक्यम् ।

atha kanyādānasaṁkalpavākyaṁ likhyate ॥ kanyādānasyaivotkṛṣṭatvamuktam । kanyādānātparaṁ dānaṁ na

पुनातु ॥ ओमद्यतत्सद्ब्रह्मणोऽह्नि द्वितीयपरार्द्धे श्रीश्वेतवाराहकल्पे जम्बूद्वीपे भरतखंडे बहुक्षेत्रान्विते सर्वसम्पत्तिसमलंकृते आर्यावर्तान्तर्गत-ब्रह्मावर्तैकदेशे वैवस्वतमन्वन्तरे अष्टाविंशतितमे कलियुगे कलिप्रथमचरणे बृहस्पतिपुण्यक्षेत्रे शुभसंवत्सरेऽस्मिन्नमुकायनगते सूर्येऽमुकऋतावमुक-मासेऽमुकपक्षेऽमुकतिथावमुकवासरे यथायोगकरणमुहूर्त्तवर्तमाने यथास्थानस्थितेषु सर्वेषु ग्रहेषु सत्सु चन्द्रताराऽनुकूले पुण्येऽहनि अमुक-गोत्रस्याऽमुकप्रवरस्याऽमुकवेदिनोऽमुकशाखिनोऽमुकसूत्रिणोऽमुकशर्मणः प्रपौत्राय १ अमुकगोत्रस्यामुकप्रवरस्याऽमुकवेदिनोऽमुकशाखिनो-ऽमुकसूत्रिणोऽमुकशर्मणः पौत्राय २ अमुकगोत्रस्यामुकप्रवरस्याऽमुक-वेदिनोऽमुकशाखिनोऽमुकसूत्रिणोऽमुकशर्मणः पुत्राय ३ एवम् अमुक-गोत्रस्यामुकप्रवरस्याऽमुकवेदिनोऽमुकशाखिनोऽमुकसूत्रिणोऽमुकशर्मणः प्रपौत्रीम् १ अमुकगोत्रस्यामुकप्रवरस्याऽमुकवेदिनोऽमुकशाखिनो-ऽमुकसूत्रिणोऽमुकशर्मणः पौत्रीम् २ अमुकगोत्रस्याऽमुकवेदिनो-ऽमुकशाखिनोऽमुकसूत्रिणोऽमुकशर्मणः पुत्रीम् ३ यथाऽभिलषित-देशनदनदीसिन्धुद्वीपदिव्यनन्दनचैत्ररथप्रभृतिसकलभोगविषयोपभोगार्थं मया सह दशपूर्वेषां दश परेषां मद्वंश्यानामग्निष्टोमातिरात्रवाजपेय-पौण्डरीकाऽश्वमेधक्रतुशतफलजन्यब्रह्मलोकावाप्तये—अमुकगोत्राया-ऽमुकप्रवरायाऽमुकवेदिनेऽमुकशाखिनेऽमुकसूत्रिणे चिरजीविने आयुष्मते कन्यार्थिनेऽमुकशर्मणे[1] वराय यथोक्तगोत्रामममुकनाम्नीमिमां कन्यां यथाशक्त्यलङ्कृतां महद्वस्त्रद्वयावृतां विवाहदीक्षितां प्रजापतिदैवतां पत्नीत्वेन

---

bhūtaṁ na bhaviṣyati । gautamaḥ । aśvamedhaḥ kratuvaro yathā yajñeṣu cottamaḥ । evaṁ sarveṣu dāneṣu kanyādānaṁ praśasyate ॥ sūtasaṁhitāyām—aśvamedhasahasrasya vājapeyaśatasya ca । ekakanyāpradānena phalamāpnoti niścitam ॥ sumanturapi । yatpuṇyaṁ koṭiyajñānāṁ vedapārāyaṇe phalam । koṭi tīrtha snānajañca kanyādāne tato'dhikamiti ॥ ekaviṁśativaṁśyā-nāmātmanā saha bhūpate । ekasmātkanyakādānādbrahmalokam-anaśvaram ॥ eka smin kanyādāne sarva karma samāpyate ॥ iti yudhiṣṭhiraṁ prati kṛṣṇavākyam ।

1. Here, again, if the bridegroom is a kṣatriya, use 'varmaṇaḥ' instead of 'śarmaṇaḥ'; if he is a vaiśya, use 'guptāva'.

तुभ्यमहं सम्प्रददे, इति शंखस्थद्रव्ययुतजलेन सह कन्या दक्षिणकराङ्गुष्ठ वरस्य दक्षिणहस्ते दद्यात् । ततः ॐ स्वस्तीति वचनमुक्त्वा 'द्यौस्त्वा ददातु, पृथिवी प्रतिगृह्णातु' इति मन्त्रेण कन्याहस्तं वरः प्रतिगृह्णीयात् । इति द्विजकन्यादानसंकल्पः ।

atha dvijavarṇakanyādāna saṁkalpaḥ

hariḥ aum viṣṇurviṣṇurviṣnurapavitraḥ pavitro vā sarvā'vasthāṅgato'pi vā । yaḥ smaretpuṇḍarīkākṣaṁ sa bāhyā'bhyantaraḥ śuciḥ ॥ śrīpuṇḍarīkākṣaḥ punātu ॥ omadyatatsadbrahmaṇo'hni dvitīyaparārdhe śrīśvetavārāhakalpe jambūdvīpe bharatakhaṁḍe bahukṣetrānvite sarvasampattisamalaṁkṛte āryāvartāntargata brahmāvartaikadeśe vaivasvatamanvantare aṣṭāviṁśatitame kaliyuge kaliprathamacaraṇe bṛhaspatipuṇyakṣetre śubhasaṁvatsare'sminnamukāyanagate śurye'mukaṛtāvamukamāse'mukapakṣe'mukatithāvamukavāśare yathāyogakaraṇa muhūrtta vartamāne yathā sthānasthiteṣu sarveṣu graheṣu satsu candratārā'nukule puṇye'hani amukagotrasyā'mukapravarasyā'mukavedino'mukaśākhino'mukasūtriṇo'mukaśarmaṇaḥ prapautrāya 1 amukagotrasyā'mukapravarasyā'mukavedino'mukaśākhino'mukasūtriṇo'mukaśarmaṇaḥ pautrāya 2 amukagotrasyāmukapravarasyā'mukavedino'mukaśākhino'mukasūtriṇo'mukaśarmaṇaḥ putrāya 3 evam amukagotrāsyāmukapravarasyā'mukavedino'mukaśākhino'mukasūtriṇo'mukaśarmaṇaḥ prapautrīm 1 amukagotrasyāmukapravarasyā'mukavedino'mukaśākhino'mukasūtriṇo'mukaśarmanaḥ pautrīm 2 amukagotrāsyā'mukavedino'mukaśākhino'mukasūtriṇo'mukaśarmanaḥ putrīm 3 yathā'bhilaṣitadeśanadanadī sindhu dvīpadivyanandana caitrarathaprabhṛti sakalabhogaviṣayopabhogārthaṁ mayā saha daśapūrveṣāṁ daśa pareṣāṁ madvaṃśyānāmagniṣṭomātirātravājapeyapauṇḍarīkā'śvamedhakratuśataphalajanyabrahmalokāvāptaye—amukagotrāyā'mukapravarāyā'mukavedine'mukaśākhinemukasūtriṇe cirajīvine āyuṣmate kanyārthine-

'mukaśarmaṇe varāya yathoktagotrāmamukanāmnīmimāṁ kanyāṁ yathāśaktyalaṅkṛtāṁ mahadvastradvayāvṛtāṁ vivāhadīkṣitaṁ prajāpatidaivatāṁ patnītvena tubhyam-ahaṁ sampradade, iti śaṁkhasthadravyayutajalena saha kanyā dakṣiṇakarāṅguṣṭhaṁ varasya dakṣiṇahaste dadyāt ı *tataḥ aum svastīti vacanamuktvā 'dyaustvā dadātu, pṛthivī pratigṛhṇātu' iti mantreṇa kanyāhastaṁ varaḥ pratigṛhṇīyāt* ı *iti dvijakanyādānasaṁkalpaḥ* ı

अथ द्विजेतरवर्णकन्यादानसंकल्पः[1]

हरिः ॐ विष्णुर्विष्णुर्विष्णुरपवित्रः पवित्रो वा सर्वावस्थां गतोऽपि वा । यः स्मरेत् पुण्डरीकाक्षं स बाह्याभ्यन्तरः शुचिः ॥ श्रीपुण्डरीकाक्षः पुनातु सर्वान् । ॐ अद्य तत्सद्ब्रह्मणोऽह्नि द्वितीयपरार्धे श्वेतवाराहकल्पे वैवस्वतमन्वन्तरेऽष्टाविंशतितमे कलियुगे प्रथमचरणे जम्बूद्वीपे भरतखण्डे आर्यावर्तान्तर्गतब्रह्मावर्तैकदेशे कुमारिकानाम्नि क्षेत्रेऽमुकनामसंवत्सरे-ऽमुकायनेऽमुकऋतावमुकमासेऽमुकपक्षेऽमुकतिथावमुकवासरे वर्तमान-नक्षत्रयोगकरणलग्नमुहूर्तवर्तमाने यथास्थानस्थितेषु सर्वेषु ग्रहेषु सत्सु अमुकगोत्रोत्पन्नोऽहं ममाऽभिलषितकामनासिद्ध्यर्थमग्निष्टोमाऽतिरात्रयाग-शतजन्यसमफलप्राप्तिकामः मम समस्तपितॄणां निरतिशयसानन्द-ब्रह्मलोकावाप्तये अनेन वरेणास्ऽस्यां कन्यायामुत्पादयिष्यमाणसंतत्या दशपूर्वान् दश परान् माञ्चैकविंशतिपुरुषानुद्धर्तुं वा पवित्रीकर्तुं ब्राह्मविवाहविधिना श्रीलक्ष्मीनारायणप्रीतये देवाऽग्निगुरुसन्निधौ अग्निसाक्षिकतयाऽमुकगोत्राय श्रीमते विष्णुरूपिणे अमुकनाम्ने वरायाऽमुकगोत्रां यथाशक्त्यलङ्कृतां प्रजापतिदैवतां यथाशक्त्युप-

---

1. Only one Saṁkalpa with its prescribed sūtras applies to all the brāhmaṇic systems and saṁskāras, it is the ignorant, however, who presume that the śūdras have another. Do the latter, too, have the 'pravara Vedas', any of the most excellent Vedas? Only in the case of dvijas (brāhmaṇas) we have gotras, gotra gradations and gotra forms, which is why two kinds of the same Saṁkalpa have been mentioned here—one for the brāhmaṇas and the other for the non-brāhmaṇas.

कल्पितयौतुकयुतां श्रीरूपिणीमायुष्मतीममुकनाम्नीमिमां कन्यां वस्त्रयुगाऽऽच्छन्नां भार्यात्वेन तुभ्यं संप्रददे तेन यज्ञपुरुषः प्रजापतिः प्रीयतामिति शंखस्थदूर्वाक्षतफलपुष्पचन्दनसुवर्णादियुतजलेन सहितं कन्यादक्षिणहस्ताङ्गुष्ठं वरस्य दक्षिणहस्ते दद्यात् । ततः ॐ स्वस्तीति-वचनमुक्त्वा । द्यौस्त्वा ददातु पृथिवी त्वा प्रतिगृह्णातु—इति मंत्रेण कन्याहस्तं वरः प्रतिगृह्णीयात् ॥ इति द्विजादन्यवर्णकन्यादानसंकल्पः ॥

atha dvijetaravarṇakanyādānasaṁkalpaḥ[1]

aum viṣṇurviṣṇurviṣṇurapavitraḥ pavitro vā sarvāvasthāṁ gato'pi vā । yaḥ smaret puṇḍarīkākṣaṁ sa bāhyābhyantaraḥ śuciḥ ॥ śrīpuṇḍarīkākṣaḥ punātu sarvān । aum adya tatsadbrahmaṇo'hni dvitīyaparārdhe śveta-vārāhakalpe vaivasvatamanvantare'ṣṭaviṁśatitame kaliyuge prathamacaraṇe jambūdvīpe bharatakhaṇḍe āryāvartāntargatabrahmāvartaikadeśe kumārikānāmni kṣetre'mukanāmasaṁvatsare'mukāyane'mukarṭāva-mukamāse'mukapakṣe'mukatithāvamukavāsare vartamāna nakṣatrayogakaraṇalagnamuhūrtavartamāne yathā-sthānasthiteṣu sarveṣu graheṣu satsu amukagotrotpanno-'haṁ mamā'bhilaṣitakāmanāsiddhyarthamagniṣṭomā-'tirātrayāgaśatajanyasamaphalaprāptikāmaḥ mama samastapitṛṇāṁ nirati śayasānandabrahmalokāvāptaye anena vareṇā'syāṁ kanyāyāmutpādayiṣyamāṇasaṁtatyā daśapūrvān daśa parān māñcaikaviṁśatipuruṣānud-dhartuṁ vā pavitrīkartuṁ brāhmavivāhavidhinā śrīlakṣmīnārāyaṇaprītaye devā'gnigurusannidhau agnisākṣikatayā'mukagotrāya śrimate viṣṇurūpiṇe amukanāmne varāyā'mukagotrāṁ yathāśaktyalaṅkṛtāṁ prajāpatidaivatāṁ yathāśaktyupakalpitayautukayutāṁ śrīrūpiṇīmāyuṣmatīmamukanāmnīmimāṁ kaṅyāṁ vastrayugā''cchannāṁ bhāryātvena tubhyaṁ saṁpradade tena yajñapuruṣaḥ prajāpatiḥ prīyatāmiti śaṁkhastha-dūrvākṣata phala puṣpa candana suvarṇādiyutajalena sahitaṁ kanyādakṣiṇahastāṅguṣṭhaṁ varasya dakṣiṇa-haste dadyāt । tataḥ aum svastītivacanamuktvā । dyaustvā dadātu pṛthivī tvā pratigṛhṇātu—iti maṁtreṇa kanyāhastaṁ varaḥ pratigṛhṇīyāt ॥ *iti dvijādanyavarṇakanyādāna-saṁkalpaḥ* ॥

"May Prajāpati, Yajñapuruṣa Viṣṇu, the soul of sacrifice as he is called, be pleased with this saṁskāra, the ritual of Kanyādāna!". Uttering the Saṁkalpa stated above, the host must pass on the conch with its contents of *dūba* grass, raw rice, fruit, flower, etc. to the bridegroom and let the latter's right hand hold the bride's right-hand thumb. "God bless you!" So saying and repeating the mantra "dyaustvā dadātu pṛthivī tvā pratigṛhṇātu," the bridegroom should hold the bride's hand. The prayer contained in the mantra has two parts:

(i) dīvyatīti dyaurlokaḥ tvā tvāmadāt tava dānena svargasādhako'bhūt—Moved by the splendid offer made, may the World of Light reward you with the attainment of heaven.

(ii) pṛthvī prathituṁ śīlā devatā tvā pratigṛhṇātu putrapautrādivistāreṇa tvāṁ prathayitrī bhavatu—May the Earth, who by nature sustains all, welcome you and bless you with a long line of sons and grandsons.

In other words, the great merit earned by the maiden's father by giving her away in marriage will be duly rewarded by letting him dwell in heaven and enjoy endless bliss. And just as the Earth deems her among those who have had a populous family, so may this bridegroom also be pleased with her and welcome her for the continuance of his ancestral line and populating his home.

If the bridegroom and the bride are kṣatriyas, then, as has been pointed out earlier, use 'varmaṇaḥ' in place of 'śarmmaṇaḥ' when mentioning their *gotras*; if they are vaiśyas, use 'guptasya' if śūdras, use 'dāsasya'. This would apply also when uttering the Saṁkalpas.

The gifts to be given by the bride's kinsfolk may be offered at this opportune moment.

ततः कन्याप्रदः देशकालौ संकीर्त्य कृतैतत्कन्यादानकर्मणः यथोक्तफलावाप्तये कन्यादानप्रतिष्ठार्थमिदं सुवर्णमग्निदैवतं रजतं चन्द्रदैवतममुकगोत्रायाऽमुकशर्मणे वराय दक्षिणां तुभ्यमहं संप्रददे इति दक्षिणां गोमिथुनं वा दद्यात् । ओ३म् स्वस्तीति वरः प्रतिब्रूयात् ।

tataḥ kanyāpradaḥ deśakālau saṁkīrtya kṛtaitatkanyādānakarmaṇaḥ yathoktaphalāvāptaye kanyādānapratiṣṭhārthamidaṁ suvarṇamagni-daivataṁ rajataṁ candradaivatamamukagotrāyā'mukaśarmaṇe varāya dakṣiṇāṁ tubhyamahaṁ saṁpradade iti dakṣiṇāṁ gomithunaṁ vā dadyāt । aum svastīti varaḥ pratibrūyat ।

Thereafter the bride's father should utter his Saṁkalpa, mentioning place and time, and for the successful completion and honour of the ceremony (of kanyādāna) give a bull and a cow (*dakṣiṇā* or *gomithuna*) or some other gift to the bridegroom. The latter should thankfully acknowledge the gift, saying, "May God bless you!"

कन्यादानप्रतिष्ठार्थं कन्याप्रदेन दक्षिणां प्रतिगृह्य वरः कामस्तुतिं कुर्यात् ।

kanyādānapratiṣṭhārthaṁ kanyāpradena dakṣiṇāṁ pratigṛhya varaḥ kāmastutiṁ kuryāt ।

Having accepted the gifts given by the person performing the kanyādāna, the bridegroom shall then eulogize Desire or Will (Kāma) with the citation of the following mantra:

ओ३म् कोऽदात् कस्मा अदात्कामो ऽदात्कामायादात्कामो दाता कामः प्रतिग्रहीता कामैतत्ते—इति वरः पठेत् ।

aum ko'dāt kasmā adātkāmo 'dātkāmāyādātkāmo dātā kāmaḥ pratigrahītā kāmaitatte—iti varaḥ paṭhet ।

"Who gives the gift to whom?" This is a question put by the bridegroom himself (kaḥ adāt dattavān iti svayameva vareṇa kṛtaḥ praśnaḥ). He replies by saying that Desire is the giver as well as the receiver (yataḥ kamo dātā kāmaḥ pratigrahītā). Therefore, O Desire, thy will is done!

Here the word 'kāma' is Will or Desire, the donor and receiver of every gift (yat incchayaiva dīyate pratigṛhate ca). This accounts for the eulogy of Desire as an indomitable and irrepressible motivating force. Considering it so mighty and overpowering, the bridegroom is filled with self-reproach and anguish. "Praise be to Desire," he says, "who as the conqueror of the world forces even kṣatriyas, reputed for their refusal to accept gifts, to yield to Desire for them. Desire overcomes all, however mighty one may be on the battleground."

Being a mantra exclusively meant for the bridegroom, this has to be intoned by him.

ततो वरस्य स्कन्धे कन्या मालासमर्पणं कुर्यात् ।

tato varasya skandhe kanyā mālāsamarpaṇaṁ kuryāt ।

Proceeding, the bride should garland the bridegroom.

ततो वरः कन्याप्रतिग्रहदोषनिवारणार्थं गोदानं कुर्यात् । तत्र सङ्कल्पः ।

tato varaḥ kanyāpratigrahadoṣanivāraṇārthaṁ godānaṁ kuryāt । *tatra saṅkalpaḥ* ।

Having done this, the bridegroom should perform the rite of Godāna for the effacement of sin caused by his acceptance of the maiden as wife. He should perform the following Saṁkalpa while offering the gift of the cow:

अद्येत्यादि० भार्याप्रतिग्रहदोषोपशमनार्थम् इमां गां तत्प्रतिनिधीभूत-कल्पितद्रव्यमयीं दक्षिणां वाऽमुकगोत्रायामुकशर्म्मणे विष्णुरूपिणे सुपूजिताय ब्राह्मणाय तुभ्यमहं सम्प्रददे । ततस्तां पाणौ गृहीत्वा—

adyetyādi० bhāryāpratigrahadoṣopaśamanārtham imāṁ gāṁ tatpratinidhībhūtakalpitadravyamayīṁ dakṣiṇāṁ vā'mukagotrāyāmukaśarmmaṇe viṣṇurūpiṇe supūjitāya brāhmaṇāya tubhyamahaṁ sampradade । *tatastāṁ pāṇau gṛhītvā—*

For taking the bride, now married off by her father with due Saṁkalpa,[1] out from the house or from the pavilion to a spot near the sacrificial fire with her both hands in his, the bridegroom should read a mantra given below, beginning with "aum yadaiṣi manasā". Here the expression "by her father" is a general statement; the person giving the maiden in marriage may be anybody,[2] including her mother or brother.

ॐ यदैषि मनसा दूरं दिशोनु पवमानो वा । हिरण्यपर्णो वैकर्णः स त्वा मन्मनसां करोतु-श्री अमुकदेवीति पठन्निष्क्रामति–

aum yadaiṣi manasā dūraṁ diśonu pavamāno va । hiraṇyaparṇo vaikarṇaḥ sa tvā manmanasāṁ karotu-śrī amukadevīti paṭhanniṣkrāmati—

O Maiden! May all the quarters, the winds that purify all, the sun whose rays are all lustrous gold, and fire may infuse you with love for me. Having taken the maiden given by her father with due Saṁkalpa, the bridegroom should step out from the house (or from the pavilion) and come near the festal fire repeating this mantra (aum yadaiṣi, etc.). If the altar is situated outside the pavilion towards the north-eastern quarter, then this rite should be performed; if it is in the pavilion itself adjacent to the Tilaka Maṁḍala in the north-eastern quarter, the couple should remain seated there itself, sliding off a little.

---

1. पित्रा प्रत्तामादाय गृहीत्वा निष्क्रामतीति सूत्रबलात्–पित्रा जनकेन प्रत्तां संकल्प्य दत्तामादाय प्रतिग्रहविधिना प्रतिगृह्य गृहीत्वा हस्ते गृहीत्वा निष्क्रामति गृहमध्यान्मंडपादग्निसमीपं गन्तुं यदैषीत्यादिना ।

pitrā prattāmādāya gṛhītvā niṣkrāmatīti sūtrabalāt—pitrā janakena prattāṁ saṁkalpya dattāmādāya pratigrahavidhinā pratigṛhya gṛhītvā haste gṛhītvā niṣkrāmati gṛhamadhyā-nmaṁḍapādagnisamīpaṁ gantuṁ yadaiṣītyādinā ।

2. पिता पितामहो भ्राता सकुल्यो जननी तथा । कन्याप्रदः पूर्वनाशे प्रकृतिस्थः परः परः ॥ इति याज्ञवल्क्येनोक्तम् ।

pitā pitāmaho bhrātā sakulyo jananī tathā । kanyāpradaḥ pūrvanāśe prakṛtisthaḥ paraḥ paraḥ ॥ iti yājñavalkyenoktam ।

ततो वेदिकाया दक्षिणस्यां दिशि वारिपूर्णकलशम् ऊर्ध्वं तिष्ठतो मौनिनो दृढ़पुरुषस्य स्कंधे अभिषेकपर्य्यन्तं धारयेत् । ततः परस्परं समीक्षेथाम् इति प्रैषानन्तरम् ।

tato vedikāyā dakṣiṇasyāṁ diśi vāripūrṇakalaśam ūrdhvaṁ tiṣṭhato maunino dṛḍhapuruṣasya skaṁdhe abhiṣekaparyyantaṁ dhārayet । tataḥ parasparaṁ samīkṣethām iti praiṣānantaram ।

On the authority of the aphorism (sūtra) already stated, the ceremony of seeing each other by the bride and the bridegroom should be performed after the bridegroom has read the following mantras right up to the one beginning with "sā naḥ pūṣā. . ." That is to say, the person who is giving away the maiden should ask the bride and the bridegroom to look at each other. They should, however, do so only after the latter has read the following mantras (up to sā naḥ pūṣā. . .).

ॐ अघोरचक्षुरपतिघ्न्येधि शिवा पशुभ्यः सुमनाः सुवर्चाः । वीरसूर्देवकामा स्योना शन्नो भव द्विपदे शं चतुष्पदे ॥

aum aghoracakṣurapatighnyedhi śivā paśubhyaḥ sumanāḥ suvarcāḥ । vīrasūrdevakāmā syonā śanno bhava dvipade śaṁ catuṣpade ॥

O maiden! May you be sinless with eyes brimful of innocent simplicity.[1] Pray never kill your husband by doing anything outrageous and improper.[2] May this marriage ceremony augur well for your protégés who, like so many animals, depend on you for help and well-being[3] and may you be jovial and light-hearted,[4] beautifully radiant and lustrous,[5] a mother of valiant sons,[6] ever ready to serve

---

1. tvaṁ aghoracakṣuḥ saumyadṛṣṭirapāpadṛṣṭiriti vā edhi ।
2. apatighnī akāryyakaraṇena patyarthaghātinī mā bhava ।
3. etasmātsaṁskārāt vivāhasaṁskārāt paśubhyaḥ paśuvadāśritebhyaḥ śivā hitaiṣiṇī bhava ।
4. sumanāḥ prasannacetā ।
5. suvarccāḥ suprabhāvayuktā ।
6. vīrasūḥ satputrajanitrī ।

such gods as the god of Fire even while being fond of flirtation,[1] by nature blissful and purveyor of bliss, a redresser of grief[2] and altruistically disposed towards all men[3] and animals.[4]

सोमः प्रथमो विविदे गन्धर्वो विविद उत्तरः । तृतीयोऽग्निष्टे पतिस्तुरो यस्ते मनुष्यजाः ॥

somaḥ prathamo vivide gandharvo vivida uttaraḥ ।
tṛtīyo'gniṣṭe patisturī yaste manuṣyajāḥ ॥

This is followed by a full-throated eulogy of the maiden whose life-span is divided into four parts, the first three being of equal duration, two and a half years each, and the fourth extending from the time she is seven and a half years old to the last day of her life. During these four periods of her life she is under the protection of four husbands—three celestial beings and one man—who not only look after her but are also responsible for her physical and intellectual growth. It is under their benign tutelege and guardianship that she ripens and attains full womanhood, ages and dies. The 'eulogy' implies that the maiden is fortunate in that she had had a protector-guardian-husband from her very childhood—from the day she was born—and that three of her husbands were gods, i.e. the Moon, the Sun and Agni, the Firegod, who looked after her, nursed and 'wound' (educated) her till she was seven and a half years old. The present bridegroom is her fourth husband, a man, who will tend and protect her like the aforesaid gods, her first husbands, for a longer period. (The task of the human guardian-protector is beset with greater

---

1. devakāmā devān agnyādīn kāmayate sevārthamicchatīti yadvā—devanaṁ krīRanaṁ kāmayate iti sā ।

2. śanno bhava no'smākaṁ saṁ sukhaṁ duḥkhavināśaśīlatvena sukharūpā bhava ।

3. dvipade manuṣyavargāya manuṣyavargamupakartum ।

4. tathā catuṣpade paśuvargāya paśuvargamupakartum ।

difficulties not only on account of the long duration of his role as the maiden's husband but also because the maiden is no longer an unthinking, immature child.)

The bride has been thus eulogized:

"O Maiden! The Moon is your protector from the day you are born and is, therefore, your first 'husband'. After two and a half years, you are placed under the charge of the god of the Gandharvas (tataḥ sārddhavarṣad-vayānantaraṁ gandharvaḥ sūryaḥ gandharvadevatāṁ balāṁ vivide), i.e. the Sun, for another period of two and a half years. Thus he becomes your second 'husband'. Then comes Agni, your third 'spouse', who continues to 'wind', look after and protect you until you are seven and a half years old. While you remain under the guardianship of these gods one after the other, you are thoroughly educated by your successive 'husbands' before they pass you on to a man[1] who has to retain you for a long duration."

'Manuṣyajāḥ', an adjective, qualifying 'turīyaḥ', is singular in the nominative case. Swami Dayanand mistakenly considered it to be plural and reasoned that not one but eleven husbands are suggested by this mantra. There is, however, no hint at all here of any promiscuity or of what is called 'niyoga' (an ancient Aryan practice according to which a childless widow or woman was permitted to have sexual intercourse with a person other than her husband to beget a child). The only note of caution sounded is that do not get a girl married unless she is more than seven and a half years old.

ॐ सोमोऽददद् गन्धर्वाय गन्धर्वोऽददग्नये । रयिञ्च पुत्रांश्चादादग्निर्मह्यमथो इमाम् ॥

aum somo'dadad gandharvāya gandharvo'dadagnaye ।
rayiñca putrāṁścādādagnirmahyamatho imām ॥

---

1. पूर्वं स्त्रियः सुरैर्भुक्ताः सोमगन्धर्ववह्निभिः । प्रतिपोष्याध्याप्य शोध्य परित्यक्तां नरो भजेत् ॥
pūrvaṁ striyaḥ surairbhuktāḥ somagandharvaṁvahnibhiḥ ।
pratipoṣyādhyāpya śodhya parityaktāṁ naro bhajet ॥

Does all this contain a detestable hint of polyandry? Does this mean that the maiden is the spouse of all the four? (nanu kimidānīṁ caturṇāmiyaṁ patnī netyāha 'somo'dadaditi') This mantra is meant to resolve this doubt. It means that, having wound the maiden (i.e. furnished her with windings or curves of the saṁskāras) and sowed firmly the seeds of her education, for thirty months, preparatory to her entrance into the second stage of life, the moon passes her on to the Gandharva Sūrya in all her radiant beauty. The Sun winds her (lays her education and saṁskāras on much surer foundations) for another thirty months. (The seeds of culture and education sown in her during the first thirty months are allowed to sprout and grow before she is transferred for similar education in saṁskāras—ideal womanhood, bashfulness, tenderness, fidelity, lovingkindness, etc.—to the Firegod, Agni.

Now the bridegroom admits with becoming candour that he has not only obtained the gift of the maiden, sanctified by righteousness, from the god of Fire but has also been rewarded with a priceless treasure and promise of an unending line of progeny. In other words, women attain their winsome beauty and charm, an enrapturing, melodious voice like the notes of a cuckoo or a nightingale, and purity (of character),[1] as if given to them by the Moon, the

---

1. somo rūpaṁ dadau strīṇāṁ gandharvastu śubhāṁ giram ı
pāvakaḥ sarvameghyatvaṁ meghyā vai yoṣito hyataḥ ıı

The interpretation of the two ṛcās (Vedic hymns), one beginning with 'somaḥ prathamo vivide' and the other with 'somo'dadadgaṁdharvāya', given by Dayananda and the trash it contains should be borne in mind. Addressing his words to the maiden, he says, "O Woman! Your first husband is Soma, the second by Niyoga is Gandharva, and the third Agni. From the fourth to the eleventh of your husbands are such (i.e. your husbands) only by Niyoga and are called men." Where Dayananda has mentioned the marriage rituals, he has cited this śruti: 'somo'dadadgandharvāya gandharvo'dadagnaye' which, he says, means, "Let Soma give the maiden to Gandharva, Gandharva to

Sun and the Agni as they ripen under the guardianship of their human husband (tathā ca somagandharvavahnibhiḥ saundaryādikadānādinā bhuktā striyo rūpasvara-medhyatvasampannāḥ).

सा नः पूषा शिवतमामैरय सा न ऊरू उशती विहर । यस्यामुशन्तः प्रहराम शेपं यस्यामु कामा बहवो निविष्ट्यै-इति वरः पठित्वा परस्परं निरीक्षेथाम् ।

sā naḥ pūṣā śivatamāmairaya sā na ūrū uśatī vihara । *yasyāmuśantaḥ praharāma śepaṁ yasyāmu kāmā bahavo niviṣṭyai-iti varaḥ paṭhitvā parasparaṁ nirīkṣethām* ।

This is the fourth mantra now being interpreted. The sun who is the light of the world, its eye, may endow this woman with winning qualities and modesty and so mould her nature that she becomes a loving wife and, wishing to be blessed with happiness and a family with sons at its centre, opens out her thighs. Wherefore will she do so? The reason lies in our pious craving for final deliverance (*mukti*)

Agni, and Agni to me." This is the bridegroom's utterance on the occasion of his marriage. Keeping the meaning of the first śruti in mind, consider the question whether the followers of Dayananda would marry only her who has married one in the first instance and then made love to two others. What a stupid gibberish all this is which has also led to the admissibility and currency in certain quarters of second marriage! Why on earth will the first legitimate husband called Soma allow his wife to desert him and go to a Niyogi husband, provisional or improvised, called Gandharva? Similarly, why will the Gandharva let her go to another Niyogi husband called Agni? Finally, why is only the fourth husband called Man? Are the first three born of animais and why should the third bear the name of Agni? It appears as though he is always in leaping flames and one wonders why the others are bereft of the qualities of tenderness, etc. discerned in the first. The mantras have indeed been misconstrued to establish the concept of Niyoga; that is, the whole theory is a monstrous hoax. The four mantras stated above have no suggestion of Niyoga at all, much less any overt reference to it.

through the purification of our conscience by the worship of the Agnihotra (oblation to Fire). Another purpose mentioned is that the woman by dilating her thighs expresses her urgings for sexual rapture and for satisfying a similar longing in man coupled with a deep-rooted yearning for the continuance of his family line. She helps her husband achieve his purpose—to combine pleasure with a sort of immortality gained in the continuance of his line.

When the bridegroom has read these four mantras, the couple then may have a look at each other.

ततोऽग्निं प्रदक्षिणीकृत्य पश्चादग्नेरहतवस्त्रवेष्टिततृणपूलकं कटं वा निवेश्य तदुपरि दक्षिणचरणं दत्वा वधूं दक्षिणतः कृत्वा तामुपवेश्य पुष्पचन्दनताम्बूलवासांस्यादाय वरः संकल्पं कुर्यात् ।

tato'gnim pradakṣiṇīkṛtya paścādagnerahatavastraveṣṭitatṛṇapūlakaṁ kaṭaṁ vā niveśya tadupari dakṣiṇacaraṇaṁ datvā vadhūṁ dakṣiṇataḥ kṛtvā tāmupaveśya puṣpacandanatāmbūlavāsāṁsyādāya varaḥ saṁkalpaṁ kuryāt ।

Thereafter the bride and the bridegroom should go around the festal fire three times as authorized by the sacramental ordinance: pradakṣiṇaṁ paryyāṇīyaike—iti sūtram । asyārthaḥ—eke ācāryyā agniṁ pradakṣiṇaṁ paryyāṇīya kanyāṁ triḥ pradakṣiṇāṁ kārayitvā vāsaḥ paridhānaṁ samañjanam samīkṣaṇañca kathayanti, eke anye tu samīkṣaṇānaṁtaraṁ kathayantītyarthaḥ. While some scholars recommend the performance of Vāsaḥparidhāna (the ceremony of donning new clothes), Samaṁjana, Samīkṣaṇa, etc. after the bride and the bridegroom have performed the sacred rite of circumambulation three times about the fire, other Ācāryas hold that these rites be performed before the couple have circumabulated.[1]

---

1. Insofar as circumambulating the ceremonial fire three times is concerned, it is authoritatively stated that such circumambulations may be silently performed unaccompanied

The controversy raised by these two schools of scholars has led to the formulation of the following simple rule ordained by the law-giver, *sūtrakāra*, who says that Samaṁjana, etc. should precede (paścādagniṁ paryyāṇīya) the circumambulations (agneḥ pascādagnikāryānantaram). Once the circumambulatory rite is over, the bridegroom should press a straw mat wrapped up in a piece of clean

---

by any loud citation of the mantras. The rest of the four circumambulations to follow added to the preceding three swell the aggregate to seven, which is the number ordained by the ceremonial code: ekā devyāḥ raveḥ sapta saptāgnergaṇapatestrayaḥ । catasro vāsudevasya śivasyārddhapradakṣiṇā ॥ catasraḥ syuḥ pitṛṇāṁ vai tisro'pyekā yadṛcchayā ॥ According to the *Padma Purāṇa*, circumambulate the various gods and manes as many times as the following: the Goddess (Devī) once; the Sun seven times; Agni as many times as the Sun; Gaṇapati three times; Viṣṇu four times; Śiva half a time; the manes one, three or four times or as many times as one wishes to circumambulate them. The Vāsaḥparidhāna and the mutual snatching of glances (*paraspara nirīkṣaṇa*) should be gone through earlier, as has been directed by the Sūtras, "tatra aghoracakṣurapatighnyedhi śivā paśubhyaḥ sumanā suvarcāḥ" ityādivarapaṭhitamantrānte parasparaṁ nirīkṣaṇā'nantaraṁ yaduktaṁ tato'gniṁpradakṣiṇīkṛtyeti । The text dealing with the mutual glimpsing of each other by the bride and the bridegroom stated at the end of the four mantras such as 'aghoracakṣuḥ', etc. is followed by the statement that the bridegroom should make the maiden circumambulate the ceremonial fire three times silently and without the repetition of a mantra. It follows, therefore, that the four circumambulations to follow with the citation of the appropriate mantras will, when added to the earlier three, make the total number of circumabulations seven. There are other pieces of evidence as well: agneḥ pradakṣiṇā sapta vivāhe tu sadā mataḥ । sarvatra yugapatkuryāt vivāhe tu yathākarmam ॥ The meaning of this is that, while performing the marriage ceremonies, the ceremonial fire should always be circumambulated seven times. Go everywhere, says the text, just once, but while performing the marital ceremony, circumambulate in due order; that is, every ceremonial rite should be performed according to its prescribed,

cloth with his right foot (tejanī korthaḥ ahatavastra-veṣṭitatṛṇapūlakaṁ vā tṛṇamayaṁ kaṭam) and, seating the bride on his right side, he should himself take his seat. He should then perform the following Saṁkalpa taking flower, sandal, betel, and cloth for the fire-act (*agnikarma*) for what is called the ceremony of Kuśakaṇḍikā (by which fire is placed on the altar or in the pit (kuṁḍa) dug for it).

---

inviolable order. The number of circumambulations is fixed at seven, for which the evidence is contained in these lines:

homātpūrvantu syustisrastisro home samantrakāḥ ।
tato bhagāya svāhetu hutvā tūṣṇiṁ pradakṣiṇā ॥
varaḥ paścādvadhūragre pūrvāsu madhyamāsvapi ।
pradakṣiṇāyamantyāyāṁ vadūḥ paścātpuro varaḥ ॥

According to this, three circumambulations should be performed by the couple before the Homa (oblation to Fire) without any citation of the mantras and three after the Homa with the relevant mantras. Thus in all the six circumambulations the bride goes ahead followed by the bridegroom. After the sixth circumambulation they sit together side by side. The next step consists in the bride uttering 'bhagāya svāhā' and offering the oblation of parched rice with the corner of a wee winnowing basket. This done, they arise and silently circumambulate without muttering any mantra, the bridegroom going ahead and the bride following him. This ritual is supported by "saptamīpradakṣiṇāyāḥ pūrvameva sūrppakoṇena tūṣṇīṁ 'bhagāya svāhe' ti pāraskaravacanāt lājāhomaṁ vadhūḥ kuryyāditi śrutisūtrānusāreṇa saptamyāṁ parikramāyāṁ na mantrapāṭhaḥ nāsyāmaṁguṣṭhagrahaṇaṁ nāśmārohaṁ na gāthāgānaṁ kuryāt । prakṣiṇāsaṁkhyāpūraṇāya tūṣṇīmeva parikramet ॥" In other words, before the seventh round is made, the oblation of parched rice is silently offered with a small winnowing basket made of the leaves of date palm. While offering oblation, 'aum bhagāya svāhā' has to be kept in mind, but no repetition of any mantra is mandatory. That is to say, while performing the seventh circumambulation, no mantra is to be read, no thumb is to be caught hold of, no 'mountaineering' is to be undertaken nor any 'encomiastic hymning'. To complete the seventh round, all they have to do is to go round silently with the bride following the bridegroom.

ॐ अद्य तत्सदित्युच्चार्य्य० अद्य कर्तव्यविवाहाङ्गभूतहोमकर्म्मणि कृताऽकृतावेक्षणरूपब्रह्मकर्म्म कर्तुममुकगोत्रममुकशर्म्माणं ब्राह्मणमेभिः फलपुष्पचन्दनद्रव्याक्षतवासोभिर्ब्रह्मत्वेन त्वामहं वृणे ।

aum adya tatsadityuccāryya० adya kartavyavivāhāṅga-bhūtahomakarmmaṇi kṛtā'kṛtāvekṣaṇarūpabrahmakarmma kartumamukagotramamukaśarmmāṇaṁ brāhmaṇamebhiḥ phalapuṣpacandanadravyākṣatavāsobhirbrahmatvena tvāmahaṁ vṛṇe ।

Having performed the Saṁkalpa especially mentioning his native place (or country) and time, the bridegroom shall say that he has employed an officiating brāhmaṇa named so-and-so, of such-and-such gotra, for supervising the sacraments, and given him fruits and flowers, sandal and raw rice, and due remuneration (money, etc.) and clothes with a view to assigning him the role of Brahmā. Having said so, the bridegroom should hold these objects—the offerings to be made to the priest—in his hand and then pronounce the following mantra:

ॐ व्रतेन दीक्षामाप्नोति दीक्षयाप्नोति दक्षिणाम् । दक्षिणया श्रद्धामाप्नोति श्रद्धया सत्यमाप्यते । इति ब्रह्माणं वृणुयात् । वृतोऽस्मीति प्रतिवचनम् । यथाविहितं कर्म्म कुर्विति वरेणोक्ते करवाणीति ब्रूयात् ।

aum vratena dīkṣāmāpnoti dīkṣayāpnoti dakṣiṇām । *dakṣiṇayā śraddhāmāpnoti śraddhayā satyamāpyate* । *iti brahmāṇaṁ vṛṇuyāt* । *vṛto'smīti prativacanam* । *yathāvihitaṁ karmma kurviti vareṇokte karavāṇīti brūyāt* ।

After he has repeated the given mantra, the bridegroom shall honour the officiating brāhmaṇa as Brahmā and tie a thread round his wrist as a mark of respect. Then the priest playing Brahmā shall say that he accepts the role assigned to him. The bridegroom should thereupon request him to perform all the rites and ceremonies prescribed by the śāstras. This should evoke from the brāhmaṇa-become-Brahmā the reply that he would abide by the rules laid down in the śāstras and do what is enjoined by them.

ततो वरोऽग्नेर्दक्षिणतः शुद्धमासनं दत्त्वा तदुपरि प्रागग्रान्कुशानास्तीर्य्य ब्रह्माणमग्निप्रदक्षिणक्रमेणानीयाऽत्र त्वं मे ब्रह्मा भवेत्यभिधाय कल्पितासने समुपवेशयेत् ।

tato varo'gnerdakṣiṇataḥ śuddhamāsanaṁ dattvā tadupari prāgagrānkuśānāstīryya brahmāṇamagnipra-dakṣiṇakrameṇānīyā'tra tvaṁ me brahmā bhavet-yabhidhāya kalpitāsane samupaveśayet ।

Thereafter in the event that such a brāhmaṇa fit to be deemed Brahmā is not available, let there be a Brahmā made of fifty blades of kuśa grass and placed on a pure seat spread with kuśas (whose front portions face the east) towards the south of the festal fire. Keeping Brahmā's seat on the left of the fire-pit, (circumambulating clockwise), the bridegroom should thus speak, "I consider your Brahmā." (Then shall he place Brahmā on the seat described above.)

तत्र क्रमः । प्रणीतापात्रं पुरतः कृत्वा वारिणा परिपूर्य्य कुशैराच्छाद्य ब्रह्मणो मुखमवलोक्य अग्नेरुत्तरतः कुशोपरि निदध्यात् ।

tatra kramaḥ । *praṇītāpātraṁ purataḥ kṛtvā vāriṇā paripūryya kuśairācchādya brahmaṇo mukhamavalokya agneruttarataḥ kuśopari nidadhyāt* ।

Now the order of the rites to follow is this:

After stationing the fancied Brahmā, keep the Praṇītāpātra[1]—the vessel for the holy water—further ahead,

---

1. प्रणीयेति प्रणीय अपः इति शेषः, अपां हि प्रणयनं सर्वार्थदृष्टं तद्वदत्रापि सर्वार्थानामपां प्रणयनम् । तद्यथा–अग्नेरुत्तरतः प्रागग्रकुशैरासनद्वयं कल्पयित्वा वारणं द्वादशाङ्गुलदीर्घं चतुरङ्गुलविस्तरं चतुरङ्गुलखातं चमसं सव्यहस्ते कृत्वा दक्षिणहस्तोद्घृतपात्रस्थोदकेन पूरयित्वा पश्चिमासने निधायालभ्य पूर्वासने स्थापयित्वा ।

praṇīyeti praṇīya apaḥ iti śeṣaḥ, apāṁ hi praṇayanaṁ sarvārthadṛṣṭaṁ tadvadatrāpi sarvārthānāmapāṁ praṇayanam । tadyathā—agneruttarataḥ prāgagrakuśairāsanadvayaṁ kalpayitvā vāraṇaṁ dvādaśāṅguladīrghaṁ caturaṅgulavistaraṁ caturaṅgulakhātaṁ camasaṁ savyahaste kṛtvā dakṣiṇahastod-ghṛtapātrasthodakena pūrayitvā paścimāsane nidhāyālabhya pūrvāsane sthāpayitvā ।

fill it, cover it with kuśas, glance at Brahmā's face, and keep it on the kuśas towards the north of the fire.[1]

ततः परिस्तरणम् । बर्हिश्चतुर्थभागमादाय आग्नेयादीशानान्तं ब्रह्मणोऽग्निपर्यन्तं नैर्ऋत्याद्वायव्यान्तम् अग्नितः प्रणीतापर्यन्तं ततोऽग्नेरुत्तरतः पश्चिमदिशि पवित्रच्छेदनार्थं कुशत्रयं पवित्रकरणार्थं साग्रमनन्तर्गर्भं कुशपत्रद्वयं प्रोक्षणीपात्रम् आज्यस्थाली संमार्जनार्थं कुशत्रयम् उपयमनार्थं वेणीरूपकुशत्रयं समिधस्तिस्रः स्रुव आज्यं षट्पञ्चाशदुत्तरवरमुष्टिशतद्वयावच्छिन्नं तंडुलपूर्णपात्रं पवित्रच्छेदनकुशानां पूर्वदिशि क्रमेणासादनीयानि ।

tataḥ paristaraṇam । *barhiścaturthabhāgamādāya āgneyādīśānāntaṁ brahmaṇo'gniparyantaṁ nairṛtyādvāyavyāntam agnitaḥ praṇītāparyantaṁ tato-'gneruttarataḥ paścimadiśi pavitracchedanārthaṁ kuśatrayaṁ pavitrakaraṇārthaṁ sāgramanantargarbhaṁ kuśapatradvayaṁ prokṣaṇipātram ājyasthālī saṁmārjanārthaṁ kuśatrayam upayamanārthaṁ veṇīrūpakuśatrayaṁ samidhastisraḥ sruva ājyaṁ ṣaṭpañcāśaduttaravaramuṣṭiśatadvayāvacchinnaṁ taṁḍulapūrṇapātraṁ pavitracchedanakuśānāṁ pūrvadiśi krameṇāsādanīyāni* ।

The next step is to spread the kuśa grass around the fire in the following manner: Take the fourth part of a 'barhi' (a handful of sixty-four pieces of kuśa grass), that is, sixteen pieces of this grass; of these keep four to the north-east and four more with their front portions pointing towards the east. The latter four should be laid down between the fire and the brāhmaṇa-in-the-role-of-Brahmā (from Brahmā to Agni). Further, another bunch of four kuśa stems should be laid between the fire and the Praṇītāpātra (the vessel for the holy water). All this is to be followed by setting apart three of the kuśas for Pavitrachedana (cutting out two blades of the kuśa grass to form a Pavitra which holds offerings or

1. See the Appendices.

sprinkles ghī) and keeping them in the north-west quarter viewed from the fire, their front portions (agra bhāga) intact for the purifying purpose. Then arrange to have the following materials: two leaves of the kuśa, Prokṣaṇīpāta[1] (the vessel for sprinkling water), Ājyasthālī[2] (the vessel for clarified butter or ghī), three blades of kuśa for cleansing the sruva[3] (the small wooden ladle), three kuśa stems braided into something like a ladle,[4] three Palāsī leaves

---

1. प्रोक्षणीयात्रं वारणं द्वादशाङ्गुलदीर्घं करतलसम्मितखातं पद्मपत्राकृति कमलमुकुलाकृति वा ।

proksạṇīpātraṁ vāraṇaṁ dvādaśāṅguladīrghaṁ karatalasammitakhātaṁ padmapatrākṛti kamalamukulākṛti vā ।

2. आज्यस्थाली तैजसी मृण्मयी वा द्वादशाङ्गुलविशाला वा प्रादेशोच्चा । तथैव चरुस्थाली तत्र देवलोक्ता: कारिका:–प्रणीता नैर्ॠते भागे तद्वायव्यगोचरे । वारणं संविजानीयात् सर्वकर्म्मसु कारयेत् ॥ सर्वसंशोधनार्थोदपात्रं वारणमिष्यते । द्वादशाङ्गुलदीर्घं च करतलोन्मितखातकम् । पद्मपत्रसमाकारं मुकुलाकारमेव वा ॥ इति ॥ तैजसी मृण्मयी वापि आज्यस्थाली प्रकीर्तिता । द्वादशाङ्गुलविस्तीर्णा प्रादेशोच्चा प्रमाणत: । चरुस्थाली तथैवापि दीर्घोंच्चा तु प्रमाणत: । नानयोरन्तरं यस्माद् द्रव्यसंस्कारणार्थक: ॥

ājyasthālī taijasī mṛṇmayī vā dvādaśāṅgulaviśālā vā prādeśoccā । tathaiva carusthālī tatra devalokatāḥ kārikāḥ—praṇītā nairṛte bhāge tadvāyavyagocare । vāraṇaṁ saṁvijānīyāt sarvakarmmasu kārayet ॥ sarvasaṁśodhanārthodapātraṁ vāraṇamiṣyate । dvādaśāṅguladīrghaṁ ca karatalonmitakhātakam । padmapatrasamākāraṁ mukulākārameva vā ॥ iti ॥ taijasī mṛṇmayī vāpi ājyasthālī prakīrtitā । dvādaśāṅgulavistīrṇā prādeśoccā pramāṇataḥ । carusthālī tathaivāpi dīrghoṁccā tu pramāṇataḥ । nānayorantaraṁ yasmād dravyasaṁskāraṇārthakaḥ ॥

3. संमार्जनार्थास्त्रयस्त्रिसंख्याका: कुशा: त्रय एव नाधिका न न्यूना: । स्रुवसंमार्जनार्थन्तु कुशत्रयमुदीरितम् । स्रुवाङ्गत्रयशुद्ध्यर्थं सूत्रे प्रोक्तास्त्रयस्तत: ।

saṁmārjanārthāstrayastrisaṁkhyākāḥ kuśāḥ traya eva nādhikā na nyūnāḥ । sruvasaṁmārjanārthantu kuśatrayamudīritam । sru vāṅgatrayaśuddhyarthaṁ sūtre proktāstrayastataḥ ।

4. उपयमनकुशा: स्त्रिप्रभृतय: । उपयमनार्थमाख्यातास्त्रिषण्णवमिता: कुशा: । वेणीरूपा निरोधार्था निरोधे बहुभि: सुखम्–इति भृगुवचनात् ॥

upayamanakuśāḥ striprabhṛtayaḥ । upayamanārthamākhyātāstriṣaṇṇavamitāḥ kuśāḥ । veṇīrūpā nirodhārthā nirodhe bahubhiḥ sukham—iti bhṛguvacanāt ॥

(samidhaḥ,[1] firewood, fuel), each of a handspan, a sruva,[2] ājya[3] (clarified butter), two hundred and fifty-six handfuls of rice measured by the fist or closed palm of the bridegroom and filled in a container. Keep all these in order towards the east of the kuśas meant for Pavitrachedana.

अथ तस्यामेव दिशि असाधारणवस्तून्युपकल्पनीयानि शमीपलाशमिस्रा लाजाः, दृषदुपलम्, सिन्दूरादिद्रव्ययुक्तं पात्रम्, कुमारीभ्राता, सूर्प्पः, दृढपुरुषः, अन्यदपि तदुपयुक्तमालेपनादि द्रव्यम् ।

---

1. समिधस्तिस्त्रः पालाश्यः । प्रदेशमात्राः । अग्रेनैंवेद्यपूजार्थं निक्षिपेत्कन्यकात्रम् ॥ पालाशजञ्च प्रादेशमात्रं दैर्घ्येण स्थूलता । कनिष्ठिकासमं ध्यात्वा विधिमग्नौ क्षिपेच्च तत् ॥

samidhastistraḥ pālāśyaḥ । prādeśamātrāḥ । agrernaiṁvedyapūjārthaṁ nikṣipetkanyakātram ॥ pālāśajañca prādeśamātraṁ dairghyeṇa sthūlatā । kaniṣṭhikāsamaṁ ghyātvā vidhimagnau kṣipecca tat ॥

2. स्रुवो ब्रह्महस्तः तस्य लक्षणमाह कात्यायनः–स्रुवस्तु ब्रह्महस्ताख्यः स्कन्धान्ते बाहुरुच्यते स्वाहाकारस्वधाकारवषट्कारसमन्वितः ॥ दण्डकारो भवेन्मूले स्यादरख्यान्तु तत्समः । सकङ्कणस्तु दण्डाग्रे हस्ताकारस्ततो बहिः ॥ अष्टाङ्गुलपरीमाणं मूलादभ्यन्तरे त्यजेत् । दशाङ्गुलपरीमाणमारभ्याऽकङ्कणावधिः ॥ हस्तमात्रं भवेद्धस्तः स्रुव इत्यभिधीयते । खादिरः शैंशपो वापि ह्यन्यो वा पुष्टवृक्षजः । धावकोऽपि समाख्यातो होमार्थं मुनिभिः कृतः ॥

sruvo brahmahastaḥ tasya lakṣaṇamāha kātyāyanaḥ—sruvastu brahmahastākhyaḥ skandhānte bāhurucyate svāhākārasvadhākāravaṣaṭkārasamanvitaḥ ॥ daṇḍakāro bhavenmūle syādarakhyāntu tatsamaḥ । sakaṅkaṇastu daṇḍāgre hastākārastato bahiḥ ॥ aṣṭāṅgulaparīmāṇaṁ mūlādabhyantare tyajet । daśāṅgulaparīmāṇamārabhyā'kaṅkaṇāvidhiḥ ॥ hastamātraṁ bhaveddhastaḥ sruva ityabhidhīyate । khādiraḥ śaiṁśapo vāpi hyanyo vā puṣṭavṛkṣajaḥ । dhāvako'pi samākhyāto homarthaṁ munibhiḥ kṛtaḥ ॥

3. आज्यं तत्तु गव्यम् । तथा च श्रुतिः–गव्यमाज्यं जुहुयात् । तदभावे माहिषेयमिति । तथा स्मृतिः–गव्यमाज्यं हुतं नित्यमभावे माहिषं स्मृतमितिचरुश्चेद्व्रीहिण्डुलाः ॥ शर्कराघृतसंयुक्ताश्चरुर्दैंवे च पैतृके । व्रीहितण्डुलसंसिद्धो मुख्यः प्रोक्तः सुरर्षिभिः ॥

ājyaṁ tattu gavyam । tathā ca śrutiḥ—gavyamājyaṁ juhūyāt । tadabhāve māhiṣeyamiti । tathā smṛtiḥ—gavyamājyaṁ hūtaṁ nityamabhāve māhiṣaṁ smṛtamiticaruścedvrīhiṇḍulāḥ ॥ śarkarāghṛtasaṁyuktāścarurdaive ca paitṛke । vrīhitaṇḍulasaṁsiddho mukhyaḥ proktaḥ surarṣibhiḥ ॥

atha tasyāmeva diśi asādhāraṇavastūnyupakalpanīyāni śamīpalāśamiṣrā lājāḥ, dṛṣadupalam, sindūrādi-dravyayuktaṁ pātram, kumārībhrātā, sūrppaḥ, dṛḍha-puruṣaḥ, anyadapi tadupayuktamālepanādi dravyam ।

All the materials—śamīpalāśa, leaves of jāṁṭī, a piece of stone, a container with vermilion in it—required for the rite of Kuśakaṁḍikā should be kept in the order and manner shown above. The bride's brother should have all these in a winnowing basket made of the leaves of date palm. The steadfast man should have all the necessary materials for the altar arranged in proper order so that they may be picked up easily when required.

ततः पवित्रच्छेदनकुशैः स्वप्रादेशमात्रे पवित्रे छित्त्वा सपवित्रकरेण त्रिवारं प्रणीतोदकं त्रिः प्रोक्षणीपात्रे निधाय अनामिकाङ्गुष्ठाभ्याम् उत्तराग्रे पवित्रे गृहीत्वा त्रिरुत्पवनम्[1] । ततः प्रोक्षणीपात्रं वामहस्ते कृत्वा अनामिकांगुष्ठाभ्यां गृहीतपवित्राभ्यां प्रोक्षणीजलं किंचिदुत्क्षिप्य प्रणीतोदकेनाभ्युक्ष्य ततः प्रोक्षणीजलेन यथासादितवस्तुसेचनं ततोग्निप्रणीतयोर्मध्ये प्रोक्षणीपात्रं निदध्यात् ।

tataḥ pavitracchedanakuśaiḥ svaprādeśamātre pavitre chittvā sapavitrakareṇa trivāraṁ praṇītodakaṁ triḥ prokṣaṇīpātre nidhāya anāmikāṅguṣṭhābhyāṁ uttarāgre pavitre gṛhitvā trirutpavanam । *tataḥ prokṣaṇīpātraṁ vāmahaste kṛtvā anāmikāṁguṣṭhābhyāṁ gṛhita-pavitrābhyāṁ prokṣaṇījalaṁ kiṁcidutkṣipya prāṇītodake-nābhyukṣya tataḥ prokṣaṇījalena yathāsāditavastusecanaṁ tatognipraṇītayormaṁdhye prokṣaṇīpātraṁ nidadhyāt* ।

Then the following rites are recommended:

First, cut the kuśas into small pieces, each as long as a handspan. Holding two kuśa blades or Pavitra (used for holding offerings or for sprinkling ghī), drop the water of the Praṇītāpātra into the Prokṣaṇīpātra three times. Again,

---

1. द्रव्यविलोडनमुत्पवमिति ।

dravyaviloḍanamutpavamiti ।

holding the two kuśa strainers with their points to the north, seizing them between the ring finger and the thumb, sprinkle water overhead three times. Then holding the Prokṣaṇīpātra in the left hand and the two kuśa blades between the ring finger and the thumb, toss up the water in the Prokṣaṇī a little bit. And then sprinkle everything with the water of the Praṇītāpātra before sprinkling them all with the water of the Prokṣaṇī. Having done so, keep the Prokṣaṇī vessel between the fire and the Praṇītā vessel.

आज्यस्थाल्यामाज्यं निरुप्य वह्नावधिश्रित्य ततो ज्वलत्तृणादिना हविर्वेष्टयित्वा प्रदक्षिणक्रमेण वह्नौ तत्प्रक्षेपः । ततः स्त्रुवः[1] प्रतपनम् । संमार्जनकुशानामग्रैरग्रं मूलैर्मूलं मध्यैर्मध्यं स्त्रुवं प्रणीतोदकेनाभ्युक्ष्य पुनः प्रतप्य स्त्रुव दक्षिणतो निदध्यात् ।

ājyasthālyāmājyaṁ nirupya vahnāvadhiśritya tato jvalattṛṇādinā havirveṣṭayitvā pradakṣiṇakrameṇa vahnau tatprakṣepaḥ । tataḥ sruvaḥ pratapanam । saṁmārjana-kuśānāmagrairagraṁ mūlairmulaṁ madhyairmadhyaṁ sruvaṁ praṇītodakenābhyukṣya punaḥ pratapya sruvaṁ dakṣiṇato nidadhyāt ।

Pour a little clarified butter (*Ājya*) in a small platter which should then be heated to cause the ghī to melt. After this, let the clarified butter be stirred round the platter with a burning straw (*tṛṇa*) which should then be thrown into the fire after waving it around (the fire). The next few instructions include heating the sruva spoon (the wooden ladle) and cleaning its front part with the point (*agra bhāga*) of the kuśa grass meant for this purpose. The middle por-

1. स्त्रुवस्यायं संस्कारो होमार्थः, एवञ्च दृष्टार्थता तत्संस्कारस्य अतः संस्कारविस्मरणे प्रायश्चित्तपूर्वकं प्रागन्त्यहोमः कार्यः । स्त्रुवे संस्कारविस्मृत्या प्रायश्चितं शतं जपः । सावित्र्याः प्राक् तथांत्ये च होमो व्याहृतिभिस्तथा । प्रायश्चित्तं विधायैव संस्कारोऽभ्युक्षणं स्मृतम् ॥

sruvasyāyaṁ saṁskāro homārthaḥ, evañca dṛṣṭārthatā tatsaṁskārasya ataḥ saṁskāravismaraṇe prāyaścittapūrvakaṁ prāgantyahomaḥ kāryaḥ । sruve saṁskāravismṛtyā prāyaścittaṁ śataṁ japaḥ । sāvitryāḥ prāk tathāṁtye ca homo vyāhṛtibhistathā । prāyaścittaṁ vidhāyaiva saṁskāro'bhyukṣaṇaṁ smṛtam ॥

tion of the sruva be cleaned with the middle of the kuśa, while the portion at the bottom should be wiped with the roots of it. Then shall the saṁskāras be performed followed by keeping the heated sruva towards the south close to Brahmā after sprinkling it with the water kept in the holy vessel Praṇītā.

ततः आज्यस्थालीमग्नेरवतार्य्य अग्रे धृत्वा प्रोक्षणीवदुत्पूय अवेक्ष्य सत्यपद्रव्ये तन्निरसनं पुनः प्रोक्षण्युत्पवनं ततः उपयमनकुशान्वामहस्ते कृत्वा उत्तिष्ठन्प्रजापतिं मनसा ध्यात्वा तूष्णीमेवाग्नौ घृताक्ताः समिधस्तिस्त्रः[1] क्षिपेत् । तत उपविश्य सपवित्रप्रोक्षण्युदकेन प्रदक्षिणक्रमेणाग्निपर्युक्षणं कृत्वा प्रणोतापात्रे पवित्रे निधाय पातितदक्षिणजानुः कुशेन ब्रह्मणान्वारब्धः[2] समिद्धतमेऽग्नो स्त्रुवेणाज्याहुतीर्जुहुयात् ।

tataḥ ājyasthālīmagneravatāryya agre dhṛtvā prokṣaṇī-vadutpūya avekṣya satyapadravye tannirasanaṁ punaḥ prokṣaṇyutpavanaṁ tataḥ upayamanakuśānvāmahaste kṛtvā uttiṣṭhanprajāpatiṁ manasādhyātvā tūṣṇīmevāgnau ghṛtāktāḥ samidhastisraḥ kṣipet । tata upaviśya sapavitra-prokṣaṇyudakena pradakṣiṇakrameṇāgniparyukṣaṇaṁ kṛtvā praṇītāpātre pavitre nidhāya pātitadakṣiṇajānuḥ

---

1. यादृश्यो समिधो निरूपितास्ताः प्रोक्ता व्यासकात्यायनवसिष्ठगौतमभरद्वाजैः ॥ पालाशखदिराश्वत्थशम्युदुम्बरजाः समित् । अपामार्गमपूर्वाग्निं कुशाश्चेत्यपरे विदुः ॥ सत्वचः समिधः स्थाप्याः ऋजुश्लक्ष्णासमास्तथा । शस्ता दशाङ्गुलास्तास्तु द्वादशाङ्गुलिकास्तु ताः ॥ आर्द्राः पक्वाः समच्छेदास्तर्जन्यङ्गुलिवर्तुलाः । अपाटिताश्च विशिखाः कृमिदोषविवर्जिताः ॥ ईदृशीर्होमयेत्प्राज्ञः प्राप्नोति विपुलां श्रियम् ॥

   yādṛśyo samidho nirūpitāstāḥ proktā vyāsakātyā-yanavasiṣṭhagautamabharadvājaiḥ ॥ pālāśakhadirāśvatthaśam-yudumbarajāḥ samit । apāmārgamapūrvāgniṁ kuśāścetyapare viduḥ ॥ satvacaḥ samidhaḥ sthāpyāḥ ṛjuślakṣṇāsamāstathā ॥ śastā daśāṅgulāstāstu dvādaśāṅgulikāstu taḥ ॥ ārdrāḥ pakvāḥ samacchedāstarjanyaṅgulivartulāḥ ॥ apāṭitāśca viśikhāḥ kṛmidoṣavivarjitāḥ ॥ īdṛśīrhomayetprājñaḥ prāpnoti vipulāṁ śriyam ॥

2. अन्वारब्धो यथा ब्रह्मणा दक्षिणहस्तेन दक्षिणहस्तस्थकुशेन वा उपस्पृष्टः ।

   anvārabdho yathā brahmaṇā dakṣiṇahastena dakṣiṇa-hastasthakuśena vā upaspṛṣṭaḥ ।

kuṣena brahmaṇānvārabdhaḥ samiddhatame'gnau sruveṇājyāhutīrjuhuyāt ।

These instructions, not yet complete, should be followed by removing the ghī jar from the fire, keeping it in front, and purifying the ghī with the Pavitras (two kuśa leaves for holding offerings or for sprinkling ghī) as one sanctifies the water contained in the Prokṣaṇī. Do not miss to have a close look at the ghī jar; if anything impure (such as an insect or a fly) has defiled it, it must be removed forthwith and the ghī be purified as one purifies the Prokṣaṇī. Then, taking the kuśa grass serving as an *upayamana* (sprinkling ladle) in the left hand and fixing the mind on Prajāpati, wet the three Samidhās (firewood, fuel) with ghī and throw them quietly into the fire. Then take your seat, with the Pavitras throw a little of the water kept in the Prokṣaṇī first into the fire; keep the Pavitras in the Praṇītā jar; bend your right knee and having touched Brahmā with kuśa, offer oblation of ghī with the Sruva to the flaming fire, thus performing the Homa (i.e. the act of making an oblation to the Devas or gods by casting clarified butter into the fire).

तत्राधारादारभ्य द्वादशाहुतिषु तत्तदाहुत्यनन्तरं स्रुवावस्थितहुतशेषघृतस्य प्रोक्षणीपात्रे प्रक्षेपः ।

tatrādhārādārabhya dvādaśāhutiṣu tattadāhutyanantaraṁ sruvāvasthitahutaśeṣaghṛtasya prokṣaṇīpātre prakṣepaḥ ।

The oblation to be performed next is called Āghāra, meaning, according to Monier-Williams, "sprinkling clarified butter upon the fire at certain sacrifices." From this Āghāra Homa to the twelfth oblation drop the residual ghī into the Prokṣaṇī jar with the Sruva.

ततः ॐ एषो ह देवः प्रदिशोऽनु सर्वाः पूर्वो ह जातः स उ गर्भे अन्तः । स एव जातः स जनिष्यमाणः प्रत्यङ् जनास्तिष्ठति सर्वतोमुखः ॥ इति मंत्रेणाग्नेः सम्मुखीकरणम् । अथ स्रुवपूजनम् । मंगलं भगवान् विष्णुर्मंगलं गरुडध्वजः । मंगलं पुण्डरीकाक्षः मंगलायतनो हरिः ॥

*tataḥ aum eṣo ha devaḥ pradiśo'nu sarvāḥ pūrvo ha
jātaḥ sa u garbhe antaḥ ı saeva jātaḥ sa janiṣyamāṇaḥ
pratyaṅ janāstiṣṭhati sarvatomukhaḥ ıı iti maṁtreṇāgneḥ
sammukhīkaraṇam ı atha sruvapūjanam ı maṁgalaṁ
bhagavān viṣṇurmaṁgalaṁ garuḍadhvajaḥ ı maṁgalaṁ
puṇḍarīkākṣaḥ maṁgalāyatano hariḥ ıı*

This pre-eminent Agnideva or the supreme Puruṣa is
immanent in all the quarters (sarvāḥ pradiśaḥ). O men, this
celebrated Deva appears as the very first being, establishes
himself in the middle of the womb (garbhe antaḥ), and then
reveals himself. It is he who enters every object and is
omnifaced, inscrutable, and omnipotent.

Pronouncing this mantra and facing the fire, do obeisance to the Sruva with the śloka 'maṁgalaṁ
bhagavānviṣṇuḥ maṁgalaṁ garuḍadhvajaḥ ı maṁgalaṁ
puṇḍarīkākṣaḥ maṁgalāyatano hariḥ ıı'

ॐ प्रजापतये स्वाहा । इदं प्रजापतये इति मनसा । ॐ इन्द्राय स्वाहा ।
इदमिन्द्राय इत्याधारौ । ॐ अग्नये स्वाहा । इदमग्नये । ॐ सोमाय
स्वाहा । इदं सोमाय इत्याज्यभागौ । ॐ भूः स्वाहा । इदमग्नये । ॐ भुवः
स्वाहा । इदं वायवे । ॐ स्वः स्वाहा । इदं सूर्य्याय । एता महाव्याहृतयः ।

*aum prajāpataye svāhā ı idaṁ prajāpataye iti manasā ı
aum indrāya svāhā ı idamindrāya ityādhārau ı aum agnaye
svāhā ı idamagnaye ı aum somāya svāhā ı idaṁ somāya
ityājyabhāgau ı aum bhūḥ svāhā ı idamagnaye ı aum bhuvaḥ
svāhā ı idaṁ vāyave ı aum svaḥ svāhā ı idaṁ sūryyāya ı etā
mahāvyāhṛtayaḥ ı*

With your mind fully focused on 'aum prajāpataye
svāhā' and muttering it, make the oblation. This and 'aum
indrāya svāhā' are the two oblations which are called
Āghāra, while 'aum agnaye svāhā' and 'aum somāya svāhā'
are called Ājyabhāga (the two portions of clarified butter
belonging to Angi and Soma). 'aum bhūḥ svāhā', 'aum
bhuvaḥ svāhā' and 'aum svaḥ svāhā'—these are three other
oblations called Mahāvyāhṛti (because they constitute the
mystical formula 'aum bhuḥ bhuvaḥ svaḥ').

ॐ त्वन्नो अन्ने वरुणस्य विद्वान्देवस्य हेडो अवयासिसीष्ठाः । यजिष्ठो वह्नितमः शोशुचानो विश्वा द्वेषाँ सि प्रमुमुग्ध्यस्मत्स्वाहा– इदमग्नीवरुणाभ्याम् ।

aum tvanno anne varuṇasya vidvāndevasya heḍo avayāsisīṣṭhāḥ । yajiṣṭho vahnitamaḥ śośucāno viśvā dveṣāṁsi pramumugdhyasmatsvāhā—idamagnīvaruṇā-bhyām ।

O Fire! If there is any flaw or imperfection (if there is anything lacking) in the performance of this ceremony, let not Varuṇa fly into rage (vaiguṇyādeva varuṇasya devasya heḍaḥ krodhaṁ avayāsisīṣṭhāḥ apanayetyarthaḥ). Considering me dull-witted (yadvā no'smān pramattān mandamatīniti jānan), let not only Varuṇa's fury (kiñca na kevalaṁ varuṇakrodhamapanaya) be quelled but also let all the sacrilege committed by me be forgiven and obtain for me all the great luxuries and objects of supreme enjoyment (kintu asmat iti asmabhyaṁ viśvā dveṣāṁsi sarvāṇi bhāgyāni pramumugdhi). You are surpassingly the greatest of all the gods of sacrifice and the most effulgent of them all (punaḥ kīdṛśastvaṁ vahnitamaḥ sakalayajñāṁśabhāgibhyaḥ sva svāṁśaprāpaṇena sātiśayaḥ).

ॐ सत्वन्नो ऽग्नेऽवमो भवोती नेदिष्ठो अस्या ऽउषसो व्युष्टौ । अवयक्ष्व नो वरुणँ रराणो व्रीहि मृडीकँ सुहवो न एधि स्वहा– इदमग्नीवरुणाभ्याम् ॥२॥

aum satvanno 'gne'vamo bhavotī nediṣṭho asyā 'uṣaso vyuṣṭau । avayakṣva no varuṇaṁ rarāṇo vrīhi mṛḍīkaṁ suhavo na edhi svāhā—idamagnīvaruṇābhyām ॥ 2 ॥

O Fire! Whatever you are, be my nourisher and sustainer. Explaining when precisely he should offer his protection and patronage, he says, he should do so from the early hours of the morning (asyā uṣaso vyuṣṭau) and not just protect (na kevalametadeva) him but also, in response to his glad invitation (kintu āgatya mṛḍīkaṁ sukhakaraṁ), willingly and happily appear and reward him with plenty of foodgrains, such as paddy, etc. (no vrīhi asmatsaṁbandhi vrīhyādikaṁ rarāṇaḥ dadānaḥ san) and let him obtain whatever food he has wished to offer to the gods and for which he has worshipped Varuṇa, the presiding Lord of Sacrifice (varuṇaṁ yajñādhiṣṭhātāram avayakṣva pūjayet-yarthaḥ).

ॐ अयाश्चाग्नेऽस्यनभिशस्तिपाश्च सत्यमित्त्वमया असि । अया नो यज्ञं वहास्यया नो धेहि भेषजँ स्वाहा-इदमग्नये ॥३॥

aum ayāścāgne'syanabhiśastipāśca satyamittvamayā asi । *ayā no yajñaṁ vahāsyayā no dhehi bheṣajaṁ svāhā-idamagnaye* ॥ 3 ॥

O Agni! You dwell everywhere, both inside and outside. (You are familiar with all the urgings and instincts of men, their intrinsic as well as extrinsic motivations.) As a purifying agent, you destroy all defilements and by purging men of their impurities, you make them pure like yourself and then protect them. (One is purged of one's sins if one sincerely repents of his transgressions and leads a life dedicated to altruistic activities, holy deeds or *karmas,* and to the performance of sacrifices, penance, etc. To be sincerely penitent is to burn in the fire of redeeming self-reproach. When one experiences the stings of conscience and burns in the fire of remorse and self-reproof, one is slowly purged of sins.) You are, O Agni, undeniably the way leading to auspicious action. Pray be so kind to me that I may perform this sacrifice with a sincere heart and may thus propitiate the celestial deities. Making me in your own image, bless me with the faculty of recognizing the real source of happiness and of destroying that which leads to suffering (*duḥkha*).

ॐ ये ते शतं वरुण ये सहस्त्रं यज्ञियाः पाशा वितता महान्तः । तेभिर्नो ऽअद्य सवितोत विष्णुर्विश्वे मुञ्चन्तु मरुतः स्वर्क्काः स्वाहा ॥ इदं वरुणाय सवित्रे विष्णवे विश्वेभ्यो मरुद्भ्यः स्वर्केभ्यः ॥४॥

aum ye te śataṁ varuṇa ye sahasraṁ yajñiyāḥ pāśā vitatā mahāntaḥ । *tebhirno 'adya savitota viṣṇurviśve muñcantu marutaḥ svarkkāḥ svāhā* ॥ *idaṁ varuṇāya savitre viṣṇave viśvebhyo marudbhyaḥ svarkkebhyaḥ* ॥ 4 ॥

O Varuṇa! The myriads of fetters which result from the irregularities in and obstructions to the performance of sacrifices and which cannot be destroyed, howsover one may try, have kept me manacled. May Savitā, Viṣṇu, Indra, Viśvedevā, Maruta, and Āditya Devatā, famed for his beautiful heart, free me and by accepting the oblation made to them in the sacrifice, be pleased with me and purify me everywhere.

ॐ उदुत्तमं वरुण पाशमस्मदवाधमं व्रिमध्यमँ् श्रथाय । अथा वयमादित्य व्रते तवानागसोऽदितये स्याम स्वाहा ॥ इदं वरुणाय ॥५॥ उदकोपस्पर्शनम् । एताः प्रायश्चितसंज्ञिकाः[1] ।

aum udduttamaṁ varuṇa pāśamasmadavādhamaṁ veimadhyamaṁ śrathāya । *athā vayamāditya vrate*

---

1. होमकर्मणि पराशरः । आघारावाज्यभागौ च महाव्याहृतयस्तथा । सर्वप्राय. . . स्तथा ॥ प्राजापत्यं स्विष्टकृतोऽग्नेर्होमश्च सर्वतः । होमकर्म्मण्याहुतीनां चतुर्द्दशकमीरितम् ॥ सर्वप्रायश्चित्तं त्वन्नोऽग्ने इत्यारभ्य उदुत्तममित्यन्तमाहुतिपञ्चकम् । प्राजापत्यं प्राजापत्याहुतिः ॥ अथ विवाहहोममप्याह सांख्यायनः–विवाहे होमयेन्नित्यं राष्ट्रभृद्द्वादशाहुतीः । जवाहुतीर्दश त्रींश्च होमयेत तत्र चेच्छया ॥ अष्टादशाऽपि जुहुयादभ्यातानाहुतीस्तथा ॥ आहुतित्रितयं दद्याद्विवाहे साक्षिकाग्नये । साक्षीदानादिपूज्यऽतोग्निं साक्षिणमाहुनेत् इति ॥ धर्म्म आत्मा सदा साक्षी धर्मो धारयते प्रजाः । अतो वैवस्वतं धर्म्ममाहुतिभ्यां प्रपूजयेत् ॥ इति वचनात् । वैवस्वतायाप्याहुतिद्वयम् ॥

homakarmaṇi parāśaraḥ । āghārāvājyabhāgau ca mahāvyāhṛtayastathā ॥ sarvaprāya. . . stathā ॥ prājāpatyaṁ sviṣṭakṛto'gnerhomaśca sarvataḥ । homakarmmaṇyāhutīnāṁ caturddaśakamīritaṁ ॥ sarvaprāyaścittaṁ tvanno'gne ityārabhya uduttamamityantamāhutipañcakam । prājāpatyaṁ prājāpatyāhutiḥ ॥ atha vivāhahomamapyāha sāṁkhyāyanaḥ—vivāhe homayennityaṁ rāṣṭrabhṛddavādaśāhutīḥ । jayāhutīrdaśa trīṁśca homayet tatra cecchayā ॥ aṣṭādaśā'pi juhuyādabhyātānahutīstathā ॥ āhutitritayaṁ dadyādvivāhe sākṣikāgnaye । sākṣīdānādipūjya'tognim sākṣiṇamāhunet iti ॥ dharmma ātmā sadā sākṣī dharmo dhārayate prajāḥ । ato vaivasvataṁ dharmmamāhutibhyāṁ prapūjayat ॥ iti vacanāt । vaivasvatāyāpyāhutidvayam ॥

tavānāgaso'ditaye syāma svāhā ॥ *idaṁ varuṇāya* ॥ 5 ॥ *udakopasparśanam* । *etāḥ prāyaścittasaṁjñikāḥ* ।

O Varuṇa ! May you protect me from your noose, which is of three kinds: the most excellent, the middling, and the vilest or the worst. Loosen the hangman's noose and save me. Having done so, O Varuṇa, son of Aditi, rid me of my sense of helplessness just as you forgave me the sins I committed in not observing the vow of celibacy.

Join all the five fingers of the right hand and touch water. These five oblations are penitential and are, therefore, called 'prāyaścitta'.

अथ छायादानम्

आज्यं तेजःसमुद्दिष्टमाज्यं पापहरं परम् । आज्ये चैव मुखं दृष्ट्वा सर्वपापैः प्रमुच्यते ॥ जानताऽजानता वापि मनोवाक्कायकर्म्मभिः । कृतं यत्पातकं तन्मे घृतस्पर्शाद्विनश्यतु ॥

atha chāyādānam

ājyaṁ tejaḥsamuddiṣṭamājyaṁ pāpaharaṁ param । *ājye caiva mukhaṁ dṛṣṭvā sarvapāpaiḥ pramucyate* ॥ *jānatā'jānatā vāpi manovākkāyakarmmabhiḥ* । *kṛtaṁ yatpātakaṁ tanme ghṛtasparśādvinaśyatu* ॥

The Ājya, which is clarified butter or ghṛta, is magnifier of brilliance, destroyer of all sins and supremely splendid. He who describes his own face mirrored in ghṛta breaks loose from the fetters of sin and all his offences, committed wittingly or unknowingly, by his mind, tongue, and spirit, are set at nought by the mere touch of this ghṛta.

ॐ तेजोऽसि शुक्रमस्यमृतमसि धाम नामाऽसि प्रियं देवानामनाधृष्टं देवयजनमसि ॥ इति मंत्रेण वरः छायापात्रे मुखं पश्येत् ।

aum tejo'si śukramasyamṛtamasi dhāma nāmā'si priyaṁ devānāmanādhṛṣṭaṁ devayajanamasi ॥ *iti maṁtreṇa varaḥ chāyāpātre mukhaṁ paśyet* ।

Having repeated this mantra, the bridegroom should

look at his face in the chāyāpātra, the small bowl filled with ghī.

ततो वरः छायापात्रं वामहस्ते गृहीत्वा संकल्पं कुर्यात् । अद्येत्यादिदेशकालौ संकीर्त्य० अमुकगोत्रोत्पन्नोऽमुकशर्म्माहं मम सर्वतापक्षयपूर्वकदीर्घायुरारोग्यादिफलप्राप्तयर्थमिदमवलोकितमाज्यं कांस्यपात्रसहितं सद्रव्यं मृत्युञ्जयदेवताप्रीतये अमुकगोत्रायाऽमुकशर्मणे ह्याचार्याय[1] तुभ्यं सम्प्रददे । स्वस्तीति ब्राह्मणो वदेत् ।

tato varaḥ chāyāpātraṁ vāmahaste gṛhītvā saṁkalpaṁ kuryāt । adyetyādideśakālau saṁkīrtya. . . amukagotrotpanno'mukaśarmmāhaṁ mama sarvapāpakṣayapūrvakadīrghāyuarārogyādiphalaprāptyarthamidamavalokitamājyaṁ kāṁsyapātrasahitaṁ sadravyaṁ mṛtyuñjayadevatāprītaye amukagotrāyā'mukaśarmaṇe hyācāryāya tubhyaṁ saapradade । svastīti brāhmaṇo vadet ।

This done, the bridegroom keeps the bowl, *chāyāpātra*, filled with ghī on his right hand and performs the following saṁkalpa. The brāhmaṇa receiving the *chāyapātra* shall say, "May God bless thee!" The bowl called *chāyāpātra* belongs to the officiating Ācārya.

ततोऽन्वारम्भं विना राष्ट्रभृद्धोमः । ॐ प्रजापतये स्वाहा । इदं प्रजापतये । ॐ अग्नये स्विष्टकृते स्वाहा । इदमग्नये स्विष्टकृते । उदकोपस्पर्शनम् ।

tato'nvārambhaṁ vinā rāṣṭrabhṛddhomaḥ । aum prajāpataye svāhā । idaṁ prajāpataye । aum agnaye sviṣṭakṛte svāhā । idamagnaye sviṣṭakṛte । udakopasparśanam ।

The repeating "aum prajāpataye svāhā", he should offer *rāṣṭrabhṛt homa,* which is a kind of prayer and oblation

---

1. आचार्याय प्रदातव्यं छायापात्रं सुसंस्कृतम् । तथैव पूर्णपात्रं च ब्रह्मणे कर्मसाक्षिणे ॥ यह नारदीय कर्माङ्ग पद्धकि में लिखा है ।

"ācāryāya pradātavyaṁ chāyāpātraṁ susaṁskṛtam । tathaiva pūrṇapātraṁ ca brahmaṇe karmasākṣiṇe ॥" This is recorded in Nārada's *Karmāṅga Paddhati.*

(offered to *rāṣṭrabhṛt*, a tributary prince, a king or a ruler) without Anvārambha (i.e. touching from behind in order to bless). This over, join the fingers of the right hand and touch water.

ॐ ऋताषाड् ऋतधामाऽग्निर्गन्धर्वः स न इदं ब्रह्म क्षत्रं पातु तस्मै स्वाहा वाट् ॥१॥

aum ṛtāṣāḍ ṛtadhāma'gnirgandharvaḥ sa na idaṁ brahma kṣatraṁ pātu tasmai svāhā vāṭ ॥ 1 ॥

Agni, who is like a Gaṁdharva (a member of the mythological community of celestial musicians), may accept the oblation offered to him. He whose habitation is truth may protect my spiritual knowledge (of Brahma) as well as my virility and potency.

ॐ ऋताषाड् ऋतधामाऽग्निर्गन्धर्वस्तस्यौषधयोप्सरसो मुदो नाम ताभ्यः स्वाहा । इदमोषधिभ्योऽप्सरोभ्यो मुद्भ्यः ॥२॥

aum ṛtāṣād ṛtadhāma'gnirgandharvastasyauṣadhayopsaraso mudo nāma tābhyaḥ svāhā । *idamoṣadhibhyo'psarobhyo mudbhyaḥ* ॥ 2 ॥

May the Gaṁdharva-like Agni, the very home of truth-abiding reality, whose celestial damsels are such pleasurable (health-restoring) herbs as barley grains, wheat, black gram, rice, green lentil, etc., protect my knowledge and strength.

ॐ सँ हितो विश्वसामा सूर्यो गन्धर्वः स न इदं ब्रह्म क्षत्रं पातु तस्मै स्वाहा वाट् । इदँ सँ हिताय विश्वसाम्ने सूर्य्याय गन्धर्वाय ॥ ३॥

aum saṁhito viśvasāmā sūryo gandharvaḥ sa na idaṁ brahma kṣatraṁ pātu tasmai svāhā vāṭ । *idaṁ saṁ hitāya viśvasāmne sūryyāya gaṁdharvāya* ॥ 3 ॥

May Gaṁdharva the Sun, who causes sunrise and sundown, day and night, and is as interminably vast as the cosmos itself and in form like the Sāmaveda, protect my knowlege and potency.

ॐ सँ हितो विश्वसामा सूर्यो गन्धर्वस्तस्य मरीचयोऽप्सरस आयुवो नाम ताभ्यः स्वाहा । इदं मरीचिभ्योऽप्सरोभ्य आयुभ्यः ॥४॥

aum saṁhito viśvasāmā sūryo gandharvastasya marīcayo'psarasa āyuvo nāma tābhyaḥ svāhā । *idaṁ marīcibhyo'psarobhya āyubhyaḥ* ॥ 4 ॥

May the celestial nymphs of the rays of Gaṁdharva the Sun, who causes day and night, receive the oblation offered and protect my knowledge and virility.

ॐ सुषुम्णः सूर्य्यरश्मिश्चन्द्रमा गन्धर्वः स न इदं ब्रह्म क्षत्रं पातु तस्मै स्वाहा वाट्–इदं सुषुम्णाय सूर्य्यरश्मये चन्द्रमसे गन्धर्वाय ॥५॥

aum suṣumṇaḥ sūryyaraśmiścandramā gandharvaḥ sa na idaṁ brahma kṣatraṁ pātu tasmai svāhā vāṭ—idaṁ suṣumṇāya sūryyaraśmaye candramase gandharvāya ॥ 5 ॥

May the celestial nymphs (apsarās) charming as the beams of Gaṁdharva the Moon, who is lighted by the Sun's rays, receive the oblation made and protect my knowledge and potency. (Knowledge or jñāna is the higher knowledge derived from meditation on the one Universal Spirit.)

ॐ सुषुम्णः सूर्य्यरश्मिश्चन्द्रमा गन्धर्वस्तस्य नक्षत्राण्यप्सरसो भेकुरयो नाम ताभ्यः स्वाहा–इदं नक्षत्रेभ्योऽप्सरोभ्यो भैकुरिभ्यः[1] ॥६॥

aum suṣumṇaḥ sūryyaraśmiścandramā gandharvastasya nakṣatrāṇyapsaraso bhekurayo nāma tābhyaḥ svāhā—idaṁ nakṣatrebhyo'psarobhyo bhekuribhyaḥ ॥ 6 ॥

May the starry nymphs, Bhanāma and Ikuri, who are sisters married to a common husband and who belong to Gandharva the Moon, an unending source of bliss, receive the oblation duly made to them.

ॐ इषिरो विश्वव्यचा वातो गन्धर्वः स न इदं ब्रह्म क्षत्रं पातु तस्मै स्वाहा वाट्–इदमिषिराय विश्वव्यचसे वाताय गन्धर्वाय ॥७॥

1. सपितृका एकपतिका इकुर्यस्ता उदीरिताः । इति गंगाधरवचनात् ।
sapitṛkā ekapatikā ikuryastā udīritāḥ । iti gaṁgādharavacanāt ।

aum iṣiro viśvavyacā vāto gandharvaḥ sa na idaṁ brahma, kṣatraṁ pātu tasmai svāhā vāṭ—idamiṣirāya viśvavyacase vātāya gandharvāya ॥ 7 ॥

May Gaṁdharva, who assumes the form of the wind enveloping the entire universe (viśvavyacāḥ sarvagataḥ visvaṁ sarvaṁ viśeṣeṇa añcatīti viśvavyacāḥ) and who is ever on the move (isiraḥ gamanasvabhāvaḥ) accept the oblation made to him (in the prescribed manner) and protect my knowledge and strength.

ॐ इषिरो विश्वव्यचा वातो गन्धर्वस्तस्यापोऽप्सरस ऊर्ज्जो नाम ताभ्यः स्वाहा । इदमद्भ्योऽप्सरोभ्यः ऊर्ग्भ्यः ॥८॥

aum iṣiro viśvavyacā vāto gandharvastasyāpo'psarasa ūrjjo nāma tābhyaḥ svāhā । *idamadbhyo 'psarobhyaḥ ūrgbhyaḥ* ॥ 8 ॥

May the celestial nymphs who are of as supreme purity as holy water (ūrjjo nāmnyaḥ[1]) and belong to Gaṁdharva the ever-moving wind, accept my offerings made in accordance with the prescribed manner.

ॐ भुज्युः सुपर्णो यज्ञो गन्धर्वः स न इदं ब्रह्म क्षत्रं पातु तस्मै स्वाहा वाट्–इदं भुज्यवे सुपर्णाय यज्ञाय गन्धर्वाय ॥९॥

aum bhujyuḥ suparṇo yajño gandharvaḥ sa na idaṃ brahma kṣatraṁ pātu tasmai svāhā vāṭ—idaṁ bhujyave suparṇāya yajñāya gandharvāya ॥ 9 ॥

May the Gaṁdharva who incarnates sacrifice (yajña) and whose movement is graceful and stately (suparṇaḥ śobhanaparṇaḥ śobhanagatiḥ) and who nurses and sustains (bhujyuḥ pālakaḥ bhunakti pālayatīti bhujyuḥ bhujadhātoryupratyayāntaḥ śabdaḥ), accept the oblation made to him with due propriety.

---

1. 'सर्वसम्पादकं तूर्ज्ज ऊर्ज्जः परमपावनम् । ऊर्ज्जा कार्तिकको मासः इति' रन्तिकोशोक्तिः ।
'sarvasampādakaṁ tūrjja ūrjjaḥ paramapāvanam । ūrjjā kārtikako māsaḥ iti'—rantikośoktiḥ ।

ॐ भुज्युः सुपर्णो यज्ञो गंधर्वस्तस्य दक्षिणा अप्सरसस्तावा नाम ताभ्यः स्वाहा–इदं दक्षिणाभ्योऽप्सरोभ्यस्तावाभ्यः ॥१०॥

aum bhujyuḥ suparṇo yajño gaṁdharvastasya dakṣiṇā apsarasastāvā nāma tābhyaḥ svāhā—idaṁ dakṣiṇābhyo-'psarobhyastāvābhyaḥ ॥ 10 ॥

May the celestial nymphs of the fee (dakṣinā) paid to the officiating priest, who belongs to Gaṁdharva, the embodiment of sacrifice, who nurses and sustains and whose gait is beautiful (tāvānāmnyaḥ yajñasya stutiyogyakarāḥ stāvāḥ), receive the oblation made to them with due devotion.

ॐ प्रजापतिर्विश्वकर्मा मनो गन्धर्वः स न इदं ब्रह्म क्षत्रं पातु तस्मै स्वाहा वाट्–इदं प्रजापतये विश्वकर्मणे मनसे गन्धर्वाय ॥११॥

aum prajāpatirviśvakarmā mano gandharvaḥ sa na idaṁ brahma kṣatraṁ pātu tasmai svāhā vāṭ—idaṁ prajāpataye viśvakarmaṇe manase gandharvāya ॥ 11 ॥

May the Gandharva, who is the Mind, whose action results in (the creation and existence of) the world and who is the very Lord—Īśvara—of his subjects, protect my knowledge and vigour.

ॐ प्रजापतिर्विश्वकर्मा मनो गन्धर्वस्तस्य ऋक्सामान्यप्सरस एष्टयो नाम ताभ्यः स्वाहा–इदमृक्सामभ्योऽप्सरोभ्य एष्टिभ्यः ॥१२॥ इति राष्ट्रभृद्धोमः ।

aum prajāpatirviśvakarmā mano gan-dharvastasya ṛksāmānyapsarasa eṣṭayo nāma tābhyaḥ svāhā—idamṛksāmabhyo'psarobhya eṣṭibhyaḥ ॥ 12 ॥ *iti rāṣṭra-bhṛddhomaḥ* ।

The celestial nymphs, who are like the hyms of the Ṛgveda and the Sāmaveda sung for the fulfilment of one's desire for progeny, who belong to Gaṁdharva the Mind, the lord of the subjects whose action is (the creation of) the universe, may have the oblation made in accordance with the prescribed code.

अथ जयासंज्ञकास्त्रयोदशमन्त्राः

ॐ चित्तं च स्वाहा । इदं चित्ताय ॥१॥

atha jayāsaṁjñakāstrayodaśamantrāḥ

aum cittaṁ ca svāhā । *idaṁ cittāya* ॥ 1 ॥

The oblation consisting of thirteen mantras beginning from 'aum cittaṁ ca svāhā' to 'aum prajāpatirjayānidrāya' is called Jayā, which means that this oblation—Homa—brings victory. The victory here referred to is the victory of Indra which he won by Prajāpati's (or Īśvara's) grace. This may be taken to be the meaning of this mantra. All the thirteen mantras given here are meant to dispel this apprehension and to show that the proper meaning is: "May Prajāpati make me victorious!" ('Cittamiti' is consciousness which is knowledge. May Prajāpati bestow that knowledge upon me!)

ॐ चितिश्च स्वाहा । इदं चित्त्यै ॥२॥

aum cittiśca svāhā । *idaṁ cittyai* ॥ 2 ॥

May Prajāpati grant me that knowledge (citti) which is worth knowing!

ॐआकूतञ्च स्वाहा । इदमाकूताय ॥३॥

aum ākūtañca svāhā । *idamākūtāya* ॥ 3 ॥

May Prajāpati grant me that knowledge which is before me (ābhimukhya)!

ॐ आकूतिश्च स्वाहा । इदमाकूत्यै ॥४॥

aum ākūtiśca svāhā । *idamākūtyai* ॥ 4 ॥

May Prajāpati grant me that special and distinctive characteristic of conscience which inclines one's mind towards auspicious actions!

ॐ विज्ञातञ्च स्वाहा । इदं विज्ञाताय ॥५॥

aum vijñātañca svāhā । *idaṁ vijñātāya* ॥ 5 ॥

May Prajāpati specially grant me the knowledge of arts and crafts!

ॐ विज्ञातिश्च स्वाहा । इदं विज्ञात्यै ॥६॥

aum vijñātiśca svāhā । idaṁ vijñātyai ॥ 6 ॥

May Prajāpati grant me the art of making ornaments and garments!

ॐ मनश्च स्वाहा । इदं मनसे ॥७॥

aum manaśca svāhā । idaṁ manase ॥ 7 ॥

May Prajāpati grant me determination to carry out all the resolutions of the mind committed to truth! (May Prajāpati help me fulfil all the honest resolutions, *satyasaṁkalpa*, of the mind!)

ॐ शक्वरीश्च स्वाहा । इदं शक्वरीभ्यः ॥८॥

aum śakvarīśca svāhā । idaṁ śakvarībhyaḥ ॥ 8 ॥

May Prajāpati grant me the vision capable of seeing the vast material universe!

ॐ दर्शश्च स्वाहा । इदं दर्शाय ॥९॥

aum darśaśca svāhā । idaṁ darśāya ॥ 9 ॥

May Prajāpati grant me devotion to, or a heart brimming over with, the love of the Lord!

ॐ पौर्णमासं च स्वाहा । इदं पौर्णमासाय ॥१०॥

aum paurṇamāsaṁ ca svāhā । idaṁ paurṇamāsāya ॥ 10 ॥

May Prajāpati grant me that particular Yajña (worship, prayer, or devotion) called Paurṇamāsa!

ॐ बृहच्च स्वाहा । इदं बृहते ॥११॥

aum bṛhacca svāhā । idaṁ bṛhate ॥ 11 ॥

May Prajāpati teach me the duty and righteousness interpreted in the Vedic language of the Sāma called Bṛhat! (A metrical hymn or song of praise, especially a particular kind of sacred text or verse, is called Sāman, intended to be changed, and forming one of the four kinds of Vedic compositions mentioned first in the Ṛgveda.)

ॐ रथन्तरञ्च स्वाहा । इदं रथन्तराय ॥१२॥

aum rathantarañca svāhā । *idaṁ rathantarāya* ॥ 12 ॥

May Prajāpati show me the particular duty and righteousness interpreted in the Vedic language of the Sāma called Rathantara (name of a Sāman said to have been created from Brahmā's mouth)!

ॐ प्रजापतिर्जयानिन्द्राय वृष्णे प्रायच्छदुग्रः पृतनाजयेषु । तस्मै विशः समनमन्त सर्वाः स उग्रः स इ हव्यो बभूव स्वाहा–इदं प्रजापतये ॥१३॥ इति जयाहोमः ।

aum prajāpatirjayānindrāya vṛṣṇe prāyacchadugraḥ pṛtanājayeṣu । *tasmai viśaḥ samanamanta sarvāḥ sa ugraḥ sa i havyo vabhūva svāhā—idaṁ prajāpataye* ॥ 13 ॥ *iti jayāhomaḥ* ।

The Lord Prajāpati communicated to the raingod Indra the twelve mantras stated above which are the basis for enlightenment. He is among the valiant warriors who conquer their enemies and force them to lick the dust. Obtaining the twelve mantras given above which form the basis for enlightenment and which were transmitted by Prajāpati, Indra became so mighty that he caused the enemy host to be utterly humiliated. He became the foremost among those who receive their legitimate portion of the sacrifice and who cause their subjects to bow to them. May the offering of the Victory mantras of Prajāpati, which made Indra so meritorious and redoubtable, reward me with victory (jayaṁ dadātu)!

Thus should oblation be made after hymning the glory of Prajāpati. (May Indra along with Prajāpati receive the oblation of clarified butter made with due propriety!)

The Homa called Victory (jayā) ends here.

अथाभ्यातानहोमः

ॐ अग्निर्भूतानामधिपतिः स मावत्वस्मिन्ब्रह्मण्यस्मिन् क्षत्रेऽस्यामाशिष्यस्यां पुरोधायामस्मिन्कर्मण्यस्यां देवहूत्याँ स्वाहा– इदमग्नये भूतानामधिपतये ॥१॥

athābhyātānahomaḥ

aum agnirbhūtānāmadhipatiḥ sa māvatvasmin-brahmaṇyasmin kṣatre'syāmāśiṣyasyāṁ purodhāyām-asminkarmaṇyasyāṁ devahūtyāṁ svāhā—idamagnaye bhūtānāmadhipataye ॥ 1 ॥

May this oblation made in accordance with the prescribed rule be acceptable to Agni, the lord of all creatures (agnirbhūtānāmiti yo'gniḥ bhūtānāṁ prāṇināmadhipatiḥ prabhuḥ)! May he bless me with success in the study of the Vedas, in the performance of such deeds as are worth doing with the strength (asminkṣatre) derived from such a study, in the attainment of this auspicious purpose, and in the evocation of the gods (asyāṁ devahūtyāṁ), and may he protect me as well as the bride.

ॐ इन्द्रो ज्येष्ठानामधिपतिः स मावत्वस्मिन् ब्रह्मण्यस्मिन् क्षत्रेऽस्यामाशिष्यस्यां पुरोधायामस्मिन्कर्मण्यस्यां देवहूत्याँ स्वाहा–इदमिन्द्राय ज्येष्ठानामधिपतये ॥२॥

aum indro jyeṣṭhānāmadhipatiḥ sa māvatvasmin brahmaṇyasmin kṣatre'syāmāśiṣyasyāṁ purodhā-yāmasminkarmaṇyasyāṁ devahūtyāṁ svāhā—idamin-drāya jyeṣṭhānāmadhipataye ॥ 2 ॥

He who is the controller of such ancient (seniormost) gods as Indra, Bṛhaspati , et al and, therefore, their sovereign master (*adhipati*) may protect me and help me perform the deeds mentioned above.

This should be followed by the recitation of 'sa māvatvasmin' and other texts which follow. Since all the sixteen mantras have an obvious sameness, the meaning of the first given here is applicable to all. The eighteen mantras are collectively called 'abhyātāna'.[1]

ॐ यमः पृथिव्या अधिपतिः स मावत्वस्मिन्ब्रह्मण्यस्मिन् क्षत्रेऽस्यामाशिष्यस्यां पुरोधायामस्मिन्कर्मण्यस्यां देवहूत्याँ स्वाहा—इदं यमाय पृथिव्या अधिपतये ॥३॥

aum yamaḥ pṛthivyā adhipatiḥ sa māvatvasmin-brahmaṇyasmin kṣatre'syāmāśiṣyasyāṁ purodhāyām-asminkarmaṇyasyāṁ devahūtyāṁ svāhā—idaṁ yamāya pṛthivyā adhipataye ॥ 3 ॥

May Yama, who is the controller of the destiny of all terrestrial creatures and who is, therefore, the sovereign ruler of the world, protect me. . .!

अत्र प्रणीतोदकस्पर्शः

atra praṇītodakasparśaḥ

While making the oblation (throwing it into the fire), wash it with the water contained in the Praṇītā jar. Now the question is: Who or what should be washed? The implied sense is that the Sruva should be abandoned and the right-hand fingers be joined together to form something like a lotus. Let these fingers be touched with the water of the

---

1. अग्निर्भूतानामित्यष्टादशमंत्रा अभ्यातानसंज्ञकाः । तथा च श्रुतिः–'यद्देवा अभ्यातानैर्मन्त्रैरसुरान् यज्ञघ्नानभ्यातन्वत'। अयमर्थः–यद्यस्माद्देवा आभ्यातानैर्मन्त्रैरसुरान् यज्ञघ्नानभ्यातन्वत आयुधानि प्रहितवन्तः घातयन्ति स्मेत्यर्थः, एतदेवाभ्यातानानामभ्यातानत्वमिति । अयं च वाक्यार्थः उपरिष्टादपि सप्तदशसु मन्त्रेषु सम्बध्यते किञ्चित्किञ्चिद्विशेषः, स च निरुपयिष्यते इति भावः ।

agnirbhūtānāmityaṣṭādaśamaṁtrā abhyātānasaṁjñakāḥ । tathā ca śrutiḥ—'yaddevā abhyātānairmantrairasurān yajñaghnānabhyātanvata' । ayamarthaḥ—yadyasmāddevā abhyā'tānairmantrairasurān yajñaghnānbhyātanvata āyudhāni prahitavantaḥ ghātayanti smetyarthaḥ, etadevābhyātānānāmabhyātānatvamiti । ayaṁ ca vākyārthaḥ upariṣṭādapi saptadaśasu mantreṣu sambadhyate kiñcitkiñcidviśeṣaḥ, sa ca nirūpayiṣyate iti bhāvaḥ ।

The word 'abhyātāna' signifies the name of certain war-songs.

Praṇītā jar. The following[1] evidence is provided to indicate the object to be touched.

ॐ वायुरन्तरिक्षस्याऽधिपतिः स माव॰ । इदं वायवेऽन्तरिक्षस्याधिपतये ॥४॥

aum vāyurantarikṣasyā'dhipatiḥ sa māva. . . । *idaṁ vāyave'ntarikṣasyādhipataye* ॥ 4 ॥

The universe, which is like a hemispherical cauldron so shaped as when the two palms are joined together, leaving some hollow space in between, has double tiers one beneath the other. The hollow space in between the two sections is called 'antarikṣa' or space. The wind being ever-moving , ever-stirring and speeding in that space is on that account the lord of the sky. May he protect me. . . !

ॐ सूर्य्यो दिवोऽधिपतिः स मा॰ । इदं सूर्य्याय दिवोऽधिपतये ॥५॥

aum sūryyo divo'dhipatiḥ sa mā. . . । *idaṁ sūryyāya divo'dhipataye* ॥ 5 ॥

May the sun who, ignoring all lights, lights itself and is, therefore, the lord of the day, protect me. . . !

ॐ चन्द्रमा नक्षत्राणामधिपतिः स मा॰ । इदं चन्द्रमसे नक्षत्राणामधिपतये ॥६॥

aum candramā nakṣatrāṇāmadhipatiḥ sa mā. . . । *idaṁ candramase nakṣatrāṇāmadhipataye* ॥ 6 ॥

---

1. हुत्वाहुतिं च क्रूराय होता होमे विवाहके । तत् क्रूरताघातपूर्वं शांतिमाङ्गल्यसिद्धये ॥ दक्षहस्ताङ्गुलीपञ्च स्त्रुवं त्यक्त्वा संमार्जयेत् । तत्र विधिः–अम्भोजमुकुलाकारं दक्षहस्तं निमन्त्रयेत् । प्रणीताप्सु सुशांत्यर्थं मनुः स्वायम्भुवोऽब्रव्रीत् ॥ इत्यग्निपुराणीयवचनात् ॥ यमो रुद्रश्च पितरः कालो मृत्युश्च पञ्चमः । पञ्च क्रूरा विवाहस्य होमे तच्छान्तिमाचरेत् ॥ प्रणीताद्भिः संहताङ्गुलिक्षालनेनेति शेषः । इत्यगस्त्यस्मृतेरिति ।

hutvāhutiṁ ca krūrāya hotā home vivāhake । tat krūratāghātapūrva śāṁtimāṅgalyasiddhaye ॥ dakṣahastāṅgulīpañca sruvaṁ tyaktvā saṁmārjayet । tatra vidhiḥ—ambhojamukulākāraṁ dakṣahastaṁ nimantrayet । praṇītāpsu suśāṁtyartha manuḥ svāyambhuvo'bravrīt ॥ ityagnipurāṅīyavacanāt ॥ yamo rudraśca pitaraḥ kālo mṛtyuśca pañcamaḥ । pañca krūrā vivāhasya home tacchāntimācaret ॥ praṇītādbhiḥ saṁhatāṅgulikṣālaneneti śeṣaḥ । ityagastyasmṛteriti ।

The Moon is the lord of all the constellations, twenty-seven in all, from Aśvinī down to Dakṣā's daughter. May he protect me. . .!

ॐ बृहस्पतिर्ब्रह्मणोऽधिपतिः स मा० । इदं बृहस्पतये ब्रह्मणोऽधिपतये ॥७॥

aum bṛhaspatirbrahmaṇo'dhipatiḥ sa mā. . . । *idaṁ bṛhaspataye brahmaṇo'dhipataye* ॥ 7 ॥

Bṛhaspati, a disciple of Rudra (Mahadeva), is like an ocean of countless words. By virtue of his special knowledge and intonation of correct words duly refined, he is the lord of the Vedas. May he protect me. . .!

ॐ मित्रः सत्यानामधिपतिः स मा० । इदं मित्राय सत्यानामधिपतये ॥८॥

aum mitraḥ satyānāmadhipatiḥ sa mā. . . । *idaṁ mitrāya satyānāmadhipataye* ॥ 8 ॥

The friendly god is the lord of all undefiled, real objects (i.e. objects in existence) made truly visible by brilliant resplendence. (It also means that friendship nourished by truth[1] which causes it to grow is the lord of truth.) May he protect me. . .!

ॐ वरुणोऽपामधिपतिः स मा० । इदं वरुणाय अपामधिपतये ॥९॥

aum varuṇo'pāmadhipatiḥ sa mā. . . । *idaṁ varuṇāya apāmadhipataye* ॥ 9 ॥

Varuṇa, who is the lord of all the element of water and aquatic creatures[2], may protect me. . .!

ॐ समुद्रः स्त्रोत्यानामधिपतिः स मा० । इदं समुद्राय स्त्रोत्यानामधिपतये ॥१०॥

aum samudraḥ srotyānāmadhipatiḥ sa mā. . . । *idaṃ samudrāya srotyānāmadhipataye* ॥ 10 ॥

---

1. मित्रत्वं जायते सत्यात्सत्यादेव प्रवर्द्धते । सत्यात्प्रफलते नित्यं सत्यहेतुर्हिमित्रता ॥ इति ।
mitratvaṁ jāyate satyātsatyādeva pravarddhate satyātpraphalate nityaṁ satyaheturhimitratā ॥ iti ।
2. 'जलानां जलजन्तूनां पाशी धात्राऽधिपः कृतः' । इति ।
'jalānāṁ jalajantūnāṁ pāśī dhātrā'dhipaḥ kṛtaḥ' । iti ।

The ocean, which is the lord of all streams flowing downward from their sources on high and of all deep, stagnant pools and ponds, may protect me. . .!

ॐ अन्नं साम्राज्यानामधिपतिः तन्मा० । इदमन्नाय साम्राज्यानामधिपतये ॥११॥

aum annaṁ sāmrājyānāmadhipatiḥ tanmā. . . । *idamannāya sāmrājyānāmadhipataye* ॥ 11 ॥

Foodgrains, which are the lord of all possessions and affluence symbolized by elephants, horses, etc., may protect me. . .!

ॐ सोम ओषधीनामधिपतिः स मा० । सोमाय ओषधीनामधिपतये ॥१२॥

aum soma oṣadhīnāmadhipatiḥ sa mā. . .। *somāya oṣadhīnāmadhipataye* ॥ 12 ॥

Soma, the lord of all remedies, may protect me. . .!

ॐ सविता प्रसवानामधिपतिः स मा० । इदं सवित्रे प्रसवानामधिपतये ॥१३॥

aum savitā prasavānāmadhipatiḥ sa mā. . .! idaṁ savitre prasavānāmadhipataye ॥ 13 ॥

Savitā, the lord of fertility, may protect me. . .!

ॐ रुद्रः पशूनामधिपतिः स मा० । इदं रुद्राय पशुनामधिपतये ॥१४॥ अत्र प्रणीतोदकस्पर्शः ।

aum rudraḥ paśūnāmadhipatiḥ sa mā. . .। *idaṁ rudrāya paśūnāmadhipataye* ॥ 14 ॥ *atra praṇītodakasparśaḥ* ।

Rudra, who incarnated himself as Nandikeśvara from the womb of the Cow of Plenty (Kāmadhenu) and is, therefore, the lord of all cattle, may protect me. . . !

ॐ त्वष्टा रुपाणामधिपतिः स मा० । इदं त्वष्ट्रे रुपाणामधिपतये ॥१५॥

aum tvaṣṭā rūpāṇāmadhipatiḥ sa mā. . .। *idaṁ tvaṣṭre rūpāṇāmadhipataye* ॥ 15 ॥

May Tvaṣṭā (Viśvakarmā, the Indian counterpart of the

Greek god Hephaestus), who is the lord of all divine forms (structures), protect me. . . !

ॐ विष्णुः पर्वतामधिपतिः स मा॰ ।इदं विष्णवे पर्वतानामधिपतये ॥१६॥

aum viṣṇuḥ parvatāmadhipatiḥ sa mā. . .। idaṁ viṣṇave parvatānāmadhipataye ॥ 16 ॥

May Viṣṇu, the lord of the periodic lunar changes (or of the time at which the moon at its conjunction or opposition passes through the node) such as Amāvasyā (the moonless night) and Vyatipāta (a particular astronomical yoga when the sun and the moon are in the opposite Ayana and have the same declination, the sum of their longitudes being=180°), and of all sacrifices such as Darśa (half-monthly sacrifice) and Paurṇamāsa (Full-Moon sacrifice), protect me. . .

ॐ मरुतो गणानामधिपतयस्ते मावन्त्वस्मिन्॰ । इदं मरुद्भ्यो गणानामधिपतिभ्यः ॥१७॥

aum maruto gaṇānāmadhipatayaste māvantvasmin . . .। idaṁ marudbhyo gaṇānāmadhipatibhyaḥ ॥ 17 ॥

Maruta, the lord of the twelve Ādityas and Viśvedevā (all the gods collectively or the sons of Viśvā, daughter of Dakṣa?, of the eight Vasus and the celestial beings called Tuṣitā, Abhāsura, Mahārājika, Sādhya and Rudra, may protect me. . .

ॐ पितरः पितामहाः परेऽवरे ततास्ततामहाः । इह मावन्त्वस्मिन् ब्रह्मण्यस्मिन्क्षत्रेऽस्यामाशिष्यस्यां पुरोधायामस्मिन् कर्मण्यस्यां देवहूत्याँ स्वाहा—इदं पितृभ्यः पितामहेभ्यः परेभ्योऽवरेभ्यस्ततेभ्यस्ततामहेभ्यः ॥१८॥

aum pitaraḥ pitāmahāḥ pare'vare tatāstatāmahāḥ । *iha māvantvasmin brahmaṇyasminkṣatre'syāmāśiṣyasyāṁ purodhāyāmasmin karmaṇyasyāṁ devahūtyāṁ svāhā—idaṁ pitṛbhyaḥ pitāmahebhyaḥ parebhyo'varebhyastatebhyastatāmahebhyaḥ* ॥ 18 ॥

May the divine manes and those of my *gotra* (lineage, family) as well as those who died earlier protect me. . .! All this is for the manes.

अत्र प्रणीतोदकस्पर्शः

इति अभ्यातानहोमः

atra praṇītodakasparśaḥ
iti abhyātānahomaḥ

The names of the authorities of Devarāja mentioned above and of those who have been reverenced with the homa called Abhyātāna are as follows: (i) Agni the lord of all living creatures; (ii) Indra the lord of all the elders and seniors; (iii) Yama the lord of earth; (iv) Vayu the lord of space; (v) the Sun the lord of the day; (vi) the Moon the lord of the stars; (vii) Bṛhaspati the lord of the Vedas; (viii) Mitra, the lord of the Satyas (the uppermost of the seven lokas or worlds, the abode of Brahmā and heaven of truth); (ix) Varuṇa the lord of waters; (x) Ocean the lord of rivers and streams; (xi) Foodgrain, the lord of empires; (xii) Soma the lord of all remedies; (xiii) Savitā the lord of procreation; (xiv) Rudra the lord of animals; (xv) Tvaṣṭā the lord of designs and structures; (xvi) Viṣṇu the lord of such periodic changes of the moon as Amāvasyā; (xvii) the forty-nine winds or Maruta the lord of such gaṇas as Āditya, Viśvedevā, etc.; and (xviii) the manes such as Aryama and the like, who are the lords of the divine manes. May they protect me!

अथाऽऽज्यहोमः

अग्निरैतु प्रथमो देवताना॑ँ सोऽस्यै प्रजां मुञ्चतु मृत्युपाशात्। तदय॑ँ राजा वरुणोऽनुमन्यतां यथेय॑ँ स्त्री पौत्रमघं न रोदात्स्वाहा–इदमग्नये ॥१॥

athā''jyahomaḥ

agniraitu prathamo devatānāṁ so'syai prajāṁ muñcatu mṛtyupāśat। tadayaṁ rājā varuṇo'numanyatāṁ yatheyaṁ strī pautramaghaṁ na rodātsvāhā—idamagnaye ॥ 1 ॥

Then perform the homa with the recitation of the five mantras extending from the one beginning with 'agniraitu' to the one whose initial words are 'paraṁ mṛtyo'. The meaning of the mantra is as follows: Agni, who is the most outstanding of all the gods like Indra that preside over sacrifice, may rid this maiden's sons and grandsons of morality (mṛtyupāśāt)[1]. May he bless her with motherhood of a rich family of children! Hunger, which rages and burns in the stomach, is pre-eminently a symbol of life and a negation of mortality. May Varuṇa command that the children of this maiden be set free from the tentacles of death, so that the maiden may not have to suffer on account of the death of her children. What the mantra means is that Agni with the approval of Varuṇa may bless the maiden with children (of undying fame) and both the gods receive the butter oblation made to them with due devotion!

ॐ इमामग्निस्त्रायतां गार्हपत्यः प्रजामस्यै नयतु दीर्घमायुः। अशून्योपस्था जीवतामस्तु माता पौत्रमानन्दमभिविबुध्यतामियँ् स्वाहा–इदमग्नये ॥२॥

aum imāmagnistrāyatāṁ gārhapatyaḥ prajāmasyai nayatu dīrghamāyuḥ । *aśūnyopasthā jīvatāmastu mātā pautra-mānandamabhivibudhyatāmiyaṁ svāhā—idama-gnaye* ॥ 2 ॥

May the Agni of the householder's sacrifice protect this maiden and bestow upon her children a blameless life and longevity. Never may the maiden's lap be empty; never may she be barren. May she be the mother of sons enjoying long lives and thus may she enjoy the blessedness resulting from the lively company of her sons and grandsons. (May the gods bless her with all the delights of life!) May the butter-oblation made with due devotional ardour be acceptable to Agni!

ॐ स्वस्ति नो अग्ने दिव आ पृथिव्या विश्वानि धेह्ययथा यजत्र। यदस्यां महि दिवि जातं प्रशस्तं तदस्मासु द्रविणं धेहि चित्रं् स्वाहा–इदमग्नये ॥३॥

aum svasti no agne diva ā pṛthivyā viśvāni dhehyayathā yajatra । *yadasyāṁ mahi divi jātaṁ praśastaṁ tadasmāsu draviṇaṁ dhehi citraṁ svāhā—idamagnaye* ॥ 3 ॥

---

1. 'मृत्युपाशस्तु मरणं निधनं मृत्युरित्यपि' इति हलायुधः।
'mṛtyupāśastu maraṇaṁ nidhanaṁ mṛtyurityapi' iti halāyudhaḥ ।

O Fire God (Agni) ! You are the saviour of all those who take refuge in you. Leave aside the question of order and let me reap all at once the fruits of life and all its blessings. May there be plenty of glory and fame, gold and cattle, which are deemed the nectar of heaven and earth, for me with all their purity and refinement!

ओ३म् सुगं नु पन्थां प्रदिशन्न एहि ज्योतिष्मद्धेह्यजरन्न आयुः । अपैतु मृत्युरमृतं न आगाद्वैवस्वतो नो ऽअभयं कृणोतु स्वाहा ॥ इदमग्नये ॥४॥

aum sugaṁ nu panthāṁ pradiśanna ehijyotiṣmad-dhehyajaranna āyuḥ । apaitu mṛtyuramṛtaṁ na āgādvaivasvato no 'abhayaṁ kṛṇotu svāhā ॥ idamagnaye ॥ 4 ॥

O Agni! May your visitation be through that glorious pathway on which all movement is an unhindered blessing. May you come with your instructions and endow me with a beautiful life of glory free from decrepitude and disease! In other words, may Agni visit our home traversing with ease and bless us with a long life free from infirmities of every kind! May death who stalls life and cuts it short be kept at bay! May the ambrosia of true bliss be ours and even Dharmarāja (Yama, the Indian counterpart of Hades, the Greek god ruling the underworld) be disposed to destroy the sufferings of hell for us! In other words, these sufferings which are consequent upon a life of depravity and sin may with Agni's wonted kindness be avoided and may he rescue us from them and accept the oblation devotedly made to him!

अथ वरवध्वोः अन्तःपटं कृत्वा मंत्रं मनसि पठित्वा जुहुयात् ।

atha varavadhvoḥ antaḥpaṭaṁ kṛtvā maṁtraṁ manasi paṭhitvā juhuyāt ।

Let there be a piece of cloth—or a cloth curtain—hung between the bride and the bridegroom on the one hand and Agni on the other. Then, having repeated the following mantra to himself, let the offerer or sacrificer make the oblation. This (oblation) relates to mortality; lest the bride and the bridegroom should see it, a cloth is hung[1] between them and Agni.

ॐ परं मृत्योऽनु परेहि पन्थां यस्ते अन्य इतरो देवयानात् । चक्षुष्मते शृण्वते ते ब्रवीमि मा नः प्रजाँ रीरिषो मोत वीरान् स्वाहा–इदं मृत्यवे ॥५॥ भूमौ त्यागः । प्रणीतोदकस्पर्शः तत आच्छादनं दूरीकृत्य लाजाहोमं कारयेत् ।

aum paraṁ mṛtyo'nu parehi panthāṁ yaste anya itaro devayānāt । *cakṣuṣmate śṛṇvate te bravīmi mā naḥ prajāṁ rīriṣo mota vīrān svāhā—idaṁ mṛtyave* ॥ 5 ॥ *bhūmau tyāgaḥ* । *praṇītodakasparśaḥ tata ācchādanaṁ dūrīkṛtya lājāhomaṁ kārayet* ।

O Death! The way leading to you is tinged bloodred and, being smeared with violence, altogether different from the way the gods like Indra, for example, tread to receive their offerings (made in the sacrifices). May you, therefore, come the divine way free from all violence in order to receive your portion of the oblation! To you who witness all the deeds or misdeeds of the world with nonchalant objectivity and non-violence. I say pray do not kill the children who may be born of this maiden, for you are the one we worship. May you be pleased with the oblation we have made, and protect us! This is our humble prayer to you and we entreat you to accept the oblation offered to you.

The remnant of the rarefied butter, not offered as oblation, should be dropped on the ground, and not in the Prokṣaṇī jar. Once again should the five fingers of the right hand be joined together to form a lotus and to touch the

---

1. There is no evidence whatsoever to prove the validity of the assertion, often made by some people nowadays, that the curtain used at the ceremony has only one purpose—to put an end to the affliction suffered by GaruRa and Śiva. If that were so, why is the practice still in vogue when there is no such bird as GaruRa except in mythology? The myths represent him as the chief of the feathered race and enemy of the serpents.

water of Praṇītā. Then removing the curtain, offer Homa of lājā (parched rice grains).

उपरि वितानं विस्तीर्य्यं ततो वधूमग्रतः कृत्वा वधूवरौ प्राङ्मुखौ स्थितौ भवतः। ततो वराञ्जलिपुटोपरि संलग्नवध्वञ्जलौ सत्यां कुमारीभ्राता घृताभिघारितशमीपलाशमिश्रान् लाजान् गृहीत्वा तान् स्वाञ्जलिना कुमार्या अञ्जलावावपति। कुमार्यपि तान् देवतीर्थेन सूर्पकोणेन वा जुहोति।

upari vitānaṁ vistīryyaṁ tato vadhūmagrataḥ kṛtvā vadhūvarau prāṅmukhau sthitau bhavataḥ । tato varāñjaliputopari saṁlagnavadhvañjalau satyāṁ kumārībhrātā ghṛtābhighāritaśamīpalāśamiśrān lājā gṛhītvā tān svāñjalinā kumāryā añjalāvāvapati । kumāryapi tān devatīrthena sūrpakoṇena vā juhoti ।

The pavilion should be tastefully structured; it may be made of cloth or else, following the popular practice, the altar should have a canopy hung over it during the circumambulation. The bride should then be made to stand at the front, followed by the bridegroom, both of them facing the east. The bride's palms, shaped like a cup to form a hollow, be joined to the bridegroom's palms, also shaped like the bride's. While they are in this position, the maiden's brother should open his cupped palms and pour into his sister's parched paddy (khīla) mixed with palāśa leaves daubed with clarified butter (ghī). The maiden, too, should keep throwing these oblatory materials into the fire, after the following mantra has been chanted, with the corner of a winnowing basket (sūrpa or bījaṇā) or with the fore part of her hand. It means that the oblation (of parched paddy, palāśa leaves, and ghī or *caru*) should be divided into ten parts. The one received in her cupped palms from her brother's hand should be made by the maiden at the beginning of the circumambulation. She should make three oblations, each time reading a mantra. Again must she make three oblations, while making the second circumambulation and three more while making the third. In this manner the number of oblations made will be nine in the course of her three circumambulations. The oblation of the remaining tenth part should be made at the end, a fact corroborated by the law-givers.[1] If that is not done, the oblation of parched paddy, palāśa leaves, and ghī (caru) should be divided into four parts, three of which should be subdivided into nine (each part having three sudivisions). Thus there would be nine subdivisions of the three parts. Offer three of these (i.e. subdivisions) with each circumambulation. The fourth part should not be subdivided; instead it should be quietly offered as oblation after the fourth circumambulation has been completed. This would be in accordance with the law governing the ceremony of marriage.[2]

ॐ अर्य्यमणं देवं कन्या अग्निमयक्षत । स नो अर्य्यमा देवः प्रेतो मुञ्चतु मा पतेः स्वाहा ॥१॥

aum aryyamaṇaṁ devaṁ kanyā agnimayakṣata । sa no aryyamā devaḥ preto muñcatu mā pateḥ svāhā ॥ 1 ॥

Aspiring to have a suitable match, this maiden did obeisance to the lustrous, fiery Surya, who, as an Aditya or as the chief of the manes (Aryamā), may accustom her to living in her husband's family, away from that of her parents'; or the bridegroom should say instead that the sun, chief of the manes and endowed with fiery resplendence, whom the maiden worships, must in no way alienate her from her husband. What the bridegroom wishes for is a peaceful home where the couple might leave without any fear of discord and dissension. Addressing her prayer to the sun, he says, "Pray let us live in close proximity to each other." The maiden, repeating the bridegroom's words, will drop the initial portion of the oblation given to her by her brother into

---

1. शमीपलाशमिश्रांश्च घृतेनाप्यभिघारितान् । सह सूर्प्यस्य कोणेन दशैवाहुतयस्तथा ॥
śamīpalāśamiśraṁśca ghṛtenāpyabhihghāritān । saha sūrpyasya koṇena daśaivāhutayastathā ॥

2. प्रस्थस्य च चतुर्भागं व्रीहीणां भर्जयेत्सुघीः । तान् लाजान् जुहुयाद्वह्नौ भ्रातृदत्तांस्तथाऽञ्जलौ ॥
prasthasya ca caturbhāgaṁ vrihiṇāṁ bharjayetsughīḥ । tān lājān juhuyādvahnau bhrātṛdattāṁstathā'ñjalau ॥

the fire. The ritual demands that the maiden should repeat the three mantras as recited by the bridegroom.

इयं नार्य्युपब्रूते लाजनावपन्तिका । आयुष्मानस्तु मे पतिरेधन्तां ज्ञातयो मम स्वाहा ॥२॥ इति द्वितीयांशं जुहोति ।

iyaṁ nāryyupabrūte lājanāvapantikā । *āyuṣmānastu me patiredhaṇtāṁ jñātayo mama svāhā* ॥ 2 ॥ *iti dvitīyāṁśaṁ juhoti* ।

The newly-wedded maiden, while praying for fecundity and offspring and with a view to propitiating the Sun-god, speaks thus near her husband even while dropping the parched rice grains into the fire, "May my husband live a long life of virility and success and may my kinsfolk be affluent! " Thus speaking, the bride should drop the second portion given by her brother into the fire.

इमाँल्लाजानावपाम्यग्नौ समृद्धिकरणं तव । मम तुभ्यं च संवननं तदग्निरनुमन्यतामियँ स्वाहा ॥३॥ इति तृतीयांशं जुहोति ।

imāṃllājānāvapāmyagnau samṛddhikaraṇaṁ tava । *mama tubhyaṁ ca saṁvananaṁ tadagniranumanyatāmiyaṁ svāhā* ॥ 3 ॥ *iti tṛtiyāṁśaṁ juhoti* ।

Let the bride say, "O may husband, I drop these parched rice grains into the fire considering that they are the source of prosperity and luck; I do so for the approval by the fire-formed Bhagadevatā (name of an Āditya bestowing wealth and presiding over love and marriage) of this overwhelming affection we have for each other." In other words, the bride prays that their love for each other may continue to grow (that they may remain inextricably attached to each other) or that there must not be any breach of trust between them. O Firegod, she says, this Svāhā (oblation personified as a daughter of Dakṣa and wife of Agni), who is your spouse, may also give her assent to this union. Having said so, the bride should drop the third portion into the fire.

अथ वध्वाः दक्षिणहस्तं साङ्गुष्ठं वरो गृह्णाति ।

atha vadhvāḥ dakṣiṇahastaṁ sāṅguṣṭhaṁ varo gṛhṇāti ।

The next step is that the bridegroom should repeat the following mantra and catch hold of the bride's right hand and its thumb.

ॐ गृभ्णामि ते सौभगत्वाय हस्तं मया पत्या जरदष्टिर्यथासः । भगो ऽअर्य्यमा सविता पुरन्धिर्मह्यं त्वाऽदुर्गार्हपत्याय देवाः ॥४॥

aum gṛbhṇāmi te saubhagatvāya hastaṁ mayā patyā jaradaṣṭiryathāsaḥ । *bhago 'aryyamā savitā purandhirmahyaṁ tvā'durgārhapatyāya devāḥ* ॥ 4 ॥

I hold your hand, dear wife, so that you may live long with me your husband. The three gods—Bhaga, Aryamā, and Savitā—have given you, an exquisitely winsome and alluring woman, as the mistress of my entire household in order that you may cause to appear such auspicious things as the sixteen[1] forms of finery (elegant dress, fine garments suitable for amorous purposes), six *rasas*, elegant jewellery, or for the supreme joy of giving birth to my sons.

ॐ अमोऽहमस्मि सा त्वँ् सा त्वमस्यमो ऽअहम् । सामाहमस्मि ऋक् त्वं द्यौरहं पृथिवी त्वम् ॥५॥

aum amo'hamasmi sā tvaṁ sā tvamasyamo 'aham । *sāmāhamasmi ṛk tvaṁ dyauraham pṛthivī tvam* ॥ 5 ॥

---

1. अथ षोडशश्रृंगाराः-पूर्व मर्दनचीरहारतिलकं नेत्राञ्जनं कुण्डलं नासामौक्तिकपुष्पमालकरणं झंङ्कारकृन्नूपुरम् । अङ्गे चन्दनलेपकञ्चुकमणिक्षुद्रावलीघण्टिका तांबुलं करकङ्कणंचतुरता शृङ्गारकाः षोडशः ॥ पुंसां श्रृंगाराः-क्षौरं मर्दनशीर्षवस्त्रतिलकं गात्रेसुचित्रार्चनं कर्णे कुण्डलमुद्रिका च मुकुटं पादौ च चर्मावृतौ । हस्ते शास्त्रपटाम्बरं कटिच्छुरी विद्याविनीतं मुखं ताम्बूलं सुरशीलवत्त्वगुणिता पुंसस्त्वमी षोडश ॥ इति ।

atha ṣodaśaśṛṁgārāḥ—pūrvaṁ mardanacīrahāratilakaṁ netrāñjanaṁ kuṇḍalaṁ nāsāmauktikapuṣpamālakaraṇaṁ jhaṅkārakṛnnu puram । aṅge candanalepakañcukamaṇikṣudrā-valīghaṇṭikā tāṁbulaṁ karakaṅkaṇaṁcaturatā śṛṁgārakāḥ ṣoḍaśaḥ ॥ puṁsāṁ sṛṁgārāḥ—kṣauraṁ mardanaśīrṣavastratilakaṁ gātresucitrārcanaṁ karṇe kuṇḍalamudrikā ca mukuṭaṁ pādau ca carmāvṛtau । haste śātsrapaṭāmbaraṁ kaṭicchurī vidyāvinītaṁ mukhaṃ tāmbūlaṁ suraśīlattvaguṇitā puṁsastvamī ṣoḍaśa ॥ iti ।

Dear wife, I am Viṣṇu (amo'hamasmi); you are Lakṣmī (sā lakṣmīstvamasi) or Brahmāṇī, Vaiṣṇavī and Rudrāṇī, the three Śaktis combined. In other words, I am Brahmā, Viṣṇu and Rudra, the three gods rolled into one. Being immanent in the universe and omniscient, I am Viṣṇu ; among the Vedas, I am the Sāma; You are the Ṛg, for the word 'Ṛc' is expressive of the feminine gender. I am the space and you are the earth. Just as the sky is infinitely vast and covers the entire terrestrial region, so will I keep you covered with my excellent attainments. In other words, if you acquit yourself with credit as an accomplished housewife I will submit myself to you and will keep you under the protection of my own excellent qualities. Just as the earth with its inimitable patience and forbearance endures great weight, digging, and other harrowing experiences, so must you suffer with mute passiveness the repression caused in my family by your mother-in-law and others like your sister-in-law. May your native endurance prompt you to serve them without uttering a single dissenting or biting word or making a scathing remark in protest.

ॐ तावेव विवहावहै सह रेतो दधावहै । प्रजां प्रजनयावहै पुत्रान्विन्दावहै बहून् ॥६॥

aum tāveva vivahāvahai saha reto dadhāvahai । prajāṁ prajanayāvahai putrānvindāvahai bahūn ॥6॥

Though we belong to two different *gotras,* we have performed the marriage ceremonies and have acquired the rights (and status) of a duly married couple. Consequently, with the passage of time our love-making will lead to the fusion in you of semen and blood which in turn will assume the form of a male child, from which again will issue forth a long line of sons, grandsons and great-grandsons.

ते सन्तु जरदष्टयः संप्रियौ रोचिष्णू सुमनस्यमानौ । पश्येम शरदः शतं जीवेम शरदः शतँ् शृणुयाम शरदः शतम् ॥७॥

te santu jaradaṣṭayaḥ sampriyau rociṣṇū sumanasyamānau । *paśyema śaradaḥ śataṁ jīvema śaradaḥ śataṁ sṛṇuyāma śaradaḥ śatam* ॥ 7 ॥

May those sons and grandsons reach old age and attain immortality (jaradaṣṭayaḥ santu jarat bṛddhatvam aśnuvantīti jaradaṣṭayaḥ)! May we also continue to love each other, faithfully accommodating and appreciating each other's views. Ideas and feelings arising in a noble heart are called 'saumanasya' (sumanaso bhāvaḥ saumanasyaṁ vā). Let my sons and grandsons cultivate such noble feelings and with perfect control and wisdom of the senses live for a hundred years with us. Thus shall we witness and experience the pleasures of life for a century and hear our children lisping and chattering which would transport us to perfect bliss.

ततः पाणिग्रहणान्तरम् एनां वधूमग्नेरुत्तरतो स्थापितमश्मानम् दृषदं दक्षिणपादे कृत्वाऽऽरोहयति वरः आरोहेममश्मानमिति मन्त्रेण ।

tataḥ pāṇigrahaṇāntaram enāṁ vadhūmagneruttarato sthāpitamaśmānam dṛṣadaṁ dakṣiṇapāde kṛtvā''rohayati varaḥ ārohemamaśmānamiti mantreṇa ।

After he has caught hold of the maiden's right-hand fingers, the bridegroom should keep the stone, already left from before towards the north of the fire altar, under the right foot of the bride. He should also keep his foot on it with the utterance of the following mantra.

'In the Śāṅkhāyana-Gṛhya-Sūtra we read:

"And after (the Ācārya) has placed a stone towards the northern direction,

"(The bridegroom) makes her rise with the words, 'Come, thou joyful one',

"And makes her tread with the tip of her right foot on the stone, with the words, 'Come, tread on the stone; like a stone be firm. . .' "

ॐ आरोहेममश्मानमश्मेव त्वं स्थिरा भव । अभितिष्ठ पृतन्यतोऽवबाधस्व पृतनायतः—इति ॥८॥

aum ārohemamaśmānamaśmeva tvaṁ sthirā bhava ।
abhitiṣṭha pṛtanyato'vabādhasva pṛtanāyataḥ—iti ॥ 8 ॥

O Wife ! May you stand firm on the stone kept in front of you (idaṁ purovartinam aśmānamāroha. . .adhitiṣṭha)! May you acquire the saṁskāra of this stone and be steady and firm like it (aśmeva pāṣāṇavat sthirā niścalā bhava). This firmness may help you tread the foes down and overcome the enemies. (What the mantra means is that the bride should attend to her household chores and duties, enduring the jibes and insinuations, howsoever pungent they may be, about her behaviour.)

अथ अश्माऽऽरूढायामेव वरो गाथां गायति ।

atha aśmā"rūḍhāyāmeva varo gāthāṁ gāyati ।

While the bride keeps standing on the stone, the bride-groom should chant the following:

सरस्वति प्रेदमव सुभगे वाजिनीवति । यां त्वा विश्वस्य भूतस्य प्रजायामस्याग्रतः १ यस्यां भूतँ् समभवद्यस्यां विश्वमिदं जगत् । तामद्य गाथां गास्यामि या स्त्रीणामुत्तमं यशः २ इति । ततो अग्रे वधूः पश्चाद्वरः प्रणीताब्रह्मसहितमग्निं प्रदक्षिणी कुरुतः 'तुभ्यमग्ने' इति मन्त्रेण । मन्त्रपाठो वरस्य ।

sarasvati predamava subhage vājinīvati । *yāṁ tvā viśasya bhūtasya prajāyāmasyāgrataḥ 1 yasyāṁ bhūtaṁ samabhavadyasyāṁ viśvamidaṁ jagat* । *tāmadya gāthāṁ gāsyāmi yā strīṇāmuttamaṁ yaśaḥ 2 iti* । *tato agre vadhūḥ paścādvaraḥ praṇītābrahmasahitamagniṁ pradakṣiṇī kurutaḥ 'tubhyamagne' iti mantreṇa* । *mantrapāṭho varasya* ।

O Sarasvati, goddess of eloquence and learning and source of all well-being, you are the very fountainhead and store-house of rice (or food in general), which is the reason why you're called 'vājinīvati'. (This is the meaning of the lines 'sarasvatī śvetavarṇā haṁsārūḍhā mahādyutiḥ । sarvebhyo'pi vicitrānnapradā vidyā'nurāgiṇī ॥') On this evidence you are the goddess of learning as well as of various food grains.

(The word 'vāja' also signifies the feathers on an arrow or on a wing. Monier-Williams gives the following meanings of the word: energy, vigour, spirit, speed, a contest, race, conflict, battle, war, the prize of a race or of battle, booty, gain, reward, any precious or valuable possession, wealth, treasure, sacrificial food, water, rice or food in general, a mantra or prayer concluding a sacrifice, etc., etc.) You are, therefore, winged and have your own feathers with which you protect this couple who have just completed the marriage ceremonies. You are Prakṛti, the very cause and source of the entire material universe, and into which it all dissolves at Doomsday. The world springs from you at the beginning of creation and into you it vanishes at the end.

The bridegroom hymns the glory of women as personifications and embodiments of Nature. He glorifies them, saying, "I will sing the glory of women born of their fidelity and other noble virtues." So saying, the bride should stand in front and the bridegroom behind her. They should then go round the festal fire, Praṇītā, and Brahma three times. While they are thus engaged, the bridegroom recites the following mantra beginning with 'tubhyamagne'.

ॐ तुभ्यमग्ने पर्य्यवहन् सूर्य्यां वहतु ना सह । पुनः पतिभ्यो जायां दाऽग्ने प्रजया सह—इति पठन् परिक्रामेत् ।

aum tubhyamagne paryyavahan sūryyāṁ vahatu nā saha । *punaḥ patibhyo jāyāṁ dā'gne prajayā saha—iti paṭhan parikrāmet* ।

O Fire! It is for you (tubhyaṁ) that the gods, such as Soma, had this maiden under their charge ever since the day she was born. There is a sentence[1] in the scriptures (dharmaśāstra) which conveys this meaning. Just as the Moon nursed this maiden for two years, endowing her with exquisite grace, and giving her to Gandharva, who nursed her

---

1. षडब्दमध्ये नोद्वाह्या कन्या वर्षद्वयं यतः । सोमो भुंक्ते च तां तद्वद्गन्धर्वोऽनल एव च ॥ इति ।
ṣaḍabdamadhye nodvāhyā kanyā varṣadvayaṁ yataḥ॥ somo bhuṁkte ca tāṁ tadvadgandharvo'nala eva ca ॥ iti ।

for another two years and blessed her with the voice as sweet as that of the cuckoo (kinnarakaṁṭhaṁ dattvā), finally giving her to Agni, in like manner, O Fire-god, nurse the maiden in her fifth and sixth years and, having made her chaste, bestow her upon me. (The subtle meaning which the bridegroom hints at is that the maiden, as fair and resplendent as the sun, should join her husband 'for human nature's daily food' before she yields to enjoyment by the gods.) Having tended and caused her to mature and yield herself to enjoyment, O Agni, bestow this protege of yours upon me, so that the union with her husband may fructify and bless her with sons and grandsons. (While the bridegroom reads this mantra, they both go round the sacrificial fire.)

एवं पश्चादग्नेः स्थित्वा लाजाहोमसाङ्गुष्ठहस्तग्रहणाश्मारोहणगाथागा- नाग्निप्रदक्षिणानि पुनरपि द्विस्तथैव कर्तव्यानि । एतेन नव लाजाहुतयः साङ्गुष्ठहस्तग्रहणत्रयम् अश्मारोहणत्रयं प्रदणित्रयं च संपद्यते ।

evaṁ paścādagneḥ sthitvā lājāhomasāṅguṣṭhahasta-grahaṇāśmārohaṇāgāthāgānāgnipradakṣiṇāni punarapi dvistathaiva kartavyāni । *etena nava lājāhutayaḥ sāṅguṣṭha-hastagrahaṇatrayam aśmārohaṇatrayaṁ pradaṇitrayaṁ ca sampadyate* ।

In this manner the couple should stand near the fire just as they had done before the first circumambulation and make the oblation of parched rice. The bridegroom should catch hold of the bride's hand with its thumb, cause the bride to keep her feet on the stone slab, hymn the glory of women, and, while reciting this mantra (tubhyamagne), let the maiden and himself circumambulate round the Praṇītā and Brahma twice. Thus the oblation of parched rice will total nine, the holding of hand with its thumb three, the placing of the feet on the stone slab three, and the circumambulation also three.

तथा आसनविपर्य्ययः ।

tathā āsanaviparyyayaḥ ।

When the three rounds are completed and the Prājāpatya

homa (sacred to Prajāpati; a form of marriage in which the father gives his daughter to the bridegroom without receiving a present from him) and the fourth round are still to be performed, their seats should be interchanged; that is, the maiden, who has been sitting on the right side of the bridegroom, will now sit on his left (so that the bridegroom sits on the right of the maiden). Unless their positions are changed, the maiden will not shed her appellation 'kumārī', which is why whole the fourth circumambulation still remains to be performed, their seats should be interchanged. The evidence for this is found in 'Rājamārtaṇḍa',[1] where it is explicitly stated that the bride and her spouse should stand facing the east and while the bridegroom's palms are joined to, the bride's, the bride should make an oblation of Śamī leaves, parched paddy (*khīla*) smeared with clarified butter given to her by her brother. This should be done with the citation of the three mantras written above. This should be followed by the bridegroom holding the thumb of the bride, causing her to keep her foot on the stone slab, and singing the glory of

---

1. वधूवरौ तु प्राक् स्थित्वा संहत्य स्वकराञ्जलिम् । त्रिभिमन्त्रैहुनेत् लाजान् भ्रातृदत्तान् यथाविधि ॥ घृताभिघारितांश्चैवमिलितांश्च शमीदलैः । साङ्गुष्ठहस्तं गृह्णीयाद्वरो वध्वा यदा पुनः ॥ अश्मन्यारोहयेद्गाथोद्गानं कुर्याद्वरस्तथा । वरोऽग्रे च वधूं कृत्वा वह्निं ब्रह्मादिसंयुतम् ॥ परिक्रमेद्विप्रयतो द्विवारन्तु पुनस्तथा । विपर्यायाऽऽसनं स्वं स्वमुपविश्य वधूवरौ ॥ पुनरुत्थाय स्थित्वा च पूर्वबद्धोमहेतवे । भातृदत्ताञ्छिलालाजान् सूर्प्पकोणेन वाञ्जलौ ॥ भगाय स्वाहेत्युक्तवा तु तांस्तु बह्नो हुनेद्वधूः । वरोऽग्रे च ततो भूत्वा वध्वास्तुष्णीं परिक्रमेत् ॥ प्राजापत्यं ततो हुत्वा उदीच्यां क्रामयेत्तु ताम् । स सप्तमण्डलेषु च वरः कन्यां प्रक्रामयेत् तदा ॥

vadhūvarau prāk sthitvā saṁhatya svakarāñjalim । tribhimantraihunet, lājān bhrātṛdattān yathāvidhi ॥ ghṛtābhighāritāṁścaivamilitaṁśca śamīdalaiḥ । sāṅguṣṭhahastaṁ gṛhlīyādvaro vadhvā yadā punaḥ ॥ aśmanyārohayedgāthodgānaṁ kuryādvarastathā । varo'gre ca vadhūṁ kṛtvā vahniṁ brahmādisaṁyuttam ॥ parikramedviprayato dvivārantu punastathā । viparyāyā"sanaṁ svaṁ svamupaviśya vadhūvarau ॥ punarutthāya sthitvā ca pūrvabaddhomahetave । bhātṛdattāñchilālājān sūrppakoṇena vāñjalau ॥ bhagāya svāhetyuktvā tu tāṁstu vahnau hunedvadhūḥ । varo'gre ca tato bhūtvā vadhvāstūṣṇīṁ parikramet ॥ prājāpatyaṁ tato hutvā udīcyāṁ krāmayettu tām । sa saptamaṇḍaleṣu ca varaḥ kanyāṁ prakrāmayet tadā ॥

women. The bride should lead him while going round the fire, Praṇītā and Brahma. Thus must another two rounds be made while reciting these mantras. When all the three rounds are completed, let the bride and the bridegroom take their seats and then interchange their positions. That is, the bride should sit on the left and the bridegroom on the right. While they are thus occupying their seats, the bride will stand up on her seat and, according to the text 'punarutthāya sthitvā ca pūrvavaddhomahetave', make oblation of parched paddy, received into her cupped palms from her brother. While making the oblation, she should utter the mantra 'aum bhagāya svāhā', after which the bridegroom will lead the bride as they quietly perform the fourth circumambulation. Last of all, the Prājāpatya Homa should be performed followed by Saptapadi or Saptapadākramaṇaṁ.[1]

ततोऽवशिष्टलाजैः कन्याभ्रातृदत्तैरञ्जलिस्थसूर्प्पकोणेन वधूर्जुहोति ।
ॐ भगाय स्वाहा । इदं भगाय ।

tato'vaśiṣṭalājaiḥ kanyābhrāṭṛdattairañjalisthasūrppa-koṇena vadhūrjuhoti । aum bhagāya svāhā । idaṁ bhagāya ।

After the exchange of seats, the bride and the bridegroom should both stand up and perform Homa with either a winnowing basket (chāja, sūpa) or a fan made of date palm of the residual parched paddy given by the bride's brother, which is left after the performance of the nine Āhutis (oblations with fire to the deities). This Homa should be performed with the mantra 'aum bhagāya svāhā'.

अथाऽग्रे वरः पश्चात्कन्या तूष्णीमेव चतुर्थपरिक्रमणं कुरुतः ।

athā'gre varaḥ paścātkanyā tūṣṇīmeva caturtha-parikramaṇaṁ kurutaḥ ।

Thereafter the bridegroom should lead the bride as they quietly perform the fourth circumambulation unaccompanied by any mantra.

---

1. The seven steps round the sacred fire at the marriage ceremony.

ततो वर उपविश्य ब्रह्मणाऽन्वारब्धः आज्येन प्राजापत्यं जुहुयात ॐ प्रजापतये स्वाहा । इदं प्रजापतये इति मनसा । अत्र प्रोक्षणीपात्रे आहुतिशेषाज्यप्रक्षेपः ।

tato vara upaviśya brahmaṇā'nvārabdhaḥ ājyena prājāpatyaṁ juhuyāt aum prajāpataye svāhā । idaṁ prajāpataye iti manasā । atra prokṣaṇīpātre āhutiśeṣājyaprakṣepaḥ ।

With the completion of the fourth round, the bride and the bridegroom should take their seats and, touching Brahma and themselves with Kuśa, make an oblation of ghī, silently uttering 'aum prajāpataye svāhā । idaṁ prajāpataye' to themselves. The remaining ghī should be dropped into the Prokṣaṇī jar with the Sruva.

तत आलेपनेनोत्तरोत्तरकृतसप्तमंडलेषु सप्तपदाक्रमणं वरः कारयेत् वक्ष्यमाणमंत्रैः ।

tata ālepanenottarottarakṛtasaptamaṁḍaleṣu saptapadākramaṇaṁ varaḥ kārayet vakṣyamāṇamaṁtraiḥ ।

After making the Prājāpatya Homa (sacred to Prajāpati) and having besmeared (whitened) the floor afresh as is done on festal occasions, draw seven circles of rice towards the north. The bride and the bridegroom should then take seven steps northward, repeating 'aum eka miṣe viṣṇustvā nayatu', etc. Each step taken should be accompanied by its own separate mantra.

एकमिषे विष्णुस्त्वा नयतु ॥१॥

ekamiṣe viṣṇustvā nayatu ॥ 1 ॥

Here the bridegroom is described as a manifestation of Viṣṇu (Viṣṇurūpa), who is the protector and sustainer of the world, including its foodgrains. By marrying the maiden, the bridegroom has placed all the rich heaps of food under her care and protection. (The terms अन्न or food has a subtle symbolical meaning. In her role as the mistress of the house, the maiden is the caretaker of its stores of food and thus of all the members of the family. This explains why she is called Lakṣmī. The seers applied the word 'anna' also to 'the lowest form in which the supreme soul is manifested'. In its mystical sense 'anna' is 'the coarsest envelope of the Supreme Spirit.[1]) The reason why the bride is asked by the bridegroom to step out and keep her feet in all the circles one by one is to enforce and strengthen amity and friendship, the bond of marriage uniting them. The Law Books testify to this: "maitrī saptapadā proktā sapta vākyā'thavā bhavet ı sattarāṇāṁ tu tripadī sattamānāṁ pade pade ıı" It is believed that men of true greatness become friends in seven steps (or seven sentences); greater men than these great ones need only three steps, and the greatest just one. The purpose and necessity of friendship has been thus stated: "pāpannivārayati yojayate hitāya guhyaṁ niguhya ca guṅān prakaṭīkaroti ı āpadgataṁ na vijahāti dadāti vittaṁ sanmitralakṣaṇamidaṁ pravadanti santaḥ ıı" A friend brings one back to perform what is good for one's well-being and wean him away from the path of unrighteousness. He con-

---

1. In the Taittirīya Upaniṣad, which contains a systematic presentation of the Vedantic teachings and is regarded as a source book of the Vedanta philosophy, we find the following lines showing the interdependence of food and life:

"Let Him (the knower of Brahman), never condemn food; that is the vow.

"The prāṇa is, verily, food; the body is the eater of food. The body rests on the prāṇa; the prāṇa rests on the body. Thus food rests on food.

"He who knows this resting of food on food is established; he becomes a possessor of food and an eater of food. He becomes great in offspring and cattle and in spiritual radiance, and great in fame." (Chapter VII)

Also see Chapters VIII and IX. (Translator's note)

"Let a twice-born man always eat his food with concentrated mind," says Manu. "Let him always worship his food and eat it without contempt . . ." See *The Laws of Manu* in *The Sacred Books of the East,* Vol. XXV, II, 54.

ceals his friend's blemishes and brings to light his merits and virtues. He never forsakes his friend in trouble but helps him in need as well as indeed. This is how excellent men have described the nature of excellent friendship. This is why friendship, which ignores the friend's petty peccadilloes and induces him to perform noble deeds, is considered so important. The meaning of the ritual is contained in the bridegroom's implied assertion that he accepts her in the first circle in order that she may look after his household property, including all the foodstuff stored there. Thus enthused after stepping out into the first circle, the bride should express her pleasure by thus replying:

धनं धान्यं च मिष्टान्नं व्यंजनाद्यं च यद् गृहे ।
मदधीनं हि कर्त्तव्यं वधूराद्ये पदेऽब्रवीत् ॥१॥

dhanaṁ dhānyaṁ ca miṣṭānnaṁ vyaṁjanādyaṁ ca yad gṛhe ।
madadhīnaṁ hi karttavyaṁ vadhūrādye pade-'bravīt ॥ 1 ॥

You have kept under my care whatever wealth and delicious food you have in your house, so that I may truly serve your parents, sister and other kinsfolk. Then the bridegroom replies:

द्वे ऊर्ज्जे विष्णुस्त्वा नयतु ॥२॥

dve ūrjje viṣṇustvā nayatu ॥ 2 ॥

Representing Viṣṇu here, I, the bridegroom, ask you to step into the second circle. In every work performed by a householder, what is required is lustiness or manly vigour. In order to strengthen myself I request you to step out a second time. Aware of the honour given her by the bridegroom, the maiden thus speaks to herself: "This husband of mine now looks upon himself as stronger than ever before; I will, therefore, be respected in my father-in-law's family." Thus delighted by the bridegroom, the bride expresses her satisfaction respectfully as follows:

कुटुम्बं प्रथयिष्यामि ते सदा मञ्जुभाषिणी ।
दुःखे धीरा सुखे हृष्टा द्वितीये साऽब्रवीद्वरम् ॥२॥

kuṭumbaṁ prathayiṣyāmi te sadā mañjubhāṣinī । *duḥkhe dhīrā sukhe hṛṣṭā dvitīye sā'bravīdvaram* ॥ 2 ॥

While nourishing your family, I will make its foundations sturdier and ever be sweet-tongued, never uttering a single biting word. In adversity I will be forbearing; in your happiness, happy, and in your unhappiness, unhappy. The bridegroom then replies:

त्रीणि रायस्पोषाय विष्णुस्त्वा नयतु ॥३॥

trīṇi rāyaspoṣāya viṣṇustvā nayatu ॥ 3 ॥

I ask you to step into the third circle for greater prosperity. In other words, I, your husband, who is for you an embodiment of Viṣṇu, request you to enter the third circle with the express purpose of making you the mistress of my property.

Hearing this (that she has now become the mistress of her husband's property), the bride in her exultation expresses her third vow.

ऋतौ काले शुचिः स्नाता क्रीडयामि त्वया सह ।
नाऽहं परपतिं यायां तृतीयं साऽब्रवीद्वरम् ॥३॥

ṛtau kāle śuciḥ snātā krīḍayāmi tvayā saha ।
nā'haṁ parapatiṁ yāyāṁ tṛtīyaṁ sā'bravīdvaram ॥ 3 ॥

The monthly course over, I will bathe and purify myself and then indulge in sex play only with you, never admitting any other person into my mind. On hearing this, the bridegroom says:

चत्वारि मायोभवाय विष्णुस्त्वा नयतु ॥४॥

catvāri māyobhavāya viṣṇustvā nayatu ॥ 4 ॥

I, your husband who embodies Viṣṇu, now ask you to step into the fourth circle for our mutual happiness. Whatever is conducive to my well-being is totally dependent on you. Thus honoured and contemplating that the speaker in love with her is none but her own husband, the bride expresses the following resolve:

लालयामि च केशान्तं गन्धमाल्यानुलेपनैः ।
काञ्चनैर्भूषणैस्तुभ्यं तुरीये साऽब्रवीद्वरम् ॥४॥

lālayāmi ca keśāntaṁ gandhamālyānulepanaiḥ ।
kāñcanairbhūṣaṇaistubhyaṁ turīye sā'bravīdvaram ॥४॥

All my adornments—the vermilion mark, the mixture of turmeric and lime powder (*rolī*), the sixteen kinds of make-up with flowers and the like or gold jewellery and clothes perfumed with sandal, etc.—will all be to please you and for our mutual flirtations and dalliance. Hearing these enrapturing words, the bridegroom thus answers:

पञ्च पशुभ्यो विष्णुस्त्वा नयतु ॥५॥

pañca paśubhyo viṣnustvā nayatu ॥ 5 ॥

I, your husband who personifies Viṣṇu, request you to enter the fifth circle for the well-being of my cattle. It is from the cows and she-buffaloes that I get milk and butter and from my horses the pleasure of a ride. You are the mistress of all my cattle wealth and of everything I possess.

Hearing this, the bride is assured of her husband's love and resolves to help him grow more prosperous, for good deeds always yield good fruit. Expressing her joy, she utters her fifth resolve.

सखीपरिवृता नित्यं गौर्याराधनतत्परा ।
त्वयि भक्ता भविष्यामि पञ्चमे साऽब्रवीद्वरम् ॥५॥

sakhīparivṛtā nityaṁ gauryārādhanatatparā ।
tvayi bhaktā bhaviṣyāmi pañcame sā'bravīdvaram ॥ 5 ॥

My friends and I will always zealously worship Gaurī for your well-being and I will always be devoted to you. To this the bridegroom thus replies:

षड् ऋतुभ्यो विष्णुस्त्वा नयतु ॥६॥

ṣaḍ ṛtubhyo viṣṇustvā nayatu ॥ 6 ॥

I, Viṣṇu, want you as your husband to step out into the sixth circle for the pleasures of the six seasons (ṣaḍ ṛtubhyaḥ). (The different seasons have their different pleasures, each its own, which have been described by a poet who, while blessing his royal patron, says: "himaśiśiravasantagrīṣmavarṣā-śaratsu stanatapanavanāmbhoharmyagokṣīrapānaiḥ । sukhamanubhava rājan । śatravo yāntu nāśaṁ divasakamala-lajjāśàrvarīreṇupaṇkaiḥ ॥" The pleasures enumerated by him are those of the 1. breast, 2. heat, 3. forest, 4. water, 5. suitable place, and 6. cow's milk.)

The bridegroom wants her to keep her foost in the sixth circle which is symbolical of the six pleasures of the seasons, all of which are for her enjoyment. Hearing this, she expectedly thinks that her husband is all too willing and ready to let her enjoy the pleasures of all the six seasons. Overjoyed, she says to herself that virtuous deeds seldom go unrewarded and then, assuring him of her unwavering dutifulness, utters the following vow:

यज्ञे होमे च दानादौ भवेयं तव वामतः ।
यत्र त्वं तत्र तिष्ठामि पते षष्ठेऽब्रवीद्वरम ॥६॥

yajñe home ca dānādau bhaveyaṁ tava vāmataḥ । *yatra tvaṁ tatra tiṣṭhāmi pade ṣaṣṭhe'bravīdvaram* ॥ 6 ॥

Wherever you are, performing sacrifices or making oblations with fire or giving alms, I will be there to serve you and render you all possible help.

The bridegroom then says to the bride after the latter has taken the sixth step:

सखे सप्तपदा भव सा मामनुव्रता भव विष्णुस्त्वा नयतु ॥७॥

sakhe saptapadā bhava sā māmanuvratā bhava viṣṇustvā nayatu ॥ 7 ॥

O Friend! I, your husband and, symbolically, Viṣṇu, request you to carry out my bidding here as well as in all the seven spheres (*lokas*). May you thus be famed for your fidelity, righteousness, and modesty! (May you be favourably disposed to me, says the bridegroom prayerfully, and be renowned in all the *lokas* for your right conduct. The emphasis here is on the loyalty to the marriage vow or on chastity being the greatest of all the virtues possessed by a woman.)

Thus honoured and encouraged by her husband, the bride, radiant with joy, expresses her feeling the seventh time.

सर्वेऽत्र साक्षिणस्त्वं हि मम भर्तृत्वमागतः ।
कृतेन ब्रह्मणा पूर्वं विधानेन कुलोत्तम ! ॥७॥

sarve'tra sākṣiṇastvaṁ hi mama bhartṛtvamāgataḥ ।
kṛtena brahmaṇā pūrvaṁ vidhānena kulottama! ॥ 7 ॥

O Kulottama! Considering that all the gentlemen present here are witnesses to our marriage and that you became my husband at this ceremony performed strictly in accordance with Vedic injunctions ordained by Brahmā, my joy knows no bounds.

ततोऽग्नेः पश्चादुपविश्य पुरुषस्कंधस्थितात्कुम्भादाम्रपल्लवेन जलमानीय तेन वरो वधूमभिषिञ्चति ।

tato'gneḥ paścādupaviśya puruṣaskaṁdhasthitātkumbhādāmrapallavena jalamānīya tena varo vadhūmabhiṣiñcati ।

Having performed the ceremony of the Saptapadī (making seven steps round the sacred fire for the conclusion of the marraige ceremony), let the bridegroom, who is seated towards the west or north of the festal fire, sprinkle, using mango leaves, the bride's head with water taken from the pot held by the person standing quietly and patiently there. The chanting of the following four mantras beginning with 'aum āpaḥ śivāḥ' should accompany the act of sprinkling.

ॐ आपः शिवाः शिवतमाः शान्ताः शान्ततमास्तास्ते कृण्वन्तु भेषजम् ।

aum āpaḥ śivāḥ śivatamāḥ śāntāḥ śāntatamāstāste kṛṇvantu bheṣajam ।

That which is the source of all well-being and ever beneficial, supremely blissful and a great blessing, the same water may keep you free from all illness! (literally, the formula means: "The blessed, the most blessed waters, the peaceful ones, the most peaceful ones, may they give medicine to you!")

Water, famous for possessing medicinal and sanctifying properties, thus sanctifies the bride's married life and frees her from physical troubles.

ॐ आपो हि ष्ठा मयोभुवस्ता न ऊर्जे दधातन । महे रणाय चक्षसे १ यो वः शिवतमो रसस्तस्य भाजयतेह नः । उशतीरिव मातरः २ तस्मा अरङ्गमाम वो यस्य क्षयाय जिन्वथ आपो जनयथा च नः ३-इति तिसृभिर्वधूमात्मानं चाभिषिञ्चति ।

aum āpo hi ṣṭhā mayobhuvastā na ūrje dadhātana । mahe raṇāya cakṣase 1 yo vaḥ śivatamo rasastasya bhājayateha naḥ । uśatīriva mātaraḥ 2 tasmā araṅgamāma vo yasya kṣayāya jinvatha āpo janayathā ca naḥ 3-iti tisṛbhirvadhūmātmānaṁ cābhiṣiñcati ।

O Water God! Renowned and experienced as you are, you have adopted us for our happiness, sturdiness and appetite for delicacies. We, therefore, entreat you to bless us with that supremely delectable *rasa* which causes happiness and well-being.

The very essence and flavour of water—milk of all varieties (obtained from the udder or from the breast), butter, etc.—is Brahmā and a boon revered by all the three varṇas. "Just as the radiant, loving mother suckles her children for their proper growth", says the bridegroom, "so must you give us your sweet essence. Pray let us have that liberating essence of yours which destroys all imperfections and bestows *mokṣa*."

Chanting these three mantras, the bridegroom shall sprinkle water both on the bride's head and on his own.

ततः सूर्य्यमुदीक्षस्वेति वधूं संबोधयति वरः । तच्चक्षुरित्यृचं पठित्वा वधूः सूर्य्यं पश्येत् ।

tataḥ sūryyamudīkṣasveti vadhūṁ saṁbodhayati varaḥ ।
taccakṣurityṛcaṁ paṭhitvā vadhūḥ sūryyaṁ paśyet ।

If the marriage ceremony is performed in broad daylight, the bridegroom shall ask the bride to look at the sun who is a witness to their union. On being directed thus, the bride should recite the following sacred verse (ṛcā) and then look at the sun.

ॐ तच्चक्षुर्देवहितम्पुरस्ताच्छुक्रमुच्चरत् । पश्येम शरदः शतं जीवेम शरदः शतँ् शृणुयाम शरदः शतं प्रब्रवाम शरदः शतमदीनाः स्याम शरदः शतं भूयश्च शरदः शतात् ॥ इति पठित्वा वधूः सूर्य्यं पश्यति ।

aum taccakṣurdevahitampurastācchukramuccarat ।
paśyema śaradaḥ śataṁ jīvema śaradaḥ śataṁ śṛṇuyāma śaradaḥ śataṁ prabravāma śaradaḥ śatamadīnāḥ syāma śaradaḥ śataṁ bhīyaśca śaradaḥ śatāt ॥ *iti paṭhitvā vadhūḥ sūryyaṁ paśyati* ।

May we look at the myriad-eyed sun for hundreds of years whose rising satiates all those gods and manes who like oblations, food or libation (*svadhā* or the sacrificial offering due to each god), whose boundless glance brings good to the gods and the senses, who, in other words, is the cause of all routine work, a dispeller of all imperfections like ignorance and cupidity and a great purifier! (May we live in affluence and prosperity, listen to your glory and hymn your praises for hundreds of years!)

अस्तं गते सूर्य्ये ध्रुवमीक्षस्व इति प्रैषानन्तरं ध्रुवं पश्यामीति ब्रूयात् । तत्र वरपठनीयो मंत्रः ।

astaṁ gate sūryye dhruvamīkṣasva iti praiṣānantaraṁ dhruvaṁ paśyāmīti brūyāt । *tatra varapaṭhanīyo maṁtraḥ* ।

If the sun has set and the ceremony is being performed at night, the bridegroom shall ask the bride to look at the Pole Star. While the maiden's eyes are fixed on the Star, the bridegroom should recite the following mantra:

ॐ ध्रुवमसि ध्रुवं त्वा पश्यामि ध्रुवैधि पोष्या मयि । मह्यं त्वाऽदाद् बृहस्पतिर्मया पत्या प्रजावती सञ्जीव शरदः शतम् ॥ इति पठेत् ।

aum dhruvamasi dhruvaṁ tvā paśyāmi dhruvaidhi poṣyā mayi । *mahyaṁ tvā'dād bṛhaspatirmayā patyā prajāvatī sañjīva śaradaḥ śatam* ॥ *iti paṭhet* ।

O Pole Star! You're immovably rooted where you are till eternity, which is why I look upon you as the best and most constant of all the celestial stars (ahaṁ tvā tvāṁ dhruvaṁ niścalaṁ tārakāviśeṣarūpaṁ vā paśyāmi).

The bridegroom praises the Pole Star for its firmness, which he wants the bride to emulate by being loyal to her husband, by being the fixed foot of the compass like the fixed Pole Star. He says in effect, "May you be unchanging in your love for me! May you be a loving mother and grandmother to my children and grandchildren! Bṛhaspati and Brahmā have caused us to be united according to their own sacred injunctions and made you my wife. May you live with me, your husband, for hundreds of years and with your sons and grandsons!"

Even in the event of the Pole Star remaining invisible to the bride, she should say, contrary to fact, that she is observing it.

अथ वरो वधूदक्षिणांसस्योपरि हस्तं नीत्वा तस्या हृदयमालभेत–मम व्रते ते हृदयं दधामि मम चित्तमनु चित्तं ते अस्तु । मम वाचमेकमना जुषस्व प्रजापतिष्ट्वा नियुनक्तु मह्यम्–इति मंत्रेण ।

atha varo vadhūdakṣiṇāṁsasyopari hastaṁ nītvā tasyā hṛdayamālabheta—mama vrate te hṛdayaṁ dadhāmi mama cittamanu cittaṁ te astu । *mama vācamekamanā juṣasva prajāpatiṣṭvā niyunaktu mahyam—iti maṁtreṇa* ।

Soon after the ritual of looking at the sun or at the Pole Star has been gone through, the bridegroom shall place his left hand on the right shoulder of the bride and, touching her heart with his right hand, shall read the mantra beginning with the words 'mama vrate', which means: "O Wife! May Bṛhaspati, who is Brahmā and who taught ethics and morality to Marīci (the eldest son of Brahmā; name of a Prajāpati) and others, adopt your heart and so regulate it that our hearts may beat in unison and your mind be attuned to mine! May you respectfully listen to me (tvaṁ ca mama vācaṁ vacanam) and carry out my instructions and may Bṛhaspati assign (attach or allot) you to me for my pleasure and happiness (tvāṁ ca sa eva bṛhaspatirmahyaṁ madarthaṁ māṁ prasādayituṁ niyunaktu)!

अथ वधूमभिमन्त्रयति वरः ।

atha vadhūmabhimantrayati varaḥ ।

Having touched the bride's heart, the bridegroom should put a mark of *rolī* (a mixture of turmeric and lime powder) with a gold ring on the bride's head. Thus should the latter be consecrated (*abhimaṁtrita*) by the mantra that follows:

सुमंगलीरियं वधूरिमाँ समेत पश्यत । सौभाग्यमस्यै दत्त्वा याथास्तं विपरेतन ॥ इति ।

sumaṁgalīriyaṁ vadhūrimāṁ sameta paśyata । *saubhāgyamasyai dattvā yāthāstaṁ viparetana* ॥ *iti* ।

O gods and goddesses[1] who preside over marriage ceremonies (he vivāhādhiṣṭhātryo gaurīpadmāśacīprabhṛtayaḥ)! This bride is exquisitely charming and auspicious. Look at this newly wed and be well-disposed towards her and before learning bestow on her prosperity as well as respectability and good luck (ata imāṁ vadhūṁ yūyaṁ sameta saṁgacchata saṁgatya ca imāṁ paśyata). Pray don't turn your back on her (astaṁ gṛhaṁ viparetana—arthāt vimukhatayā mā parā); instead, bless her with children and other propitious things and if you are constrained to go, please do so only to come back again.

अथ स्विष्टकृद्धोमः

ॐ अग्नये स्विष्टकृते स्वाहा । इदमग्नये स्विष्टकृते । अत्र स्रुवावशिष्टाऽज्यस्य प्रोक्षणीपात्रे प्रक्षेपः । अयं च होमो ब्रह्मणाऽन्वारब्धकर्तृकः । अथ संस्रवप्राशनम् । तत आचम्य पूर्णपात्रं

1. They are Gaurī, Padmā, Śacī, et al.

दक्षिणां वा ब्रह्मणे दद्यात् । संकल्पं च एवं कुर्यात् ॐ तत्सदिति कालज्ञानं कृत्वा कृतैतद्धोमकर्मकृताकृतावेक्षणरूपब्रह्मकर्मप्रतिष्ठार्थमिदं पूर्णपात्रं प्रजापतिदैवतममुकगोत्रायाऽमुकशर्मणे ब्राह्मणाय ब्रह्मणे दक्षिणां तुभ्यमहं सम्प्रददे–इति ब्रह्मणे दक्षिणां दद्यात् । स्वस्तीति प्रतिवचनम् । ततो ब्रह्मग्रन्थिविमोकः ।

atha sviṣṭakṛddhomaḥ

aum agnaye sviṣṭakṛte svāhā ı idamagnaye sviṣṭakṛte ı atra sruvāvaśiṣṭājyasya prokṣaṇīpātre prakṣepaḥ ı ayaṁ ca homo brahmaṇā'nvārabdhakartṛkaḥ ı atha saṁsrava-prāśanam ı tata ācamya pūrṇapātraṁ dakṣiṇāṁ vā brahmaṇe dadyāt ı saṁkalpaṁ ca evaṁ kuryāt aum tatsaditi kālajñānaṁ kṛtvā kṛtaitaddhomakarmakṛtākṛtāvekṣaṇarūp-abrahmakarmapratiṣṭhārthamidaṁ pūrṇapātraṁ prajāpati-daivatamamukagotrāyā'mukaśarmaṇe brāhmaṇāya brahmaṇe dakṣiṇāṁ tubhyamahaṁ sampradade—iti brahmaṇe dakṣināṁ dadyāt ı svastīti prativacanam ı tato brahmagranthivimokaḥ ı

Then perform the Sviṣṭakṛt Homa in the following manner:

Muttering 'aum agnaye sviṣṭakṛte svāhā ı idamagnaye sviṣṭakṛte'; make an oblation to the consecrated fire, and drop with the Sruva the clarified butter (still left after the Āhuti) into the Prokṣaṇī jar. This offering of oblation into the consecrated fire should, however, be made by touching Brahmā (i.e. Kuśā). Then lick the remaining ghī left in the Sruva. This should be followed by Ācamana (sipping water before the ceremony), the utterance of the following Saṁkalpa, and offering of the full jar along with the fee to Brahmā. Finally bless the person ("May thou be blessed", Brahmā will say in return) who offers the fee and then unite the brahma-knot.

अथ ग्रामवचनं कुर्याद्वरः ।

atha grāmavacanaṁ kuryādvaraḥ ı

The bridegroom will now welcome the benedictory

words of the old gentle ladies and then consecrate them by the following mantra:

ॐ सुमित्रिया न आप ओषधयः सन्तु–इति प्रणीताजलेन पवित्रे गृहीत्वा शिरः समृज्य–दुर्मित्रियास्तस्मै सन्तु योऽस्मान्द्वेष्टि यञ्च वयं द्विष्मः–इत्यैशान्यां सपवित्रां सजलां प्रणीतां न्युब्जीकुर्यात् । तत आस्तरणक्रमेण बर्हिरुत्थाप्य आज्येनावघार्य वक्ष्यमाणमन्त्रेण हस्तेनैव जुहुयात् ।

aum sumitriyā na āpa oṣadhayaḥ santu—iti praṇītājalena pavitre gṛhītvā śiraḥ saṁmṛjya—durmitriyāstasmai santu yo'smāndveṣṭi yañca vayaṁ dviṣmaḥ—ityaiśānyāṁ sapavitrāṁ sajjalāṁ praṇītāṁ nyubjīkuryāt । tata āstaraṇakrameṇa barhirutthāpya ājyenāvaghārya vakṣyamāṇamantreṇa hastenaiva juhuyāt ।

May such drinkables as water and milk and such edibles as foodgrains, etc. give us supreme happiness! So saying, the bridegroom shall throw some drops of Praṇītā water upon his head with a couple of Kuśa leaves. While doing so, he should thus speak, "To him who is hostile to me and is deemed my enemy (yañca[1] vayaṁ dviṣmaḥ), all drinkables and edibles may cause unhappiness." With the recitation of this mantra throw away the Praṇītā with all its water in the north-eastern direction, picking up the Kuśas[2]

1. ननु निषिद्धस्य द्वेषस्य करणे विधिः कथम् । तत्राह । स्वयं द्वेषकरणे निषेधेऽपि य आत्मानं द्वेष्टि तं प्रति द्वेषोऽदोषायैवेति । तदुक्तं राजनीतौ–'शठं प्रतिशठं कुर्यादादरं प्रति चादरम् । त्वया मे लुण्ठितौ पक्षौ मया ते मुण्डितं शिरः ॥' इति गृहस्थे राजनीतिवृत्तिवद्वर्त्तमानत्वेन दोषोऽपि विधिरेवेति ।

nanu niṣiddhasya dveṣasya karaṇe vidhiḥ katham । tatrāha । svayaṁ dveṣakaraṇe niṣedhe'pi ya ātmānaṁ dveṣṭi taṁ prati dveṣo'doṣāyaiveti । taduktaṁ rājanītau—'śaṭhaṁ pratiśaṭhaṁ kuryādādaraṁ prati cādaram । tvayā me luṇṭhitau pakṣau mayā te muṇḍitaṁ śiraḥ ॥' iti gṛhasthe rājanītivṛttivadvarttamānatvena doṣo'pi vidhireveti ।

2. यज्ञे विवाहे होमे तु कुशानास्तृणुयात्सदा । अग्नेर्दोषविनाशाय पुण्यस्याऽतिशयाय च ॥ ततः स्तरणक्रमेणैतद्वर्हिरुत्थापयेत्सुधीः । अभिघार्य घृतेनैतद्धुनेदग्नौ करेण वै । इति वशिष्ठवचनम् ।

yajñe vivāhe home tu kuśānāstṛṇuyātsadā । agnerdoṣavināśāya puṇyasyā'tiśayāya ca ॥ tataḥ staraṇakrameṇaitad-varhirutthāpayetsudhīḥ । abhighārya ghṛtenaitaddhunedagnau kareṇa vai ॥ iti vaśiṣṭhavacanam ।

in the order in which they were kept here and there when the first Kuśakaṁḍikā (i.e. the placing of fire on the sacrificial altar or into the sacrificial pit or kuṁḍa) was being performed, and smearing them with ghī. With the citation of the following mantra make oblation to the consecrated fire with hand.

ॐ देवा गातुविदो गातु वित्त्वा गातुमित । मनसस्पत देव इमं यज्ञँ स्वाहा वातेधाः–स्वाहा–इति बर्हिर्होमः ।

aum devā gātuvido gātu vittvā gātumita । *manasaspata deva imaṁ yajñaṁ svāhā vātedhāḥ—svāhā—iti barhirhomaḥ* ।

O Gods! You are the possessor of the knowledge of the sacrifice called Gātu; you are like Viṣṇu, the preserver of all and you know all the various beneficent sacrifices. May you happily go, regarding the Gātu sacrifice as Viṣṇu! O Lord! O Brahmā the Controller of the Inner Self! May you have the fruit of the sacrifice and my you offer it to the winds! ('Svāhā' is an exclamation used in making oblations to the gods.)

तत उत्थाय वध्वा दक्षिणहस्तेन स्पृष्टैः स्रुवस्थघृतपुष्पफलैः पूर्णाहुतिं कुर्यात् । तत्र मन्त्रः–

tata uthāya vadhvā dakṣiṇahastena spṛṣṭaiḥ sruvastha-ghṛtapuṣpaphalaiḥ pūrṇāhutiṁ kuryāt । *tatra mantraḥ—*

Then, rising, keep flower, fruit and butter into the Sruva touched by the bride's right hand. With the following mantra perform the last oblatory ritual, the *Pūrṇāhuti.* The word 'Pūrṇāhuti' may also signify the oblation (with fire) made to the Supreme Lord—Īśvara—who stands for perfection.[1] The law-givers do enjoin the making of the last Āhuti (or Pūrṇāhuti), but there are also proofs to the contrary in

---

1. वधूदक्षकरस्पृष्टे स्रुवे संस्थापयेद्वरः । घृतपुष्पफलांदीनि पूर्णार्थश्चाहुतिं ददेत् ॥
vadhūdakṣakaraspṛṣṭe sruve saṁsthāpayedvaraḥ । ghṛta-puṣpaphalādīni pūrṇārthāścāhutiṁ dadet ॥

which such Pūrṇāhutis in relation to marriage are prohibited. The reason is that right to adult action is obtained only after marriage; so making Pūrṇāhuti is rather odious and uncalled for. Witness these lines as evidence to show how marriage Pūrṇāhutis had not the approbation of all: "pūrṇāhutihomo barhirhomaśca kālyāyanasūtrādāvanuktatvānnādaraṇīyaḥ । pramāṇañcaivamvivāhādikriyāyāṁ ca śālāyāṁ vāstupūjane । nityahome vṛṣotsarge pūrṇāhutiṁ na kārayet iti ।" On the evidence of this no Pūrṇāhuti is to be made. I have, however, followed the practice in vogue and have given the relevant mantra.

ॐ मूर्द्धानं दिवो अरतिं पृथिव्या वैश्वानरमृत आ जातमग्निम् ।
कवि॑ँ सम्राजमतिथिं जनानामासन्ना पात्रं जनयन्तु देवाः—स्वाहा इदमग्नये ।

aum mūrddhānaṁ divo aratiṁ pṛthivyā vaiśvānaramṛta ā jātamagnim ׀ kaviṁ samrājamatithiṁ janānāmāsannā pātraṁ janayantu devāḥ—svāhā idamagnaye ׀

May the Supreme Lord, Parameśvara, who is unapproachable by or beyond the three worlds, who is unattached to the elements and the senses, but who animates the entire universe, who is true Īśvara, unborn, immaculate, radiant, all-knowing, the creator and destroyer of all the three worlds, nameless and timeless, bliss, abode of all, the progenitor even of all the gods, and being the controller of the inmost beings of all creatures, induces them (the gods) to perform their several duties—may He receive this sacrificial offering!

So saying, drop the Pūrṇāhuti into the consecrated fire.

तत उपविश्य स्रुवेण भस्मानीय दक्षिणाऽनामिकाग्रेण—त्र्यायुषं जमदग्नेः—इति ललाटे । कश्यपस्य त्र्यायुषम्—इति ग्रीवायाम् । यद्देवेषु त्र्यायुषम्—इति दक्षिण-बाहुमूले । तन्नो अस्तु त्र्यायुषम्—इति हृदये । अनेनैव मंत्रेण वध्वा अपि त्र्यायुषं कुर्यात् । तत्र तन्नो इत्यस्य स्थाने तत्ते इति विशेषः ।

tata upaviśya sruveṇa bhasmānīya dakṣiṇā'nāmikāgreṇa—tryāyuṣaṁ jamadagneḥ—iti lalāṭe ׀ kaśyapasya tryāyuṣam—iti grīvāyām । yaddeveṣu tryāyuṣam—iti dakṣiṇabāhumūle । tanno astu tryāyuṣam—iti hṛdaye । anenaiva maṁtreṇa vadhvā api tryāyuṣaṁ kuryāt । tatra tanno ityasya sthāne tatte iti viśeṣaḥ ।

Once the Pūrṇāhuti has been performed, the bridegroom should pick up the ashes of the Homa (burnt offering) with the Sruva and with the ring finger of his right hand mark his forehead repeating 'aum tryāyuṣaṁ jamadagneḥ', his neck repeating 'aum kaśyapasya tryāyuṣaṁ', his right shoulder with the repetition of 'aum yaddeveṣu tryāyuṣaṁ', and his bosom, reciting 'aum tanno astu tryāyuṣaṁ' with these ashes. He should, however, use the word 'tatte' instead of 'tanno' while applying the ash mark to the bride.

तत आचाराच्छणशंखशमीपुष्पार्द्राक्षतारोपणरूपसिंदूरकरणं वरः कुर्यात् ।

tata ācārācchaṇaśaṁkhaśamīpuṣpārdrākṣatāropaṇa-rūpasiṁdūrakaraṇaṁ varaḥ kuryāt ।

In keeping with the custom in vogue and family traditions the bridegroom should thereafter mark the line where the bride parts her hair with vermilion pounded with conch shell, hemp, palāśa leaves, and gold leaves. Bṛhadvasiṣṭha has this in support of this practice: "suvarṇaśaṇayuktena vadhvāḥ śaṁkhena mūrddhani ॥ siṁdūrakaraṇaṁ kuryāt suvarṇārthaṁ svayaṁ varaḥ ॥" Ladies and gentlemen should show respect to the bride on this occasion. Another instruction recorded is: "na vai vijahyātkuladeśadharmān ।"

अथ वारुणमहाकलशाभिषेकः

तत्र पूर्वस्थापितकलशे वरुणं गङ्गादितीर्थानि चावाहयेत् । एवम्-भो भो जलेश वरुण सर्वकार्य्यप्रसाधक! इहागच्छ इह तिष्ठ सन्निधानं कुरु प्रभो ॥ एवं तत्रैव तीर्थान्यावाहयेत्-गंगाद्याः सरितः सर्वाः समुद्राश्चं सरांसि च । आयान्तु यजमानस्य दुरितक्षयकारकाः ॥१॥ अथ वारुणकलशाज्जलमानीय पञ्चपल्लवैः कुशैरेव वा वरं वधूं च ब्राह्मणा अभिषिञ्चेयुर्वक्ष्यमाणमन्त्रैः–

सुरास्त्वामभिषिञ्चन्तु ब्रह्मविष्णुमहेश्वराः । वासुदेवो जगन्नाथस्तथा संकर्षणो विभुः ॥१॥ प्रद्युम्नश्चाऽनिरुद्धश्च भवन्तु विजयाय ते । आखण्डलोऽग्निर्भगवान् यमो वै नैर्ऋतिस्तथा ॥२॥ वरुणः पवनश्चैव धनाध्यक्षः शिवस्तथा । ब्रह्मणा सहितः शेषो दिक्पालाः पान्तु ते सदा ॥३॥ कीर्तिर्लक्ष्मीर्धृतिर्मेधा पुष्टिः सदा क्रिया रतिः । बुद्धिर्जातिर्वपुर्ऋद्धि-स्तुष्टिर्हृष्टिश्च मातरः ॥४॥ एतास्त्वामभिषिञ्चन्तु देवपत्न्यः समागताः । आदित्यचन्द्रभौमाश्च बुधजीवसितार्कजाः ॥५॥ ग्रहास्त्वामभिषिञ्चन्तु राहुः केतुस्तथैव च । देवदानवगन्धर्वा यक्षराक्षसपन्नगाः ॥६॥ ऋषयो मनवो गावो देवमातर एव च । देवपत्न्यो द्रुमा नागा दैत्याश्चाप्सरसां गणाः ॥७॥ अस्त्राणि चैव शस्त्राणि शतशो वाहनानि च । औषधानि च रत्नानि कालस्यावयवाश्च ये ॥८॥ सरितः सागराः शैलास्तीर्थानि जलदास्तथा । एते त्वामभिषिञ्चन्तु धर्मकामार्थसिद्धये ॥९॥ इति वारुणकलशा-ऽभिषेकः ।

atha vāruṇamahākalaśābhiṣekaḥ

tatra pūrvasthāpitakalaśe varuṇaṁ gaṅgāditīrthāni cāvāhayet । evam-bho bho jaleśa varuṇa sarvakāryya-prasādhaka! ihāgaccha iha tiṣṭha sannidhānaṁ kuru prabho ॥ evaṁ tatraiva tīrthānyāvāhayet-gaṁgādyāḥ saritaḥ sarvāḥ samudrāśca sarāṁsi ca । āyāntu yajamānasya duritakṣayakārakāḥ ॥ 1 ॥ atha vāruṇakalaśājjalamānīya pañcapallavaiḥ kuśaireva vā varaṁ vadhūṁ ca brāhmaṇā abhiṣiñce yurvakṣyamāṇamantraiḥ:—

surāstvāmabhiṣiñcantu brahmaviṣṇumaheśvarāḥ । vāsudevo jagannāthastathā saṁkarṣaṇo vibhuḥ ॥ 1 ॥ pradyumnaścā'niruddhaśca bhavantu vijayāya te । ākhaṇḍalo'gnirbhagavān yamo vai nairṛtistathā ॥ 2 ॥ varuṇaḥ pavanaścaiva dhanādhyakṣaḥ śivastathā । brahmaṇā sahitaḥ śeṣo dikpālāḥ pāntu te sadā ॥ 3 ॥ kīrtirlakṣmīrdhṛtirmedhā puṣṭiḥ sadā kriyā ratiḥ । buddhirjātirvapurṛddhistuṣṭirhṛṣṭiśca mātaraḥ ॥ 4 ॥ etāstvāmabhiṣiñcantu devapatnyaḥ samāgatāḥ । ādityacandrabhaumāśca budhajīvasitārkajāḥ ॥ 5 ॥ grahāstvāmabhiṣiñcantu rāhuḥ ketustathaiva ca ।

devadānavagandharvā yakṣarākṣasapannagāḥ ॥6॥ *ṛṣayo manavo gāvo devamātara eva ca* । *devapatnyo drūmā nāgā daityāścāpsarasāṁ gaṇāḥ* ॥7॥ *astrāṇi caiva śastrāṇi śataśo vāhanāni ca* । *auṣadhāni ca ratnāni kālasyāvayavāśca ye* ॥8॥ *saritaḥ sāgarāḥ śailāstīrthāni jaladāstathā* । *ete tvāmbhiṣiñcantu dharmakāmārthasiddhaye* ॥9॥ *iti vāruṇakalaśā'bhiṣekaḥ* ।

अथ पुष्पार्द्राक्षतारोपणम्

आशीर्वचनपूर्वकं सर्वे सामाजिकाः स्त्रियः पुरुषाश्च पुष्पाणि संगृह्य एकैकं पुष्पमादाय ब्राह्मणकर्तृकमन्त्राऽध्ययनं श्रुत्वा तथा त्वं भव भर्तरीति ब्राह्मणोक्तमंत्रान्ते स्वयमप्युक्त्वा प्रथमं वध्वा उपरि क्षिपेयुरिति ।

atha puṣpārdrākṣatāropaṇam

āśīr vacanapūrvakaṁ sarve sāmājikāḥ striyaḥ puruṣāśca puṣpāṇi saṁgṛhya ekaikaṁ puṣpamādāya brāhmaṇakartṛkamantrā'dhyayanaṁ śrutvā tathā tvaṁ bhava bhartarīti brāhmaṇoktamantrānte svayamapyuktvā prathamaṁ vadhvā upari kṣipeyuriti ।

अथ मन्त्राः

गायत्री च विधौ यद्वल्लक्ष्मीर्देवपतौ यथा । उमा यथा महेशाने तथा त्वं भव भर्तरि ॥१॥ सुवर्चला यथा चार्के यथा चन्द्रे तु रोहिणी । मदने च रतिर्यद्वत्तथा त्वं भव भर्तरि ॥२॥ सुदक्षिणा दिलीपे तु राघवे तु विदर्भजा । अरुन्धती वसिष्ठे च तथा त्वं भव भर्तरि ॥३॥ राघवेन्द्रे यथा सीता उर्मिला लक्ष्मणे यथा । पावके च यथा स्वाहा तथा त्वं भव भर्तरि ॥४॥ अनिरुद्धे यथैवोषा दमयन्ती नले यथा । श्यामली ऋतुपर्णे च तथा त्वं भव भर्तरि ॥५॥ पुलोमजा च देवेन्द्रे वसुदेवे च च देवकी । लोपामुद्रा यथाऽगस्त्ये तथा त्वं भव भर्तरि ॥६॥ छाया यथैव चादित्ये कुशे कुमुद्वती यथा । रोहिणी वसुदेवेऽपि तथा त्वं भव भर्तरि ॥७॥ शान्तनौ च यथा गंगा सुभद्रा च यथाऽर्जुने धृतराष्ट्रे च गान्धारी तथा त्वं भव भर्तरि ॥८॥ गौतमे च यथाऽहल्या द्रौपदी पाण्डवेषु च । यथा बालिनि तारा च तथा त्वं भव भर्तरि ॥९॥ मन्दोदरी दशग्रीवे विनता कश्यपे यथा ।

पाण्डुराजे यथा कुन्ती तथा त्वं भव भर्तरि ॥१०॥ अत्रौ यथाऽनसूया च जमदग्नौ च रेणुका । श्रीकृष्णे रुक्मिणी यद्वत्तथा त्वं भव भर्तरि ॥११॥ भास्करे च प्रभा यद्वज्ज्योतिष्णा च यथा पतौ । नदीशे च यथा गङ्गा तथा त्वं भव भर्तरि ॥१२॥ मेना हिमालये यद्वन्मेरौ मरुवती यथा । शिशुमारे भ्रमीर्यद्वत्तथा त्वं भव भर्तरि ॥१३॥ संवरे तपती यद्वद् दुष्यन्ते च शकुन्तला । मरुदेवी यथा नाभौ तथा त्वं भव भर्तरि ॥१४॥ ईश्वरे प्रकृतिर्यद्वत्कालिका भैरवे यथा । अम्बिका च मृडे यद्वत्तथा त्वं भव भर्तरि ॥१५॥ रेवती बलभद्रे च शाम्बे च लक्ष्मणा यथा । रुक्मिसुता कृष्णपौत्रे तथा त्वं भव भर्तरि ॥१६॥ सर्पराज़सुताऽनन्ते भारती च प्रजापतौ । सत्यभामा यथा कृष्णे तथा त्वं भव भर्तरि ॥१७॥ धनपुत्रवती साध्वी सततं भर्तृवत्सला । मनोज्ञा ज्ञानसहिता तिष्ठ त्वं शरदां शतम् ॥१८॥ जीवत्सूर्वीरसूर्भद्रे भव सौख्यसमन्विता । भाग्यारोग्यसुसम्पन्ना यज्ञपत्नी पतिव्रता ॥१९॥ अतिथीनागतान्साधून्बालान्वृद्धान् गुरूँस्तथा । पूजयन्त्या यथान्यायं शश्वद्गच्छन्तु ते समाः ॥२०॥ पृथिव्यां यानि रत्नानि गुणवन्ति गुणान्विते । त्वं तान्याप्नुहि कल्याणि सुखिनी शरदां शतम् ॥२१॥

एभिर्मन्त्रैर्वधूमाशीर्भिः संवर्ध्य पुष्पार्द्राक्षतारोपणं स्त्रियः पुरुषाश्च वरस्याऽपि कुर्युः वक्ष्यमाणमन्त्रैः ।

atha mantrāḥ

gāyatrī ca vidhau yadvallakṣmīrdevapatau yathā । umā yathā maheśāne tathā tvaṁ bhava bhartari ॥ 1 ॥ suvarcalā yathā cārke yathā candre tu rohiṇī । madane ca ratiryadvattathā tvaṁ bhava bhartari ॥ 2 ॥ sudakṣiṇā dilīpe tu rāghave tu vidarbhajā । arundhatī vasiṣṭhe ca tathā tvaṁ bhava bhartari ॥ 3 ॥ rāghavendre yathā sītā urmilā lakṣmaṇe yathā । pāvake ca yathā svāhā tathā tvaṁ bhava bhartari ॥ 4 ॥ aniruddhe yathaivoṣā damayantī nale yathā । śyāmalī ṛtuparṇe ca tathā tvaṁ bhava bhartari ॥ 5 ॥ pulomajā ca devendre vasudeve ca ca devakī । lopāmudrā yathā'gastye tathā tvaṁ bhava bhartari ॥ 6 ॥ chāyā yathaiva cāditye kuśe kumudvatī yathā । rohiṇī vasudeve'pi tathā tvaṁ bhava bhartari ॥ 7 ॥ śāntanau ca yathā gaṁgā subhadrā ca yatha'rjune । dhṛtarāṣṭre ca gāndhārī tathā tvaṁ bhava bhartari ॥ 8 ॥ gautame ca yathā'halyā draupadī pāṇḍaveṣu ca । yathā bālini tārā ca tathā tvaṁ bhava bhartari ॥ 9 ॥ mandodarī daśagrīve vinatā kaśyape yathā । pāṇḍurāje yathā kuntī tathā tvaṁ bhava bhartari ॥ 10 ॥ atrau yathā'nasūyā ca jamadagnau ca reṇukā । śrīkṛṣṇe rukmiṇī yadvattathā tvaṁ bhava bhartari ॥ 11 ॥ bhāskare ca prabhā yadvajjyotiṣṇā ca yathā patau । nadīśe ca yathā gaṅgā tathā tvaṁ bhava bhartari ॥ 12 ॥ menā himālaye yadvanmerau maruvatī yathā । śiśumāre bhramīryadvattathā tvaṁ bhava bhartari ॥ 13 ॥ saṁvare tapatī yadvad duṣyante ca śakuntalā । marudevī yathā nābhau tathā tvaṁ bhava bhartari ॥ 14 ॥ īśvare prakṛtiryadvatkālikā bhairave yathā । ambikā ca mṛḍe yadvattathā tvaṁ bhava bhartari ॥ 15 ॥ revatī balabhadre ca śāmbe ca lakṣmaṇā yathā । rukmisutā kṛṣṇapautre tathā tvaṁ bhava bhartari ॥ 16 ॥ sarparājasutā'nante bhāratī ca prajāpatau । satyabhāmā yathā kṛṣṇe tathā tvaṁ bhava bhartari ॥ 17 ॥ dhanaputravatī sādhvī satataṁ bhartṛvatsalā । manojñā jñānasahitā tiṣṭha tvaṁ śaradāṁ śatam ॥ 18 ॥ jīvatsūrvīrasūrbhadre bhava saukhyasamanvitā । bhāgyārogyasusampannā yajñapatnī pativratā ॥ 19 ॥ atithīnāgatānsādhūnbālānvṛddhān gurūṃstathā । pūjayantyā yathānyāyaṁ śaśvadgacchantu te samāḥ ॥ 20 ॥ pṛthivyāṁ yāni ratnāni guṇavanti guṇānvite । tvaṁ tānyāpnuhi kalyāṇi sukhinī śaradāṁ śatam ॥ 21 ॥

ebhirmantrairvadhūmāśīrbhiḥ saṁvardhya puṣpārdrākṣatāropaṇaṁ striyaḥ puruṣāśca varasyā'pi kuryuḥ vakṣyamāṇamantraiḥ ।

अथ मन्त्राः

ब्रह्मा वेदपतिः शिवः पशुपतिः शक्रः सुराणां पतिः प्राणो देहपतिः सदागतिरयं ज्योतिष्पतिश्चन्द्रमाः । अम्भोधिः सरितां पतिर्जलपतिः सुर्य्यो ग्रहाणां पतिः सर्वे ते पतयः कुबेरसहिताः कुर्वन्तु ते मंगलम् ॥१॥ मत्स्यः कूर्म्मतनुर्वहारनृहरी श्रीवामनो भार्गवस्तद्वद्दाशरथिश्च यादवपतिर्बुद्धोऽथ कल्की पतिः । अन्ये चाऽपि सनत्कुमारकपिलप्राणाः कलांशा हरेः सर्वे

ते कलिकल्मषापहरणाः कुर्वन्तु ते मङ्गलम् ॥२॥ आदित्योऽग्नियुतः शशी सवरुणो भौमः कुवेरान्वितः सौम्यो विश्वयुतो गुरुः समघवा देव्या युतो भार्गवः । सौरिः केतुयुतः सदा सुरवरो राहुर्भुजङ्गेश्वरो मांगल्यं सुखदुःखदाननिरताः कुर्वन्तु सर्वे ग्रहाः ॥३॥ गंगा सिन्धु सरस्वती च यमुना गोदावरी नर्मदा कावेरी सरयूर्महेन्द्रतनया चर्मण्वती वेदिका । क्षिप्रा वेत्रवती महासुरनदी ख्याता च या गण्डकी पूर्णाः पूर्णजलैः समुद्रसहिताः कुर्वन्तु ते मंगलम् ॥४॥ आयुर्द्रोणसुते श्रियो दशरथे शत्रुक्षयो राघवे ऐश्वर्यं नहुषे गतिश्च पवने मानं च दुर्योधने । शौर्यं शान्तनवे बलं हलधरे सत्यं च कुन्तीसुते विज्ञानं विदुरे भवन्तु भवतः कीर्तिश्च नारायणे ॥५॥ आयुष्मान्भव पुत्रवान्भव भव श्रीमान् यशस्वी भव प्रज्ञावान्भव भूरिभूतिकरणो दानैकनिष्ठो भव । तेजस्वी भव वैरिदर्प्पदलनो व्यापारदक्षो भव श्री शम्भोर्भव पादपूजनरतः सर्वोपकारी भव ॥६॥ आयुर्बलं विपुलमस्तु सुखित्वमस्तु सौभाग्यमस्तु विशदा तव कीर्तिरस्तु । श्रेयोऽस्तु धर्म्ममतिरस्तु रिपुक्षयोस्तु सन्तानवृद्धिरपि वाञ्छितसिद्धिरस्तु ॥७॥ दीर्घायुर्भव जीव वत्सरशतं नश्यन्तु सर्वापदः, स्वस्थं संभुज मुञ्च चञ्चलधियं लक्ष्यैकनाथो भव । किं ब्रूमो भृगुगौतमात्रिकपिल-व्यासादिभिर्भाषितं यद्रामस्य पुराभिषेकसमये तच्चाऽस्तु ते मङ्गलम् ॥८॥ यावदिन्द्रादयो देवा यावच्चन्द्रदिवाकरौ । यावद्धर्म्मक्रिया लोके तावद् भूयात्स्थितिस्तव ॥९॥ एवं वरस्याऽप्याद्रक्षितारोपणं विदध्युरिति ।

atha mantrāḥ

brahmā vedapatiḥ śivaḥ paśupatiḥ śakraḥ surāṇāṁ patiḥ prāṇo dehapatiḥ sadāgatirayaṁ jyotiṣpatiścandramāḥ । ambhodhiḥ saritāṁ patirjalapatiḥ sūryyo grahāṇāṁ patiḥ sarve te patayaḥ kuverasahitāḥ kurvantu te maṁgalaṁ ॥ 1 ॥ *matsyaḥ kūrmmatanurvarāhanṛharī śrīvāmano bhārgava-stadvaddāśarathiśca yādavapatirbuddho'tha kalkī patiḥ । anye cā'pi sanatkumārakapilaprāṇāḥ kalāṁśā hareḥ sarve te kalikalmaṣāpaharaṇāḥ kurvantu te maṅgalam* ॥ 2 ॥ *āditye'gniyutaḥ śaśī savaruṇo bhaumaḥ kuverānvitaḥ saumyo viśvayuto guruḥ samaghavā devyā yuto bhār-gavaḥ* । *sauriḥ ketuyutaḥ sadā suravaro rāhurbhujaṅgeśvaro māṁgalyaṁ sukhaduḥkhadānaniratāḥ kurvantu sarve grahāḥ* ॥3॥ *gaṁgā sindhu sarasvatī ca yamunā godāvarī narmadā kāverī sarayūrmahendratanayā carmaṇvatī vedikā* । *kṣiprā vetravatī mahāsuranadī khyātā ca yā gaṇḍakī pūrṇāḥ pūrṇajalaiḥ samudrasahitāḥ kurvantu te maṁgalam* ॥4॥ *āyurdroṇasute śriyo daśarathe śatrukṣayo rāghave aiśvaryaṁ nahuṣe gatiśca pavane mānaṁ ca duryodhane* । *śauryaṁ śāntanave balaṁ haladhare satyaṁ ca kuntīsute vijñānaṁ vidure bhavantu bhavataḥ kīrtiśca nārāyaṇe* ॥5॥ *āyuṣmānbhava putravānbhava bhava śrīmān yaśasvī bhava prajñāvānbhava bhūribhūtikaraṇo dānaikaniṣṭho bhava* । *tejasvī bhava vairidarppadalano vyāpāradakṣo bhava śrīśambhorbhava pādapūjanarataḥ sarvopakārī bhava* ॥6॥ *āyurbalaṁ vipulamastu sukhitvamastu saubhāgyamastu viśadā tava kīrtirastu* । *śreyo'stu dharmmamatirastu ripukṣayo'stu santānavṛddhirapi vāñchitasiddhirastu* ॥7॥ *dīrghāyurbhava jīva vatsaraśataṁ naśyantu sarvāpadaḥ, svasthaṁ saṁbhujya muñca cañcaladhiyaṁ lakṣmyaikanātho bhava* । *kiṁ brūmo bhṛgugautamātrikapilavyāsādibhirbhāṣitaṁ yadrāmasya purā'bhiṣekasamaye taccā'stu te maṅgalaṁ* ॥8॥ *yāvadindrādayo devā yāvaccandra-divākarau* । *yāvaddharmmakriyā loke tāvad bhūyātsthitistava* ॥9॥ *evaṁ varasyā'pyārdrākṣatāropaṇaṁ vidadhyuriti* ।

ततो वरः आचार्य्याय गां सुवर्णं दक्षिणां दद्यात् । अद्येत्यादि देशकालौ संकीर्त्य० मम विवाहकर्मसाङ्गतासिद्ध्यर्थं न्यूनाऽतिरिक्तदोषपरिहारार्थं ब्राह्मणश्चेद्गां क्षत्रियश्चेद्ग्रामं वैश्यश्चेदश्वं शूद्रश्चेत्सुवर्णादिद्रव्यं अमुकगोत्रायाऽमुकशर्म्मणे आचार्याय तुभ्यमहं संप्रददे । ततो नानानामगोत्रेभ्यो ब्राह्मणेभ्यो भूयसीं दक्षिणां च दद्यात् । तत आशीर्वादग्रहणं वरः कुर्यात् ।

tato varaḥ ācāryyāya gāṁ suvarṇaṁ dakṣiṇāṁ dadyāt । *adyetyādi deśakālau saṁkīrtya. . . mama vivāhakarmasāṅgatāsiddhyarthaṁ nyūnā'tiriktadoṣaparihārārthaṁ brāhmaṇaścedgāṁ kṣatriyaścedgrāmaṁ vaiśyaścedaśvaṁ śūdraścetsuvarṇādidravyaṁ amukagotrāyā'muka-*

śarmmaṇe ācāryāya tubhyamahaṁ saṁpradade । *tato nānānāmagotrebhyo brāhmaṇebhyo bhūyasīṁ dakṣiṇāṁ ca dadyāt* । *tata āśīrvādagrahaṇaṁ varaḥ kuryāt* ।

After all this (and before the conclusion of the marriage ceremony) the bridegroom should give the nuptial fees to the priest who conducts the nuptial. He should be given a cow by a brāhmaṇa bridegroom, a village by a kṣatriya, a horse by a vaiśya, and a fee of gold, etc. by a śūdra. The offering should be made by uttering the above saṁkalpa. This done, the bridegroom should distribute dakṣiṇā among other brāhmaṇas and receive their blessings.

अथ तां दृढपुरुषो ब्राह्मणोऽन्यो वा उन्मथ्य प्राग्वोदग्वाऽनुगुप्त आगारे आनडुहे आर्षभ रोहिते उत्तरलोम्नि चर्म्मण्युपवेशयति–ॐ इह गावो निषीदन्त्विहाश्वा इह पूरुषाः । इहो सहस्त्रदक्षिणो यज्ञ इह पूषा निषीदतु–इति मन्त्रेण ।

atha tāṁ dṛḍhapuruṣo brāhmano'nyo vā unmathya prāgvodagvā'nugupta āgāre ānaḍuhe ārṣaṁbhe rohite uttaralomni carmmaṇyupaveśayati—aum iha gāvo niṣīdantvihāśvā iha pūruṣāḥ । *iho sahasradakṣino yajña iha pūṣā niṣīdatu—iti mantreṇa* ।

After the completion of the ceremony of marking the line of demarcation (of the locks of hair) on the bride's head with vermilion, a steady and robust brāhmaṇa, a maternal uncle or the bridegroom himself should lift the bride and set her down on a hairy piece of deerskin spread on the floor of a room exquisitely decorated as enjoined by the ancient seers. This is the view of the Smārtas, albeit different from that of the Vaiṣṇavas who hold that the bride should be seated on a red hemp seat, the colour of which resembles the red lac solution (*mahāvara*) on the hands and feet of the women present there. The hemp carpet approved by the peace-loving seers, such as Vyāsa, Vasiṣṭha, Nārada, Gautama, Parāśara, etc., and not deerskin, symbolical of diabolical cruelty of demons and fiends, should be laid out in the brightly and auspiciously lit Kautukāgāra. The bridal chamber is called 'anaḍuha' and the hemp carpet laid in the middle of it is called 'ānaḍuha'. The word 'carmmaṇi' implies that hemp is fleeced out like skin, which is why a carpet made of hemp is called 'ānaḍuha carma'. Here is an evidence: "anaḍvān vṛṣabhaḥ prokta-stvanaḍvānmukhya ālaye । nārīyukprajvaladdīpa-manuḍutkautukaṁ gṛham । iti rantikośe ।"

The mantra "iha gāvo niṣīdantu" means that here in the bride's house there are thousands of cows, etc. ready for being offered as fees; may, therefore, this all-satisfying sacrifice be held at this place! The bride should sit on the hemp carpet with the muttering of the above mantra.

त्रिरात्रमक्षारालवणाशिनौ स्यातामधः शयीयाताम् निर्मिथुनौ स्याताम् ।

trirātramakṣārālavaṇāśinau syātāmadhaḥ śayīyāṭām nirmithunau syātām ।

'Both the bride and the bridegroom should refrain from taking salty food and, avoiding copulation, sleep on the floor for three days and nights from the wedding day. Coitus is forbidden because the maiden does not become a wife (*bhāryā*) in the true sense of the term before the Caturthī Karmma is performed. Here is the evidence: "āpradānād-bhavetkanyā pradānānantaraṁ vadhūḥ । pāṇigrahe tu patnī syādbhāryā cāturthakarmaṇi ॥"

Here ends Karmasubodhinībhāṣāṭīkāsahitā vivāha-paddhatiḥ by Kaviratnavaidyaśāstrī Paṇḍita Bhaiyārāma of Karahaṁsanagara, Karanāla.

अथ चतुर्थीकर्म्म

ततष्चतुर्थ्यां अपररात्रे चतुर्थीकर्म्म । तच्च गृहाभ्यन्तर एव कार्यम् । तत उद्वर्त्तनादि कृत्वा युगकाष्ठमुपविश्य स्नात्वा शुद्धवस्त्रं परिधाय गृहं प्रविश्य वधूवरौ प्राङ्मुखौ भवतः । ॐ गणपत्यादिदेवतापूजनम् । ततः कुशकण्डिकारम्भः । तत्र क्रमः जामातृहस्तपरिमितां वेदीं कुशैः परिसमुह्य तान्कुशानैशान्यां परित्यज्य गोमयोदकेनोपलिप्य स्फ्योन स्त्रुवेण वा

प्रागग्रप्रदेशमात्रं त्रिरुत्तरोत्तरक्रमेणोल्लिख्योल्लेखनक्रमेणानामिका-ङ्गुष्ठाभ्यां मृदमुद्धृत्य जलेनाभ्युक्ष्य तत्र तूष्णीं कांस्यपात्रेणाग्निमानीय स्वाभिमुखं निदध्यात् । ततः पुष्पचन्दनताम्बूलवस्त्राण्यादाय ॐ अस्यां रात्रौ कर्त्तव्यचतुर्थीहोमकर्म्मणि कृताकृतावेक्षणरूपब्रह्मकर्म्म कर्त्तुं होतृ-कर्म्म कर्त्तुममुकगोत्रममुकशर्माणं ब्राह्मणमेभिः पुष्पचन्दनादिभिर्ब्रह्मत्वेन होतृत्वेन च त्वामहं वृणे इति ब्राह्मणं वृणुयात् । ॐ वृतोऽस्मीति प्रतिवचनम् । यथाविहितं कर्म्म कुरु इति वरेणोक्ते ॐ करवाणीति ब्राह्मणो वदेत् । ततोऽग्नेर्दक्षिणतः शुद्धमासनं दत्त्वा तदुपरि प्रागग्रान् कुशानास्तीर्य्य ब्रह्माणमग्निं प्रदक्षिणक्रमेणानीय ॐ अत्र त्वं मे ब्रह्मा भवेत्यभिधाय ॐ भवानीति ब्राह्मणेनोक्ते कल्पितासने उदङ्मुखं ब्राह्मणमुपवेशयेत् । ततः पृथूदकपात्रमग्नेरुत्तरतः प्रतिष्ठाप्य प्रणीतापात्रं पुरतः कृत्वा वारिणा परिपूर्य्य कुशैराच्छाद्य ब्रह्मणो मुखमवलोक्याग्नेरुत्तरतः कुशोपरि निदध्ययात् । ततः परिस्तरणम् । बर्हिषश्चतुर्थभागमादायाग्नेयादीशानान्तं ब्रह्मणोऽग्निपर्य्यन्तं नैर्ऋत्याद्वायव्यान्तम् अग्नितः प्रणीतापर्य्यन्तम् । ततोऽग्नेरुत्तरतः पश्चिम-दिशि पवित्रच्छेदनार्थं कुशत्रयम् । पवित्रकरणार्थं साग्रमनन्तर्गर्भंकुशपत्र-द्वयम् । प्रोक्षणीपात्रम् । आज्यस्थाली । सम्मार्जनार्थं कुशत्रयम् । उपयमनार्थं वेणीरूपकुशत्रयम् । समिधस्तिस्रः । स्रुवः आज्यम् । षट्पञ्चाशदुत्त-रवरमुष्टिशतद्वयावच्छिन्नामतण्डुलपूर्णपात्रम् एतानि पवित्रच्छेदनकुशाहर्ां पूर्वपूर्वदिशि क्रमेणासादनीयानि । ततः पवित्रच्छेदनकुशैः पवित्रे च्छित्वा प्रदेशमितपवित्रकरणम् । ततः सपवित्रकरेण प्रणीतोदकं त्रिःप्रोक्षणीपात्रे निधाय अनामिकाङ्गुष्ठाभ्यामुत्तराग्रे पवित्रे धृत्वा त्रिरुत्पवनम् । ततः प्रोक्षणीपात्रस्य सव्यहस्तकरणम् । पवित्रे गृहीत्वा त्रिरुद्दिङ्गनम् । प्रणीतोदकेन प्रोक्षणीप्रोक्षणम् । ततः प्रोक्षणीजलेन यथासादितवस्तुसेचनम् । ततोऽग्निप्रणीतयोर्मध्यो प्रोक्षणीपात्रं निधाय आज्यस्थाल्यामाज्यनिर्वापः । ततोऽधिश्रयणम् । ततो ज्वलत्तृणादिना हविर्वेष्टयित्वा प्रदक्षिणक्रमेण पर्य्यग्निकरणम् । ततः स्रुवं प्रतप्य संमार्जनकुशानामग्रैरन्तरतो मूलैर्बाह्यतः स्रुवसंमार्ज़नं प्रणीतोदकेनाभ्युक्ष्य पुनः प्रतप्य स्रुवं दक्षिणतो निदध्यात् । तत आज्यस्याग्नेरवतारणम् । तत आज्ये प्रोक्षणीवदुत्पवनम् । अवेक्ष्य

सत्यपद्रव्ये तन्निरसनम् । पुनः पूर्ववत् प्रोक्षण्युत्पवनम् उपयमन-कुशान्वामहस्तेनादाय उत्तिष्ठन् प्रजापतिं मनसा ध्यात्वा तूष्णीमग्नौ घृताक्ताः समिधस्तिस्त्रः क्षिपेत् । तत उपविश्य प्रोक्षणीजलेनाग्निं प्रदक्षिणं पर्युक्ष्य पवित्रं प्रणीतापात्रे धृत्वा ब्रह्मणान्वारब्धः पातितदक्षिणजानुर्जुहुयात् । तत्राघारादारभ्याहुतिचतुष्टयेन तत्तदाहुत्यनन्तरं स्त्रुवावस्थिताज्यं प्रोक्षिण्यां क्षिपेत् । ॐ प्रजापतये स्वाहा इदं प्रजापतये इति मनसा । ॐ इन्द्राय स्वाहा इदमिन्द्राय । इत्याघारौ । ॐ अग्नये स्वाहा इदमग्नये । ॐ सोमाय स्वाहा इदं सोमाय । इत्याज्यभागौ । तत आज्याहुतिपञ्चतये स्थालीपाकाहुतौ च प्रत्याहुत्यनन्तरं स्त्रुवावस्थितहुतशेषघृतस्य प्रोक्षणीपात्रे प्रक्षेपः । ततो ब्रह्मणान्वारब्धं विना ॐ अग्ने प्रायश्चित्ते त्वं देवानां प्रायश्चित्तिरसि ब्राह्मणस्त्वा नाथकाम उपधावामि यास्यै पतिघ्नी तनूस्तामस्यै नाशय स्वाहा । इदमग्नये ॥१॥ ॐ वायो प्रायश्चित्ते त्वं देवानां प्रायश्चित्तिरसि ब्राह्मणस्त्वा नाथकाम उपधावामि यास्यै प्रजाघ्नी तनूस्तामस्यै नाशय स्वाहा । इदं वायवे ॥२॥ ॐ सूर्य्य प्रायश्चित्ते त्वं देवानां प्रायश्चित्तिरसि ब्राह्मणस्त्वा नाथकाम उपधावामि यास्यै पशुघ्नी तनूस्तामस्यै नाशय स्वाहा । इदं सूर्य्याय ॥३॥ ॐ चन्द्र प्रायश्चित्ते त्वं देवानां प्रायश्चित्तिरसि ब्राह्मणस्त्वा नाथकाम उवधावामि यास्यै गृहघ्नी तनूस्तामस्यै नाशय स्वाहा । इदं चंद्राय ॥४॥ ॐ गंधर्व प्रायश्चित्ते त्वं देवानां प्रायश्चित्तिरसि ब्राह्मणस्त्वा नाथकाम उपधावामि यास्यै यशोघ्नी तनूस्तामस्यै नाशय स्वाहा । इदं गन्धर्वाय ॥५॥ ततः स्थालीपाकेन जुहुयात् । ॐ प्रजापतये स्वाहा । इदं प्रजापतये । इति मनसा । अग्न्याहुतिनवके हुतशेषघृतस्य प्रोक्षणीपात्रे प्रक्षेपः । अयञ्च होमो ब्रह्मणान्वारब्धकर्तृकः तत्र आज्यस्थालीपाकाभ्यां स्विष्टकृद्धोमः । ॐ अग्नये स्विष्टकृते स्वाहा । इदमग्नये स्विष्टकृते । तत आज्येन ॐ भूः स्वाहा इदं भूः । ॐ भुवः स्वाहा इदं भुवः । स्वः स्वाहा इदं स्वः । एता महाव्याहृतयः । ॐ त्वन्नो अग्ने वरुणस्य विद्वान् देवस्य हेडो अवयासिसीष्ठाः । यजिष्ठो वह्नितमः शोशुचानो विश्वा द्वेषाँ्सि प्रमुमुग्ध्यस्मत् स्वाहा इदमग्नीवरुणाभ्याम् । ॐ स त्वन्नो अग्नेऽवमो भवोती नेदिष्ठोऽस्या उषसो व्युष्टा । अवयक्ष्व नो वरुणँ् रराणो वीहि मृडीकँ् सुहवो न एधि–स्वाहा इदमग्नीवरुणाभ्याम् ।

ॐ अयाश्चाग्नेस्यनभिशस्तिपाश्च सत्यमित्त्वमया असि। अया नो यज्ञं वहास्यया नो धेहि भेषज ँ् स्वाहा । इदमग्नये । ॐ ये ते शतं वरुण ये सहस्त्रं यज्ञियाः पाशा वितता महान्तः तेभिर्न्नो अद्य सवितोत विष्णुर्विश्वे मुञ्चन्तु मरुतः स्वर्क्काः स्वाहा ॥ इदम् वरुणाय सवित्रे विष्णवे विश्वेभ्योदेवेभ्यो मरुद्भ्यः स्वर्क्केभ्यः । ॐ उदुत्तमं वरुणपाशमस्मदवाधमं विमध्यम ँ् श्रथाय । अथा वयमादित्य व्रते तवानागसो अदितये स्याम स्वाहा इदम् वरुणाय । एताः प्रायश्चित्तसंज्ञकाः । ॐ प्रजापतये स्वाहा ॥ इदं प्रजापतये । इति मनसा । इदं प्राजापत्यम् । ततः संस्त्रवप्राशनम् । ततः आचम्य ॐ अस्यां रात्रौ कृतैतच्चतुर्थीहोमकर्मणि कृताकृतावेक्षण-रूपब्रह्मकर्म्मप्रतिष्ठार्थमिदं पूर्णपात्रं प्रजापतिदैवतकममुकगोत्रा-यामुकशर्म्मणे ब्राह्मणाय दक्षिणात्वेन तुभ्यमहं संप्रददे । इति दक्षिणां दद्यात् । स्वस्तीति प्रतिवचनम् । ततो ब्रह्मग्रन्थिविमोकः । ततः ॐ सुमित्रिया न आप ओषधयः सन्तु इति पवित्राभ्यां शिरः संमृज्य ॐ दुर्मित्रियास्तस्मै सन्तु योस्मान् द्वेष्टि यञ्च वयं द्विष्मः–इत्यैशान्यां दिशि प्रणीतां न्युब्जीकुर्य्यात् । ततस्तरणक्रमेण बर्हिरुत्थाप्य घृताक्तं हस्तेनैव जुहुयात् । ॐ देवा गातुविदो गातु वित्वा गातुमित । मनसस्पत इमं देवयज्ञ ँ् स्वाहा वाते धाः ॥ ततः पृथूदकपात्रस्थं आम्रपल्लवेन जलमानीय मूर्ध्नि वरो वधूमभिषिञ्चति ॐ या ते पतिघ्ना प्रजाघ्नी पशुध्नी गृहघ्नी यशोघ्नी निन्दिता तनूः । जारघ्नी तत एनां करोमि । सा जीर्य्य त्वं मया सह श्री अमुकदेवि इति मन्त्रेण । ततो वधूं स्थालीपाकं प्राशयति वरः । ॐ प्राणैस्ते प्राणान् सन्दधामि । ॐ अस्थिभिस्तेऽस्थीनि सन्दधामि । ॐ मांसैस्ते मांसानि सन्दधामि । ॐ त्वचा ते त्वचं सन्दधामि । इति मन्त्रचतुष्टयेन प्रतिमन्त्रान्तमन्नं प्राशयेत् । ततो वधूं स्थालीपाकं प्राशयति वरः । ततो वधू हृदयं स्पृष्ट्वा वरः पठेत् । ॐ यत्ते तुसीमे हृदयं दिवि चन्द्रमसि श्रितम् वेदाहं तन्मां तद्विद्यात् पश्येम शरदः शतं जीवेम शरदः शत ँ् शृणुयाम शरदः शतम् ॥ इति । अथ कङ्कणमोक्षणादीनि युतग्रन्थिविमोकादीनि आचारप्राप्तानि । तत उत्थाय वधू-दक्षिणहस्तस्पृष्टस्त्रुवेण घृतफलपुष्पपूर्णेन पूर्णाहुतिं कुर्यात् । ॐ मूर्द्धानं दिवो अरतिं पृथिव्या वैश्वानरमृत आ जातमग्निम् । कवि ँ् सम्राजमतिथिं

जनानामासन्ना पात्रं जनयन्तु देवाः स्वाहा ॥ इति मन्त्रेण पूर्णाहुतिः ततः स्रुवेण भस्मानीय दक्षिणानामिकाग्रगृहीतभस्मना ॐ त्र्यायुषं जमदग्नेः इति ललाटे ॐ कश्यपस्य त्र्यायुषम्–इति ग्रीवायाम् ॐ यद्देवेषु त्र्यायुषम् इति दक्षिणबाहुमूले ॐ तन्नोऽस्तु त्र्यायुषम् इति हृदये । एवं वध्वा अपि त्र्यायुषं कुर्यात् । तन्नो इत्यस्य स्थाने तत्ते इति विशेषः । तत आचार्याय दक्षिणां दद्यात् होत्रे च दक्षिणां दद्यात् भूयसीम् ।

इति चतुर्थीकर्म्म समाप्तम्

atha caturthīkarmma

tataścaturthyā apararātre caturthīkarmma । tacca gṛhābhyantara eva kāryyam । tata udvarttanādi kṛtvā yugakāṣṭhamupaviśya snātvā śuddhavastraṁ paridhāya gṛhaṁ praviśya vadhūvarau prāṅmukhau bhavataḥ । aum gaṇapatyādidevatāpūjanam । tataḥ kuśakaṇḍikārambhaḥ । tatra kramaḥ jāmātṛhastaparimitāṁ vedīṁ kuśaiḥ parisamuhya tānkuśānaiśānyāṁ parityajya gomayodakenopalipya sphyena sruveṇa vā prāgagraprādeśamātraṁ triruttarottarakrameṇollikhyollekhanakrameṇānāmikāṅguṣṭhābhyāṁ mṛdamuddhṛtya jalenābhyukṣya tatra tūṣṇīṁ kāṁsyapātreṇāgnimānīya svābhimukhaṁ nidadhyāt । tataḥ puṣpacandanatāmbūlavastrāṇyādāya aum asyāṁ rātrau karttavyacaturthīhomakarmmaṇi kṛtākṛtāvekṣaṇarūpabrahmakarmma karttuṁ hotṛkarmma karttumamukagotramamukaśarmmāṇaṁ brāhmaṇamebhiḥ puṣpacandanādibhirbrahmatvena hotṛtvena ca tvāmahaṁ vṛṇe iti brāhmaṇaṁ vṛṇuyāt । aum vṛto'smīti prativacanam । yathāvihitaṁ karmma kuru iti vareṇokte aum karavāṇīti brāhmaṇo vadet । tato'gnerdakṣiṇataḥ śuddhamāsanaṁ daṭtvā tadupari prāgagrān kuśānāstīryya brahmāṇamagniṁ pradakṣiṇakrameṇānīya aum atra tvaṁ me brahmā bhavetyabhidhāya aum bhavānīti brāhmaṇenokte kalpitāsane udaṅmukhaṁ brāhmaṇanupaveśayet । tataḥ pṛthūdakapātramagneruttarataḥ pratiṣṭhāpya praṇītāpātraṁ purataḥ kṛtvā vāriṇā paripūryya kuśairācchādya brahmaṇo mukhamavalokyāgneruttarataḥ kuśopari nidadhyāt । *tataḥ paristaraṇam* । *barhiṣaścaturthabhāgamād-āyāgneyādīdāśānāntaṁ brahmaṇo'gniparyyantaṁ nairṛtyā-dvāyavyāntam agnitaḥ praṇītāparyyantam* । *tato-'gneruttarataḥ paścimadiśi pavitracchedanārthaṁ kuśatrayam* । *pavitrakarṇārthaṁ sāgramanantar-garbhaṁkuśapatradvayam* । *prokṣaṇīpātram* । *ājyasthālī* । *sammārjanārthaṁ kuśatrayam* । *upayamanārthaṁ veṇīrūpakuśatrayam* । *samidhastisraḥ* । *sruvaḥ ājyam* । *ṣaṭpañcāśaduttaravaramuṣṭiśatadvayāvacchinnā-mataṇḍulapūrṇapātram etāni pavitracchedanakūśārhāṁ pūrvapūrvadiśi krameṇāsādaṇīyani* । *tataḥ pavitra-cchedanakuśaiḥ pavitre cchitvā prādeśamitapavitra-karaṇam* । *tataḥ sapavitrakareṇa praṇītodakaṁ triḥ-prokṣaṇīpātre nidhāya anāmikāṅguṣṭhābhyāmuttarāgre pavitre dhṛtvā trirutpavanam* । *tataḥ prokṣaṇīpātrasya savyahastakaraṇam* । *pavitre gṛhītvā triruddiṅganam* । *praṇītodakena prokṣaṇīprokṣaṇam* । *tataḥ prokṣaṇījalena yathāsāditavastusecanam* । *tato'gnipraṇītayormadhye prokṣaṇīpātraṁ nidhāya ājyasthālyāmājyanirvāpaḥ* । *tato'dhiśrayaṇam* । *tato jvalattṛṇādinā havirveṣṭayitvā pradakṣiṇakrameṇa paryyagnikaraṇam* । *tataḥ sruvaṁ pratapya saṁmārjanakuśānāmagrairantarato mūlair-bāhyataḥ sruvasaṁmārjanaṁ praṇītodakenābhyukṣya punaḥ pratapya sruvaṁ dakṣiṇato nidadhyāt* । *tat ājyasyā-gneravatāraṇam* । *tata ājye pokṣaṇīvadutpavanam* । *avekṣya satyapadravye tannirasanam* । *punaḥ pūrvavat prokṣaṇyutpavanam upayamanakuśānvāmahastenādāya uttiṣṭhan prajāpatiṁ manasā dhyātvā tūṣṇīmagnau ghṛtāktāḥ samidhastisraḥ kṣipet* । *tata upaviśya prokṣaṇījalenāniṁ pradakṣiṇaṁ paryyukṣya pavitraṁ praṇītāpātre dhṛtvā brahmaṇānvārabdhaḥ pātitadakṣiṇa jānurjuhuyāt* । *tatrāghārādārabhyāhuticatuṣṭayena tattadāhutyanantaraṁ sruvāvasthitājyaṁ prokṣiṇyāṁ kṣipet* । *aum prajāpataye svāhā idaṁ prajāpataye iti manasā* । *aum indrāya svāhā idamindrāya* । *ityāghārau* । *aum agnaye svāhā idamagnaye* । *aum somāya svāhā idaṁ somāya* । *ityājyabhāgau* । *tata ājyāhutipañcataye sthālīpākāhutau ca pratyāhutyanantaraṁ sruvā vasthitahutaśeṣaghṛtasya prokṣaṇīpātre prakṣepaḥ । tato brahmaṇānvārabdhaṁ vinā aum agne prāyaścitte tvaṁ devānāṁ prāyaścittirasi brāhmaṇastvā nāthakāma upadhāvāmi yāsyai patighnī tanūstāmasyai, nāśaya svāhā । idamagnaye ॥ 1 ॥ aum vāyo prāyaścitte tvaṁ devānāṁ prāyaścittirasi brāhmaṇastvā nāthakāma upadhāvāmi yāsyai prajāghnī tanūstāmasyai nāśaya svāhā । idaṁ vāyave ॥ 2 ॥ aum sūryya prāyaścitte tvaṁ devānāṁ prāyaścittirasi brāhmaṇastvā nāthakāma upadhāvāmi yāsyai paśughnī tanūstāmasyai nāśaya svāhā । idaṁ sūryyāya ॥ 3 ॥ aum candra prāyaścitte tvaṁ devānāṁ prāyaścittirasi brāhmaṇastvā nāthakāma upadhāvāmi yāsyai gṛhaghnī tanūstāmasyai nāśaya svāhā । idaṁ caṁdrāya ॥ 4 ॥ aum gaṁdharva prāyaścitte tvaṁ devanāṁ prāyaścittirasi brāhmaṇastvā nāthakāma upadhāvāmi yāsyai yaśoghnī tanūstāmasyai nāśaya svāhā । idaṁ gandharvāya ॥ 5 ॥ tataḥ sthālīpākena juhuyāt । aum prajāpataye svāhā । idaṁ prajāpataye । iti manasā । agnyāhutinavake hutaśeṣaghṛtasya prokṣaṇīpātre prakṣepaḥ । ayañca homo brahmaṇānvārabdhakartṛkaḥ tatra ājyasthālīpākābhyāṁ sviṣṭakṛddhomaḥ । aum agnaye sviṣṭakṛte svāhā । idamagnaye sviṣṭakṛte । tata ājyena aum bhūḥ svāhā idaṁ bhūḥ । aum bhuvaḥ svāhā idaṁ bhuvaḥ । svaḥ svāhā idaṁ svaḥ । etā mahāvyāhṛtayaḥ । aum tvanno agne varuṇasya vidvān devasya heḍo avayāsisīṣṭhāḥ । yajiṣtho vahnitamaḥ śośucāno viśvā dveṣāṁsi pramu-mugdhyasmat svāhā idamagnīvaruṇābhyam । aum sa tvanno agne'vamo bhavotī nediṣṭho'syā uṣaso vyuṣṭhā । avayakṣva no varuṇaṁrarāṇo vīhi mṛḍīkaṁsuhavo na edhi—svāhā idamagnīvaruṇābhyām । aum ayāścāgnesyana-bhiśastipāśca satyamittvamayā asi । ayā no yajñaṁ vahāsyayā no dhehi bheṣajaṁ svāhā । idamagnaye । aum ye te śataṁ varuṇa ye sahasraṁ yajñiyāḥ pāśā vitatā mahāntaḥ । tebhirnno adya savitota viṣṇurviśve muñcantu marutaḥ svarkkāḥ svāhā ॥ idaṁ varuṇāya savitre viṣṇave viśvebhyo-devebhyo marudbhyaḥ svarkkebhyaḥ । aum uduttamaṁ varuṇapāśamasmadavādhamaṁ vimadhyamaṁśrathāya ।*

athā vayamāditya vrate tavānāgaso aditaye syāma svāhā idaṁ varuṇāya । etāḥ prāyaścittasaṁjñakāḥ । aum prajāpataye svāhā ॥ idaṁ prajāpataye । iti manasā । idaṁ prājāpatyam । tataḥ saṁsravaprāśanam । tataḥ ācamya aum asyāṁ rātrau kṛtaitaccaturthīhomakarmmaṇi kṛtākṛtāvekṣaṇarūpabrahmakarmmapratiṣṭhārthamidaṁ pūrṇapātraṁ prajāpatidaivatakamamukagotrāyāmukaśarmmaṇe brāhmaṇāya dakṣiṇātvena tubhyamahaṁ sampradade । iti dakṣiṇāṁ dadyāt । svastīti prativacanam । tato brahmagranthivimokaḥ । tataḥ aum sumitriyā na āpa oṣadhayaḥ santu iti pavitrābhyāṁ śiraḥ saṁmṛjya aum durmitriyāstasmai santu yo'smān dveṣṭi yañca vayaṁ dviṣmaḥ—ityaiśānyāṁ diśi praṇītāṁ nyubjīkuryyāt । tatastaraṇakrameṇa barhirutthāpya ghṛtāktaṁ hastenaiva juhuyāt aum devā gātuvido gātu vitvā gātumita । manasaspata imaṁ devayajñaṁsvāhā vāte dhāḥ ॥ tataḥ pṛthūdakapātrasthaṃ āmrapallavena jalamānīya mūrdhni varo vadhūmabhiṣiñcati aum yā te patighnī prajāghnī paśughnī gṛhaghnī yaśoghnī ninditā tanūḥ । jāraghnī tata enāṁ karomi । sa jīryya tvaṁ mayā saha-śrī amukadevi iti mantreṇa । tato vadhūṁ sthālīpākaṁ prāśayati varaḥ । aum prāṇaiste prāṇān sandadhāmi । aum asthibhiste'sthīni sandadhāmi । aum māṁsaiste māṁsāni sandadhāmi । aum tvacā te tvacaṁ sandadhāmi । iti mantracatuṣṭayena pratimantrāntamannaṁ prāśayet । tato vadhūṁ sthālīpākaṁ prāśayati varaḥ । tato vadhūhṛdayaṃ spṛṣṭvā varaḥ paṭhet । aum yatte tusīme hṛdayaṁ divi candramasi śritam vedāhaṁ tanmāṁ tadvidyāt paśyema śaradaḥ śataṁ jīvema śaradaḥ śataṁśṛṇuyāma śaradaḥ śatam ॥ iti । atha kaṅkaṇamokṣaṇādīni yutagranthivimokādīni ācāraprāptāni । tata utthāya vadhūdakṣiṇahastaspṛṣṭasruveṇa ghṛtaphalapuṣpapūrṇena pūrṇāhutiṁ kuryāt । aum mūrddhānaṁ divo aratiṁ pṛthivyā vaiśvānaramṛta ā jātamagnim । kaviṁsamrājamatithiṁ janānāmāsannā pātraṁ janayantu devāḥ svāhā ॥ iti mantreṇa pūrṇāhutiḥ । tataḥ sruveṇa bhasmānīya dakṣiṇānāmikāgragṛhītabhasmanā aum tryāyuṣaṁ jamadagneḥ iti lalāṭe aum kasyapasya tryāyuṣam—iti grīvāyām aum yaddeveṣu tryāyuṣam iti dakṣiṇabāhumūle aum tanno'stu tryāyuṣaṁ iti hṛdaye ı *evaṁ vadhvā api tryāyuṣaṁ kuryyāt* ı *tanno ityasya sthāne tatte iti viśeṣaḥ* ı *tata ācāryāya dakṣiṇāṁ dadyāt hotre ca dakṣiṇāṁ dadyāt bhūyasīm* ı

iti caturthīkarmma samāptam ı

APPENDICES

APPENDIX I

PREPARATORY RITUAL AND FORMULAS

Some of the often-repeated formulas used in all nuptial ceremonies are listed here in order to provide the rationale for their recurring use. One such formula is Aum or Om—the Oṁkāra. Aum, according to Manu, must be pronounced at the beginning and at the end of a lesson in the Veda; for unless the syllable Om precede the lesson will slip way from the student and unless it follow it will fade away. In some of the subsequent verses he says:

> Seated on blades of Kuśa grass with their points to the east, purified by Pavitras (blades of Kuśa grass), and sanctified by three suppressions of the breath (Prāṇāyāma), he is worthy to pronounce the syllable Om.
> Prajāpati (the lord of creatures) milked out as it were from the three Vedas the sound A, U and M, and the Vyāhṛtis Bhuḥ, Bhuvaḥ, Svaḥ. . . .
> Know that the three imperishable Mahāvyāhṛtis, preceded by the syllable Om, and followed by the three-footed Sāvitrī are the portal of the Veda and the gate leading to union with Brahman. . .
> The monosyllable Om is the highest Brahman, three suppressions of the breath are the best form of austerity, but nothing surpasses the Sāvitrī; truthfulness is better than silence.
> All rites ordained in the Veda, burnt oblations and other sacrifices, pass away; but know that the syllable Om is imperishable, and it is Brahman, and the Lord of all creatures (Prajāpati).[1]

---

1. Concluding this salutation to Om, Mani adds: "An offering, consisting of muttered prayers, is ten times more efficacious than a

Om (Aum), says the Muṇḍaka Upaniṣad , is the bow; the ātman is the arrow; Brahman is said to be the mark. It is to be struck by an undistracted mind. Then the ātman becomes one with Brahman, as the arrow with the target:

प्रणवो धनुः शरो ह्यात्मा ब्रह्म तल्लक्ष्यमुच्यते ।
अप्रमत्तेन वेद्धव्यं शरवत्तन्मयो भवेत् ॥

praṇavo dhanuḥ śaro hyātmā brahma tallakṣyamucyate ।
apramattena veddhavyaṁ śaravattanmayo bhavet ॥ (II.ii.4)

As the bow is the cause of the arrow's entering into the target, so Om is the cause of the ātman's entering into Brahman. The ātman becomes purified through the constant repetition of Om, and then with the support of this mystic syllable is absorbed in Brahman. The seers ask the aspirant to take the bow of our sacred knowledge, to lay against it the arrow of devotion, to pull the string of concentration, and to strike the target. To the seers the single-syllabled Om is the Brahman hidden in the cavity of the heart. This Om is the set of the three Vedas, three worlds, three fires, three steps of Viṣṇu, and the Ṛk, Sāman and Yajur mantras. According to the Vāyu Purāṇa, the Oṁkāra is a set of the three worlds; its head is the heavens; it is the entire universe and the region of Brahmā.

No less important and often recited than Om is the Gāyatrī, the most celebrated and exalted mantras of the Vedas that is addressed to the divine law-giver as Supreme God, symbolized in Savitṛ, the Sun. It is for this reason that this mantra is recited daily at sunrise and at sunset and is called Sāvitrī. Composed according to tradition by the sage Viśvāmitra, its name is derived from the metre in which it is written, the *gāyatrī* being a Vedic poetic metre of twenty-four syllables. Lest the word 'mantra' should be misinterpreted, authoritative commentators remind us that

---

sacrifice performed according to the rules of the Veda; a prayer which is inaudible to others surpasses it a hundred times, and the mental recitation of sacred texts a thousand times."

mantras are neither magic formulas nor merely logical sentences; their function is to 'connect, in a very special way, the objective and subjective aspects of reality'. As a matter of fact, the word 'mantra' stands for "that which has been thought or known or that which is privately—or even secretly by initiation (*dīkṣā*)—transmitted" and in which inheres power to liberate. The sacred Gāyatrī reads as follows:

ॐ तत्सवितुर्वरेण्यं भर्गोदेवस्य धीमहि धियो योनः प्रचोदयात् ॥

Om tat savitur vareṇyaṁ bhargo devasya dhīmahi dhiyo yonaḥ pracodayāt ॥

What this sacred mantra means can be best expressed thus: "We meditate on the adorable light of the radiant Sun. May he himself illumine our minds!" It is identical with the vital breath (prāṇa), because the vital breath as the Kṣatra protects the body by healing wounds. Giving a reason for the meditation on the Gāyatrī and for particularly enjoining it, Swami Nikhilananda says: "...There is another reason. The brāhmiṇ caste forms the highest caste in Hindu society. Entitled to the study of the Vedas and the performance of the Vedic rituals, a brāhmiṇ is pre-eminently equipped for Self-knowledge and Liberation. But a brāhmiṇ is regarded, at the time of his birth, as a śūdra. It is only when he is invested with the sacred thread that he is considered to have had his second birth (*dvija*) and to have become a real brāhmiṇ. At the time of this second birth he is taught the sacred Gāyatrī mantra, which he repeats regularly thereafter. Hence the importance of the gāyatrī."[1]

Numerous hymns are found in the Atharva Veda which allude to the exalted position occupied by the Gāyatrī mantra. In the *Bṛhadāraṇyaka Upaniṣad* the following eulogistic story is narrated:

> On this subject, Janaka, Emperor of Videha, said to Buḍila, son of Aśvatarāśva: "Well, how is it that you, who called

1. *The Upanishads* (A Third Selection), London, 1957, p. 339.

yourself a knower of the Gāyatrī, have come to be an elephant and are carrying me?"

He replied: "Because, Your Majesty, I did not know its mouth."

Janaka said, "Fire is its mouth. If people put a large quantity of fuel into the fire, it is all burnt up. Similarly, a man who knows this, even if he commits a great many sins, consumes them all and becomes pure, clean, and free from decay and death."[1]

This profound parable shows that "the knowledge of the Gāyatrī, being deficient in one part, had been fruitless" and that he who knows the mantra "becomes identified with the Gāyatrī and has fire for his mouth, which consumes the sins such as those resulting from the acceptance of gift."[2]

The *Chāndogya Upaniṣad* (III.xii) describes the Gāyatrī as everything:

गायत्री वा इदँ सर्वं भूतं यदिदं किं च वाग्वै ।
गायत्री वाग्वा इदँ सर्वं भूतं गायति च त्रायते च ॥

gāyatrī vā idaṁsarvaṁ bhūtaṁ yadidaṁ kiṁ ca vāgvai ।
gāyatrī vāgvā idaṁ sarvaṁ bhūtaṁ gāyati ca trāyate ca ॥

"Whatever here exists is the Gāyatrī. Speech is verily the Gāyatrī, for speech sings forth (gāya-ti) and protests (trāya-tē) everything, whatever here exists." The *Chāndogya* regards the Gāyatrī and speech as non-different. Etymologically also they are the same. Speech sings forth an object, that is to say, gives it a name. It also protects others from fear by pointing out the name of the object and exhorting them to give up fear. Speech is able to perform these two functions because it is one with the Gāyatrī. In the *Maitrī Upaniṣad*, again, we have an account of the Gāyatrī and an explanation of its symbolism verse by verse.

It is clear from what the Upaniṣads say that the mantra is

1. *Ibid.*, pp. 343-44.
2. *Ibid.*, p. 344.

not necessarily connected with a sacrificial rite; it is also murmured or repeated on other occasions as well without the accompaniment of ritual offering. Daily, the student of sacred lore must stand at dawn and recite the Gāyatrī until the sun rises. At dusk he, seated, should recite it until he catches sight of the budding stars. From another source we learn that "While facing the East at the morning twilight and the West in the evening, one may control his breath while reciting the Gāyatrī a hundred times." The seers do not tire of telling the devotee that the chanting of the Gāyatrī harmonizes the chanter's heart and mind with the cosmic powers and that, when the mantra is chanted at dawn it purifies from the sins of the previous night. The evening recitation of the mantra is conducive to purification from the sins committed during that day.

APPENDIX II

ŚĀṄKHĀYANA GṚHYASŪTRA

The following lines taken from Śāṅkhāyana Gṛhyasūtra provide a typical example of how the old manuals deal with the Vivāha saṁskāras:

During the northern course of the sun, in the time of the increasing moon, on an auspicious day he shall seize the hand of a girl, who should possess the auspicious characteristics required, whose limbs should be proportionate, whose hair should be smooth, who should also have at her neck two curls turned to the right. Of such a girl he shall know that she will give birth to six men.

If he will acquire a wife, let him recite over the wooers whom he sends to the girl's father when they go away, the verse, 'Thornless'. When they arrive, they take flowers, fruits, barley and a pot of water. They say thrice, 'Here I am, sir!' When these words have been uttered, they ask the girl in marriage, reciting the clan names, the dwellers turning their faces to the east, the visitors to the west. When the matter pleases both sides, let them touch a full vessel into which have been put flowers, fried grain, fruits, barley and gold, and let them recite the formula, 'Undisturbed art thou, the undisturbable vigour of the gods, not cursed, protecting against a curse, unexposed to a curse. Might I straightway attain to truth. Put me into prosperity.' With the verse, 'Offspring may produce us,' the Ācārya of the girl's family, standing up, places the vessel on her head saying, 'Offspring I put into thee, cattle I put into thee, splendour and holy lustre I put into thee'.

When assent has been declared by the girl's father, the bridegroom sacrifices. He besmears a quadrangular space with cowdung. Let him consider in the ceremonies to be performed, of the two eastern intermediate directions, the southern one as that to which the rites should be directed, if the rites belong to the Manes, the northern one, if the rites belong to the gods, or rather the east itself according to some teachers. He draws in the middle of the sacrificial ground aline from south to north, upwards from this, turned upwards, to the south one line, in the middle one, to the north one. These he sprinkles with water, carries forward the fire with the verse, 'I carry forward Agni with genial mind; may he be the assembler of goods. Do no harm to us, to the old nor to the young; be a saviour to us, to men and animals', or he carries it forward silently, then he wipes with his wet hand three times around the fire, turning his right side to it. This they call Samūhana sweeping together. Once, turning his left side to it, in the rites belonging to the Manes.

Now follows the strewing of grass around the fire. He strews eastward-pointed Kuśa grass around it, in three layers or in five layers. Beginning on the east side, then to the west, then to the west. He covers the roots of the grass-blades with the points. And all kinds of rites are to be performed beginning south, ending north. He places the Brahman south with the words, Bhūr Bhuvaḥ Svaḥ, adorns him with flowers, carries forward on the north side the Praṇītā waters with the words, 'Who carries ye forward?'—takes up with the left hand the Kuśa blades, and arranges them on ground with the right hand, bending his right knee, the left when worshipping the Manes. The strewing around of the grass is not necessary in the Ājya offerings, nor in the standing offerings, according to Manḍukeya. He now measures off with the span of his hand two Kuśa blades, which are not unequal, with unbroken points, bearing no young shoots in them, and severs them from their roots with a Kuśa blade, saying, 'Purifiers are ye'. There are two or three of these Kuśa strainers. He holds them with their points to the east and sprinkles them with water, saying, 'Belonging to Vishnu'. With the two Kuśa blades he sprinkles water around the fire three times, keeping his right side turned towards it, takes up the Ājya pot with the words, Milk of the cow art thou; puts into the fire with the words,'For sap thee'; takes it from the fire towards the north with the words, 'For juice thee'; and holding the two Kuśa strainers with their points to the north, seizing them on both sides with his two thumbs and fourth fingers, he bends them down, the points upwards, and dips them into the Ājya with the words, 'By the impulse of Savitar I purify thee with this uninjured purifier, with the rays of the good sun.' This preparation of the Ājya takes place each time. Let him not offer Ājya which has not been thus prepared. Also the waters in the Sruva spoon he purifies with the words, 'By the impulse of Savitar I purify you'. This is called the Praṇītā and the Prokṣaṇī water.

The Sruva spoon serves as a vessel. According to the purpose the properties of the different things to be used at each oblation should be chosen. Taking up Kuśa blades with the left, and the Sruva at its bottom with the right hand, with the words, 'The hand of Viṣṇu art thou'—he offers with the Sruva the Ājya oblations. Beginning from the north-west side of the fire he offers the Ājya unintermittingly on the south side of the fire with the verse, 'Thou Agni art full of foresight'. Beginning from the south-west side of the fire he unintermittingly offers on the north side with the verse, 'To whom these snowy mountains'. To Agni belongs the northern Ājya portion, to Soma the southern. In the middle are made the other oblations, with the words, 'Agni is the begetter; may he give to me N.N. as my wife; svāhā! Soma is rich in wives; may he make me rich in wives, by N.N. svāhā! 'Pushan is rich in kindred; may he make me rich in kindred by the father, the mother, the brothers of N.N. svāhā!' At the Ājya oblations the offering of the two Ājya portions and of the Sviṣṭakṛt oblation is not standing, nor in the standing oblations, according to Māṇḍūkeya. The place for the insertion is the interval between the Mahāvyāhṛtis, the general expiation, and the oblation of Prajāpati. If the oblation consists in Ājya, let him seize the Kuśa blades in his left hand with his right hand at their points and with the left at their roots, and let him wet their point with Ājya in the Sruva, the middle and the roots in the Ājya pot; in the oblations of cooked food, however, the points in the Sruc, the middle in the Sruva, the roots in the Ājya pot. When he then has thrown them into the fire with the words, 'Agni's garment art thou', and has put on the fire three pieces of wood, water is sprinkled round the fire as stated above. Oblations for which only the deities are indicated, but no texts prescribed, are to be made merely with the word Svāhā, 'To such and such a deity svāhā! To such and such a deity svāhā!' The ritual here declared of the sacrifice to be performed when the father's assent to give away his daughter has been declared—

Forms the standard for all sacrifices that procure happiness, and for all Ājya offerings, for the sacrifice of animals which are tied to a branch, and for the offerings of boiled rice grains and of cooked food. These are performed, all the offerings of cooked food, without Prayāga and Anuyāga oblations, without the invocation of the Ilā, without Nigada recitation, and without Sāmidhenī verses. There are also the following ślokas: 'An oblation is called Huta, if made by the performing of the Agnihotra; Ahuta, i.e. unsacrificed, if by the Bali offering; Prahuta, i.e. sacrificed up, if by a sacrifice to the Manes; Praśita, i.e. tasted, if deposited as an offering in a Brāhmaṇa. Without raising his knees, with spread knees let him always offer his oblation; for the gods never accept an offering that has been made holding the hand not between the knees. 'But when he has repeated a text sacred to Rudra, to the Rākṣas to the Manes, to the Asuras, or that contains an imprecation, let him touch water, and so also when he has touched his own body.'

Now when the bride is to be carried away to the bridegroom's house that night, or on the next, or on the third night, on that night, when the darkness of night is gone, they wash the girl up to her head with water that has been made fragrant by all sorts of herbs and the choicest fruits together with scents; they put on her a newly-dyed garment or a new one which has not yet been washed; then the Ācārya of the bride's family makes the girl sit down behind the fire, and while she takes hold of him he sacrifices with the Mahāvyāhṛtis, and then he makes Ājya oblations to Agni, to Soma, to Prajāpati, to Mitra, to Varuṇa, to Indra, to Indrānī, to the Gandharva, to Bhaga, to Pūṣan, to Tvaṣṭar, to Bṛhaspati, to the king Pratyānīka. After they have regaled four or eight women, who are not widows, with lumps of vegetables, Sura, and food, these should perform a dance four times. The same deities they worship also on behalf of the man, and Vaiśravaṇa and Īśāna. Then follows the distribution of food to Brāhmaṇas.

The bridegroom, who has bathed and for whom auspicious ceremonies have been performed, is escorted by happy young women, who are not widows, to the girl's house. To these he shall not behave unobsequiously, except where forbidden food or a transgression is concerned. Having obtained their permission, he then gives her the garment with the verse, 'The Raibhī was'. With the verse, 'Mind was the cushion' he takes up the salve-box. The verse for the anointing is, 'May the Viśvedevās anoint or, unite', 'As this has protected Śacī the beloved one, and Aditi the mother of noble sons, and Apālā who was free from widowhood, may it thus here protect thee, N.N.!'—with these words the bridegroom gives her into her right hand the quill of a porcupine and a string of three twisted threads, with the verse, 'Shape by shape' a mirror into the left. Her relations tie to her body a red and black, woollen or linen cord with three amulet gems, with the verse, 'Dark-blue and red'. With the verse, 'Full of honey the herbs', the bridegroom ties to her body Madhūka flowers. At the wedding one cow, when the Argha ceremony has been performed; in the house one cow: these are the two Madhuparka cows. The bridegroom makes the girl sit down behind the fire, and while she takes hold of him he makes three oblations with the Mahāvyāhṛtis. A fourth oblation with the three Mahāvyāhṛtis together is to be understood from this rule. In this way, where no express rule is stated, in all sacrifices that procure happiness, one is to sacrifice before and afterwards with these same Mahāvyāhṛtis.

'Be queen with the father-in-law', with this verse her father or brother sacrifices with a sword's point on her head, or with the Sruva, standing while she is sitting, with his face turned to the west, while her face is turned to the east. 'I seize thy hand for the sake of happiness', with these words the bridegroom seize with his right hand her right hand with the thumb, both hands being turned with the palms upwards, he standing while she is sitting, with his face turned to the west, while her face is turned to the east. And when he has murmured the following five verses, he continues thus, 'This am I, that art thou; that art thou, this am I; the heaven I, the earth thou; the Ṛc art thou, the Saman I. So be thou devoted to me.' Well! Let us here marry. Let us beget offspring. Let us acquire many sons who may reach old age. The Ācārya fills, with the words bhur bhuvaḥ svaḥā, a new water-pot, throws into it branches with milky sap and leaves, of a tree the name of which is masculine, together with Kuśa grass, and gold, according to some teachers, and hands it over to a student who observes silence. They should walk round this Stheyā water, placed to the north-east, so that they turn their right sides towards it. And after Ācārya has placed a stone towards the northern direction, the bridegroom makes her rise with the words, 'Come, thou joyful one', and makes her tread with the tip of her right foot on the stone, with the words, 'Come, tread on the stone; like a stone be firm. Tread the foes down; overcome the enemies.' He then leads her round the fire so that their right sides are turned to it, and gives her a second garment with the same text. Her father or brother pours out of a basket fried grain mixed with Śamī leaves into her joined hands. The spreading under, the sprinkling over, and the second sprinkling over are done with Ājya. She sacrifices those fried grains.

'This woman, strewing grains, prays thus, "May I bring bliss to my relations; may my husband live long. Svāhā!" '—while the husband murmurs this text, she sacrifices standing. All the ceremonies, beginning from the treading upon the stone, are repeated in the same way for a second time, and in the same way a third time. Silently, if they like, a fourth time. The Ācārya makes them step forward in a north-eastern direction seven steps with the words, 'For sap with one step, for juice with two steps, for the prospering of wealth with three steps, for comfort with four steps, for cattle with five steps, for the seasons with six steps. Friend be with seven steps.' The Ācārya 'appeases' those foot-steps with water. With the three Āpohiṣṭhīyā verses he wipes them with the Stheyā water, and sprinkles it on their heads. The bridegroom then says, 'I give you a cow'. Let him give something to the Brāhmaṇas each time at the Sthālīpākas and other rites; to him who knows the Sūrya hymn the bride's shift. A cow is the optional gift to be given by a Brāhmaṇa, a village by a Rājanya, a horse by a Vaiśya. A hundred cows with a chariot he gives to a father who has only daughters. To those versed in the sacrificial rites he gives a horse.

The three verses, 'I loosen thee', when she departs from the house. 'The living one they bewail', if she begins to cry. The wife then smears the axle of the chariot with clarified butter with this verse, 'They feasted, they got drunk', and with the two verses, 'Pure are thy wheels', 'Thy two wheels', of the two wheels the first with the first verse and the second with the second verse, and the two bulls. After the wife has put, with this verse, 'In the box of the wheel', a branch of a fruit-bearing tree into each of the holes destined for the pins, or, if such branches are already fixed, has recited that verse over them, they then harness the two bulls with the two verses, 'Harnessed be thy right one', the bridegroom reciting the half-verse, 'White the two bulls', over them when they have been harnessed. Now should any part of the chariot break or burst, let him take the girl to the house of one who keeps the sacred fires, and repair the damage with the verse,

'Cover thyself with the Khadiras'. A knot with the verse, 'Him like a horse'. He then murmurs the five verses, 'May prosperity give us'. 'Adorned with Kiṁśuka flowers', when she mounts the chariot; 'May no waylayers meet us', at a cross-way; 'Which the woman's, near a cemetery'; the half-verse, 'O tree with thy hundred branches', he mutters near a big tree; 'The good protectress', when she ascends a ship; 'Carrying stones', when she crosses a river; optionally he also murmurs the same verse, if that is done with the harnessed chariot; 'Up may your wave', at deep places in the river; and at such places let her not look out. The seven verses, 'Here may delight', when she has reached the house, omitting the verses already employed.

'A bull's hide'—this has been declared. On that hide the husband makes her sit down and sacrifices, while she takes hold of him, four oblations with the following formulas, 'With god Agni, with the earth-world of the worlds, and the Ṛgveda of the Vedas: therewith I appease thee, N.N., svāhā!' With god Vāyu, with the air-world of the worlds, with the Yajurveda of the Vedas: therewith I appease thee, N.N., svāhā!' 'With god Sūrya, with the heaven-world of the worlds, with the Sāmaveda of the Vedas: therewith I appease thee, N.N., svāhā!' 'With god Candra, with the world of the quarters of the horizon of the worlds, with the Brahmaveda of the Vedas: therewith I appease thee, N.N., svāhā!' or, 'Bhūḥ! What harm dwells in thee, bringing death to thy husband, death to thy husband's brother, that I make death-bringing to thy paramour, N.N., svāhā!'—thus the first of the before-mentioned formulas may be joined with the first Mahāvyāhṛti , the second with the second, the third with the third, the fourth with the three Mahāvyāhṛtis together. With the verse, 'With no evil eye', let him besmear her eyes with Ājya salve. The bridegroom, having touched the ends of her hair with the three verses, 'How may us the resplendent one. . .', and having quickly recited the four verses, 'And those divine medicines', at the end of that text with the word svāhā pours out the remainder on her head. Here some place a boy of good birth on both sides, in her lap, with this verse, 'Into thy womb', or also silently. Into this boy's joined hands the bridegroom gives fruits and causes the Brāhmaṇas to wish an auspicious day. Thus she becomes the mother of male children. With the rest of the hymn, 'Stay ye here both', they make them enter the house.

With the verse, 'I praised Dadhikrāvan', let them drink together curds. Let them sit silent, when the sun has set, until the polar-star appears. He shows her the polar-star with the words, 'Firm be thou, thriving with me!' Let her say, 'I see the polar-star; may I obtain offspring'. Through a period of three nights let them refrain from conjugal intercourse. Let them sleep on the ground. Let them eat together boiled rice with curds, with the three verses, 'Drink and satiate yourselves'. Let them serve the nuptial fire in the evening and in the morning with the words, 'To Agni svāhā! To Agni Sviṣṭakṛt svāhā!' 'Let the two men Mitra and Varuṇa, let the two men, the Aśvins both, let the man Indra and also Agni make a man grow in me. Svāhā!' —with these words she offers the first oblation if she is desirous of pregnancy. For ten days they are not to set out from home.

Now the rites of the fourth day. When the three nights have elapsed, he makes offerings of cooked food with the texts, 'Agni! Thou art expiation; thou art the expiation of the gods. What substance dwells in her that brings death to her husband, that drive away from her.' Vāyu! Thou art expiation; thou art the expiation of the gods. What substance dwells in her that brings sonlessness, that drive away from her. 'Sūrya! Thou art expiation; thou art the expiation of the gods. What substance dwells in her that brings destruction to the cattle, that drive away from her.' To god Aryaman the girls have made sacrifice, to Agni; may he, god Aryaman, loosen her from this, and not from that place. To god Varuṇa the girls have made sacrifice, to Agni; may he, god Varuṇa, &c. 'To god Pūṣan the girls have made sacrifice, to Agni; may he, god Pūṣan, &c.' The seventh oblation with the verse, 'Prajāpati'. The eighth to Agni Sviṣṭakṛt.

Let him pound the root of the Adhyāṇḍā plant and sprinkle it at the time of her monthly period with the two verses, 'Speed away from here; a husband has she', with svāhā at the end of each, into her right nostril. 'The mouth of the Gandharva Viśvāvasu art thou'—with these words let him touch her, when he is about to cohabit with her. When he has finished, let him murmur, 'Into thy breath I put the sperm, N.N.!' or, 'As the earth is pregnant with Agni, as the heaven is with Indra pregnant, as Vāyu dwells in the womb of the regions of the earth, thus I place an embryo into thy womb, N.N.!' or, 'May a male embryo enter the womb, as an arrow the quiver; may a man be born here, a son after ten months.' Give birth to a male child; may after him another male be born; their mother shalt thou be, of the born, and to others mayst thou give birth. 'In the male verily, in the man dwells the sperm; he shall pour it forth into the woman: thus has said Dhātar, thus Prajāpati has said.' Prajāpati has created him, Savitar has shaped him. Imparting birth of females to other women may he put here a man. 'From the auspicious sperms which the men produce for us, produce thou a son; be a well-breeding cow.' Roar, be strong, put into her an embryo, achieve it; a male, thou male, put into her; to generation we call thee. 'Open thy womb; take in the man's sperm; may a male child be begotten in the womb. Him thou shalt bear; having dwelt ten months in the womb may he be born, the most excellent of his kin.'

In the third month the Puṁsavana, i.e. the ceremony to secure the birth of a male child, under the Nakṣatra Puṣya or Sravaṇa. Having pounded a Soma stalk, or a Kuśa needle, or the last shoot of a Nyagrodha trunk, or the part of a sacrificial post which is exposed to the fire, or having taken after the completion of a sacrifice the remnants from the Juhū ladle, let him sprinkle it into her right nostril with the four verses, 'By Agni may good', 'That sperm to us', 'May he succeed who lights fire', 'Of tawny shape', with Svāhā at the end of each verse.

APPENDIX III

SANSKRIT GLOSSARY*

Aṁguṣṭha (aṁgūṭhā)	:	the thumb.
Aṁjali	:	the open hands placed side by side and slightly hollowed; a libation to the manes; when raised to the forehead, a mark of supplication; reverence, salutation.
Aditi	:	personified as mother of the Gods called Ādityas; Aditi is the symbol of unbound, divine freedom and generosity, of inexhaustible fullness.
Agni	:	the fire of sacrifice and the divine Fire, one of the most important Gods or divine manifestations, the mediator or priest to Men and Gods.
Agnihotra	:	daily fire-sacrifice which was performed morning and evening in every household of the higher castes, consisting in an oblation of milk sprinkled on the fire.
Agnikuṁḍa	:	fire-pit.
Agnisthāpana	:	installation of fire.
Agniṣṭoma	:	Soma sacrifice, lasting for several (usually five) days; one of the most important Vedic sacrifices.
Aham	:	'I', the first person.
Ahiṁsā	:	'non-violence'; respect for life; non-killing.

* Only those words are listed here which, besides being technical, have been frequently used in the text or in the rendition.

Akṣata	:	raw rice grains; unhusked barley-corns.
Akṣara	:	syllable; smallest part of speech; imperishable.
Amṛta	:	immortal, imperishable; the sacred drink (ambrosia), the nectar of immortality.
Aṁtarikṣa	:	the 'in-between', the airy space between heaven and earth, atmosphere, midspace.
Antaryāmī	:	the 'inner Controller' (*antar-yam*).
Anāmikā	:	the ring finger.
Aśmārohaṇa	:	the ceremony of placing the foot on a stone.
Ācamana	:	sipping water from the palm of the hand (before religious ceremonies, before meals) for purification.
Āditya	:	son of Aditi.
Ājya	:	clarified butter (ghī) used for oblations, or for pouring into the holy fire at the sacrifice, or for anointing anything sacrificed or offered.
Ājyasthālī	:	a vessel for clarified butter.
Āhūti	:	calling, invoking; an oblation or offering, especially to a deity; a sacrifice.
Īṣāna koṇa	:	north-eastern quarter.
Kanyā rāśi	:	Virgo.
Kamalāsana	:	Lotus posture.
Karka, rāśi	:	Cancer.
Kalaśa	:	sacrificial (festal) vessel.
Kula	:	clan, lineage.
Kuśa	:	the sacred grass used at certain religious ceremonies.
Kumbha rāśī	:	Aquarius

Kautukāgāra	:	a room for festivity; a pleasure-house.
Khīla	:	parched rice.
Gotra	:	a family, race, lineage; a name, appellation.
Candana	:	sandal.
Chāyāpātra	:	a small bowl, plate, platter, etc. filled with clarified butter in which one sees his face reflected.
Tulā rāśi	:	Libra.
Tṛṇa	:	blade of grass; straw.
Dūrvā	:	bent grass.
Dhanu rāśi	:	Sagittarius.
Parikramā	:	circumambulation; walking round or about.
Pavitre	:	a small sieve or strainer; two kuśa leaves for holding offerings or for sprinkling and purifying ghī.
Purohita	:	family priest.
Praṇītā pātra	:	the vessel for the holy water.
Prokṣaṇī pātra	:	a vessel for sprinkling water.
Maṁḍapa	:	a temporary shed erected on festive occasions; pavilion; tent.
Makara rāśi	:	Capricorn.
Mithuna rāśi	:	Gemini.
Mīna rāśi	:	Pisces.
Meṣa rāśi	:	Aries.
Yajña	:	act of worship or devotion; offering: oblation; sacrifice.
Yajamāna	:	the person paying the cost of a sacrifice; the institutor of a sacrifice (who to perform it employs a priest

		or priests, who are often hereditary functionaries in a family); host.
Lājā	:	fried or parched rice.
Vedi	:	an elevated piece of ground serving for a sacrificial altar (generally strewn with kuśa grass, and having receptacles for the sacrificial fire).
Vṛścika rāśi	:	Scorpio.
Vṛṣa rāśi	:	Taurus.
Saṁkalpa	:	a solemn vow or determination to perform any ritual observance; definite intention.
Siṁha rāśi	:	Leo.
Sruva	:	a wooden ladle shaped like a spoon.
Havi	:	an oblation or burnt offering; anything offered as an oblation with fire (as clarified butter, milk, Soma, grain etc.).
Havya	:	anything to be offered as an oblation; sacrificial gift or food.
Havana	:	a hole made in the ground for the sacrificial fire which is to receive a burnt oblation; the act of offering an oblation with fire.